W9-AAJ-460

Welcome to My Kitchen

Welcome to My Kitchen

A NEW YORK CHEF SHARES HIS ROBUST RECIPES AND SECRET TECHNIQUES

TOM VALENTI AND ANDREW FRIEDMAN

HARPERCOLLINSPUBLISHERS

WELCOME TO MY KITCHEN. Copyright © 2002 by Tom Valenti and Andrew Friedman. All rights reserved. Printed in the United States of America. No part of this book may be used or reproduced in any manner whatsoever without written permission except in the case of brief quotations embodied in critical articles and reviews. For information, address HarperCollins Publishers Inc., 10 East 53rd Street, New York, NY 10022.

HarperCollins books may be purchased for educational, business, or sales promotional use. For information, please write: Special Markets Department, HarperCollins Publishers Inc., 10 East 53rd Street, New York, NY 10022.

FIRST EDITION

DESIGNED BY DEBORAH KERNER/DANCING BEARS DESIGN

Printed on acid-free paper

Library of Congress Cataloging-in-Publication Data
Valenti, Tom
Welcome to my kitchen : a New York chef shares his robust recipes and secret techniques / Tom Valenti and Andrew Friedman.
p.   cm.
Includes index.
ISBN 0-06-019819-2
1. Cookery.   I. Friedman, Andrew   II. Title.
TX651 . V35   2002
641.5—dc21   2001026473

02   03   04   05   06   ❖/RRD   10   9   8   7   6   5   4   3   2   1

For my grandparents,
whose garden and pots and plates
helped form my foundation
of family and food.

For my mother, who forgave me for not pursuing
a law degree.

For my father.
Yes, Dad, there were a couple of dishes I stole from you.

For my brigades, past and present,
for their hard work, diligence, enthusiasm, and ideas.
This book would have many blank pages without them.

And to my darling wife, Abigail.
You make my spirits soar.

—T. V.

For Caitlin,
a great wife.

—A. F.

Contents

Acknowledgments

We'd like to offer our thanks to the following people who helped make this book a reality:

our editor, Susan Friedland, for believing in the book and encouraging us along the way;

our agent, Judith Weber, who watches out for us and who let us use her home kitchen to test the recipes;

Nat Sobel, Judith's husband and business partner (it's his kitchen, too);

the Sobel Weber Associates group, past and present—Laura Nolan, Anna Bliss, Michelle Somers, Liz Bukac, and Catherine Crawford—for being fun to work with;

Lisa Reilly, who tested the dessert recipes;

Vanessa Stich, Monica Meline, Carrie Weinberg, and Kate Stark at HarperCollins, for their help and support.

—T. V. and A. F.

Thanks to my good friends, the too-many-to-mention great chefs (and their brigades) of New York City, where I have the honor and privilege of dining at their tables. You, ladies and gentlemen, now set the culinary pace for this planet.

—T. V.

Thanks to Phillip Baltz and Steve Naidich for daily support and encouragement. Thanks always to Alfred Portale for getting me started. And thanks to Caitlin Connelly, who reads things first and cuts out the embarrassing stuff.

—A. F.

INTRODUCTION:
Welcome to My Kitchen
(IT'S A LOT LIKE YOURS)

Allow me to introduce myself. I am a New York City chef. I'm not known for one particular restaurant, but I have cooked in several prominent ones over the years, including Alison on Dominick Street, Cascabel, Butterfield 81, and the restaurant where I now cook, Ouest, on the Upper West Side. I am known for a very distinct style of food that I've carried with me and developed from kitchen to kitchen. My cooking has been described as robust, hearty, rustic, and intense, and I'm especially associated with slow-cooking techniques such as roasting, stewing, and braising that produce soul-nourishing flavors, textures, and aromas.

Cooking was something that grew organically out of my life. Like a lot of contemporary American chefs, I am the proud product of an Italian heritage. My grandmother raised me on hearty food remembered from the Old Country, and some of my favorite memories are of the dishes she cooked and the powerful aromas that wafted out of the kitchen and filled our home. I learned to love and respect food—delicious, lusty, unabashedly full-flavored food. And my grandmother was my first instructor.

As a kid the first things I cooked were hamburgers, chili, and pasta, which I'd make for my friends while they were hanging out at our house. Because I didn't want to spend too much time away from them, I became adept at organizing my time and my kitchen, forming habits that stay with me to this day and that are represented in this book. And because kids like to be excited by their food, I spent most of my time focusing on seasoning and technique, making those burgers as juicy, that chili as complex, and that pasta as tasty as possible.

I learned something important in those days: If you master the art of seasoning and learn how to control heat properly, you can create dishes that have great impact without a lot of complicated recipes.

In my late teens and early twenties I had the honor of cooking with many great chefs in many great restaurants, including Guy Savoy at his restaurant in Paris and Alfred Portale at the Gotham Bar and Grill in New York City. As sophisticated as those settings were, I never stopped remembering what it was like when the powerful scent of garlic and rosemary first tickled my nose at my grandmother's house. And of how great that chili tasted when I made it for my friends on a cold winter afternoon. And of how simple the recipes of my youth were. I'm always trying to create a flavor that has an impact comparable to those I enjoyed when I was a kid, with recipes that are just as user-friendly and have the same pure intimacy of something cooked at home.

The Nightly Dinner Party

The professional environments I've worked in for the last fifteen years have made it easy for me to relate to the home cook's frame of mind.

If you were to drop by my restaurant and poke your head into the kitchen in the midst of dinner service, when things are really swinging, you'd see five or six cooks supporting me—grilling meats, fussing over little salads, plating desserts, and so on.

But if you were to drop by my kitchen at eight o'clock in the morning, you'd see a very different sight: me, by myself, readying the components of almost every dish on the menu, wrapping them and placing them in the refrigerator or freezer, where they'll stay until dinner that night or some other night later in the week.

There is no other way I'd rather spend my day. Although I have the title of "executive chef," I am also a proud cook who loves turning raw ingredients into delicious food. And it's a good thing because almost all of the kitchens where I've cooked have been small, cramped spaces with very little room for people to move around. (At night everyone pretty much sticks to his or her station, so it's less of a problem.)

In order to control the quality of the food and continue to do the work that I love in these settings, I have developed a repertoire of recipes that can be prepared in advance and then heated, finished, and served in a matter of minutes at the dinner hour. It's not unlike a home cook getting ready for a big dinner party by cooking ahead of time and having all the dishes ready to go when the guests arrive. In fact, I often compare a restaurant to a nightly dinner party where the guests just happen to have a choice of what they'd like to eat. And in my mind's eye when I'm standing there at eight in the morning—slicing salmon or making white bean puree or braising a dozen lamb shanks—I still envision myself in a home kitchen.

In my conversations with home cooks I've learned that there are three things they think prevent them from creating restaurant-level dishes at home. One is the complicated *mise en place*, or ingredients and preparations, required to prepare the recipes we enjoy in restaurants. Another is time and manpower—simply not having enough hours or hands available to make the recipes. A third is chef cookbooks that make it seem as if you have to spend an entire day in the kitchen just to get dinner on the table or that don't allow any room for flexibility.

The recipes in this book will help you with all three of these obstacles and enable you to create restaurant-caliber flavors and meals in your own home kitchen.

Cooking Ahead of Time

The most important thing this book has to offer, outside of the recipes themselves, is a philosophy of cooking centered around the ability to prepare recipes in advance. You'll learn in the following pages that you can get your dishes ready ahead of time at home just as I do at my restaurants. Not just obvious recipes like soups, pasta sauces, and slow-cooked meats, but also lobster, risotto, chicken, pork tenderloin, and others that one usually regards as being prepared *à la minute*.

If you flip through this book, you'll see a number of dishes that *look* very elaborate and complicated. But if you look more closely, you'll notice that many of the components are actually very easy to prepare and that most of the work can be done the day before or several days before you plan to serve and eat them.

Take, for example, the Seared Tuna with Chickpea-Eggplant Puree and Tomato Vinaigrette (page 166). In that dish the puree and tomato vinaigrette can be made more than a day in advance, leaving you to simply sear the tuna when ready to serve. Similarly, the Poached Chicken Breast Stuffed with Goat Cheese and Spinach (page 202) can be made days early, sealed in plastic, and then plopped into a pot of boiling water for a last-minute dinner, or paired with a salad for a very satisfying lunch.

To really drive this point home, there are a few visual aids that make it easy to take advantage of this aspect of the recipes. (See "How to Use this Book," page 5.)

Component Cooking

Many of the recipes in this book, especially the main-course dishes, are organized component by component. I've done this for a number of reasons:

1. To facilitate preparation and planning. If you want to prepare a dish ahead of time, having the recipes broken down into components allows you to work at your own pace. Take, for example, the Herb Risotto with Lobsters and Chanterelles (page 149). The preparation of the herb puree, the lobster, and the chanterelles each takes just a few minutes, and each may be refrigerated for up to twenty-four hours. Having the components separated invites you to make them at your leisure and breaks down the cooking process into simple steps.

2. To facilitate mixing and matching. If you want to use the component of one dish in another context (maybe as a side dish or accompaniment), having the components broken out makes this very easy to do.

3. To facilitate the omission of a component. For example, if you're not inclined to make the herb puree in the aforementioned risotto, you can simply skip it and not have to recalculate the quantities of ingredients in the recipe.

Shortcuts to Flavor

Over the years, because of my limited staff and time, I have also come to depend on a few key ingredients and preparations to provide a certain effect in my cooking or to accent dishes with bursts of flavor. So in addition to the recipes themselves, this book shares my favorite little tricks of the trade. For example, I'll show you how to get the most out of white vinegar and the acidic undercurrent it adds to so many dishes, how to season with sugar with almost as much frequency as salt and pepper, and an insane number of uses for pork products. You'll also learn unconventional ways of making gravlax, consommé, and other recipes. Since I never went to cooking school, many of these techniques are not the same as those you might find in a textbook. But they work, and I think they make cooking a lot easier than the traditional methods, and in some cases a lot more fun.

In short, what follows are the recipes that I love and the secrets of how to cook them. Enjoy yourself, don't skimp on the garlic, and remember that the most important lesson is no secret at all: Follow your own personal taste and instinct.

TOM VALENTI

How to Use This Book

This book is organized the same way as most cookbooks you own, but a few elements merit a brief explanation:

My Favorite Ingredients, Controlling the Elements, and Seasoning

This section constitutes an orientation of sorts, explaining a number of themes that run through the book. They will call your attention to the ingredients I use most frequently and explain why I love them as much as I do: they will also offer some general cooking guidance and explain my philosophy of seasoning. Basically, what follows includes the information and advice that is too abstract or cumbersome to address over and over in the individual recipes.

Headnotes

Each recipe is preceded by a little introduction, or headnote, that describes the dish and any points of interest, such as where I got the idea for it or any special attention you might need to pay to an aspect of cooking it.

Recipes

Because I am a big proponent of make-ahead cooking, most of the recipes in this book feature advice on how to cook and store components—or, in many cases, the entire dish—a day or two in advance, if not longer. There's also direction on how to pick up where you left off when you're ready to serve. I encourage you to take advantage of this information. There's nothing like waking up on the day of a dinner party and having time to go to the movies because the entire meal is all in the fridge and ready to go, or of having a great dinner on tap all week long because you did a little make-ahead cooking on Sunday afternoon.

To help you determine which recipes best suit your schedule, the make-ahead portion and the final preparation are divided by a ❖ symbol.

One other note about the recipes: I often instruct you to chop or dice a quantity of ingredients rather than offer a specific volume of the final product. For example, rather than saying "1 cup cubed carrots," I say "1 small carrot, cut into 1/4-inch dice." My style of cooking isn't so precise that you need to fuss over measuring items like this too carefully. The same is true of lemon juice. I usually suggest that you use the "juice of 1 lemon" rather than specify "2 tablespoons lemon juice." Since the strength of these ingredients varies based on their freshness and individual intensity, you may need to adjust the amount at the end of the cooking process anyway, so I've leaned toward keeping the use of measuring vessels to a minimum.

Flexibility and Substitutions

One of the things I love about cooking at home is flexibility, so I've kept a lot of recipes very loose and adaptable. You'll notice that many of the headnotes tell you to use whatever herbs you like or have on hand, or that you can vary the ratio of meat to tomato in a sauce, or that you can substitute any kind of fish in a particular dish.

I have also indicated several possible accompaniments or substitutions for given accompaniments in many of the recipes. The recipes presented are the way I would serve and eat them, but if you find that your personal taste calls for some minor adjustments or makes a replacement side dish desirable, by all means suit yourself.

There's a chapter toward the end of the book that gathers many side dishes and accompaniments together in one place—such as Red Lentil Mash (page 252), Leek Puree (page 262), Potato Gratin (page 256), and White Bean Puree (page 259). These are my favorite accompaniments and are presented on their own to provide you with easy reference should you want to use them in other contexts.

Food for Thought

This is where I include points of interest, perhaps explaining the historical inspiration for a dish, sharing a fun fact about an ingredient, or offering a helpful tip about a technique.

Options

This is where I let you know of possible substitutions for ingredients or ways to take a dish in a slightly different direction.

Beer or Wine

Where I have a strong feeling about what should be drunk with a particular dish, this is where I let you know. Here, as elsewhere, I have kept my suggestions open to your interpretation, offering up types of beer and varietals of wine without getting too specific.

My Favorite Ingredients

Over the years I have come to rely on the following ingredients and simple preparations, either to enhance the overall flavor of a dish or to provide little bursts of flavor.

Acids

In my opinion, acid is one of the most important elements in brightening a dish. When placed in the proper context, it makes flavors come alive the way nothing else can. There are very few preparations, even a dessert or two, where I do not reach for my trusty vinegar bottle or add a squeeze of lemon or a drop of vermouth to make the flavors in a dish register as round in the mouth.

What do I mean by "round in the mouth"? This refers to a complete sensation that makes something feel substantial, yet light and vibrant. The best example I can give involves a simple experiment: Make yourself a cup of tea with lemon and another with honey. Taste them separately. The first will register as acidic; the second as sweet. But when you stir both lemon *and* honey into a cup of tea, they complement and complete each other, becoming what I think of as round in the mouth. (Another, more sophisticated example is the use of rice wine vinegar in seasoning sushi rice. That vinegar—comprising sweetness and acidity—ties the rice and fish together. Without it, sushi would lack the complexity that makes it so special.)

Acidity is often the missing link in attaining this completeness in cooking. Part of the reason is that many people do not understand how to use it. Just as the use of salt doesn't mean something should taste salty, the use of an acidic agent doesn't mean a dish should taste acidic. Rather, it's the *sensation* acids provide that is so useful.

Traditionally, acid is used in cooking as a last-minute seasoning—most commonly with a lemon being squeezed into a salad dressing, mayonnaise, or sauce to liven it. In my food it is part of the structure, a key player in the culinary DNA of a dish. In this book you will see that I use white vinegar constantly in an effort to round out the flavor of a recipe. You'll even find it in such seemingly unlikely places as Braised Lamb Shanks (page 225) and Autumn Fruit Compote (page 272).

I find that white vinegar is especially valuable for attaining an instant result in the preparation of stocks and sauces. Some vinegar added at the beginning will register right away and will not dissipate as the liquid simmers; the high note it provides survives the cooking process.

Regarding whether to employ lemon or white vinegar, a good rule of thumb is that lemon should be used when seeking a specific lemon *flavor;* white vinegar should be used when a more neutral, though unmistakably acidic, boost is called for. Of course there are times when acid is inappropriate. For the most part it has no place in starchy foods such as white bean puree, polenta, and potato dishes. These components often serve to ground a dish by offering relief from the more vibrantly flavored ones, and trying to tack some acidity onto them goes against their character.

Bacon

When I was the chef at Butterfield 81, *New York* magazine's Gael Greene reviewed us and posed the question, "What is it with this guy and Porky?" But she wasn't really confused by my love affair with bacon. As Ms. Greene herself once declared, "Everything tastes better with bacon."

I use bacon and pork products a lot. In this book you'll find them scattered on salads and atop risotto, wrapped around scallops and pork tenderloin, and infusing Smoked Pork Jus (page 25), a broth that I use even for such non-pork dishes as Smoky Lobster Minestrone (page 108).

I first fell in love with bacon when I was nineteen and coming out of a pastry apprenticeship. I was working as a cook at a Greek restaurant, side by side with the owner, and he had me making clams casino. My role in this assembly line was to put the bacon over each piece as it arrived before me. I ate quite a few of those clams myself, and one taste of how the salinity of the clams interacted with the smokiness of the bacon was all I needed to know about how much I adored the effect. It was love at first sight (or is it first bite?) if ever there was such a thing.

In my own home kitchen it soon got to the point where I was wrapping everything in bacon—fish, meats, you name it. Over the past ten years I've explored the possibilities of bacon in a vast array of dishes and have come to regard it as one of the most versatile resources in the kitchen.

SOME OF MY FAVORITE USES FOR BACON INCLUDE THE FOLLOWING:

- As a basting element for lean meats. In the Bacon-Wrapped Pork Tenderloin (page 229), for example, the bacon doesn't just add flavor; its fattiness helps keep the lean tenderloin moist as it cooks.

- As a punctuation mark. In salads, such as the Endive and Roquefort Salad with Lardons (page 62), and on top of risotto, such as the Corn and Green Onion Risotto (page 189), the presence of bacon adds an unmistakable accent to dishes that might otherwise become a bit monotonous. The ultimate example of this effect is a BLT. It's the bacon that makes that little classic work.

- To infuse an entire dish with smoky flavor. Often I'll begin a dish by rendering some bacon in the pan and cooking the garlic and onions in the fat rather than in butter or oil. This lends the finished dish tremendous flavor. Try the Tubetti with Clams and Bacon (page 117), which was actually inspired by those clams casino days, and imagine how much of the dish's personality would be lost without the bacon.

- To add complexity to a one-dimensional ingredient. Wrapping a scallop in bacon, as I do with the Bacon-Wrapped Sea Scallops (page 178), balances its creamy richness with smokiness and just a bit of a crunch.

THERE ARE A VARIETY OF GUISES IN WHICH BACON APPEARS:

Simple Cured Bacon

This is what we are used to seeing at the supermarket. It is good for utilitarian applications (such as Sunday breakfast) but doesn't lend much, if any, smokiness to dishes. It also tends to be rather fatty, so I avoid it in more sophisticated recipes.

Smoked Bacon and Double-Smoked Bacon

These are the varieties I use most often because the smoking process not only melts away some of the fat but also intensifies the flavor of the cured meat. Most important, the sweet, smoky character provides a great anchoring "bottom" in many recipes. This is particularly valuable as a counterpoint when there's a prominence of acid in a dish.

Pancetta

This is Italian bacon that has been rolled and cured, giving it its cylindrical shape. I find pancetta a little too salty and so don't use it much, but many of my friends, particularly Mario Batali, are expert in its applications. By all means experiment with it and decide for yourself whether or not it belongs in your own bag of tricks.

A Note on Lardons: Throughout the book you'll see that I call for lardons in recipes. *Lardon* is a general French term that refers to a nugget of bacon, most commonly browned and scattered on salads. To make lardons, take a slab or piece of bacon, cut it into 1/2-inch strips, then cut the strips crosswise into 1/2-inch-square pieces comprising both meat and fat.

Garlic

There is a famous scene in the movie *Goodfellas* where the lead characters are doing a turn in the joint and we see that, connected guys that they are, they have been placed in a very comfortable cell complete with a working kitchen. Paul Sorvino, as Paulie the don, makes dinner every night, and for the meal we watch him prepare, we see that he slices his garlic with a razor blade. Well, everyone who knows about garlic nods when they see that moment because one thing is clear about Paulie: He may be a killer and a thief, but the guy knows how to cook.

Of course all chefs use garlic, so the fact that I employ it isn't as original as the way I deploy white vinegar. But I do use it a lot, in about 80 to 90 percent of my recipes.

And here is the Great Garlic Paradox: Although I put garlic in almost all my dishes, all of them do not taste garlicky. That is a shorthand way of saying that the taste we associate with raw garlic isn't what garlic is all about. The use of garlic as a flavor-building component is based on knowing how to cut it, how to cook it, and when to add it or take it out of a dish.

In this book the disparate effects of garlic are on display just about everywhere, but most dramatically in such dishes and components as Garlic Soup with Poached Egg, Black Pepper, and Chives (page 98), Roasted Garlic Mayonnaise (page 280), and Garlic Confit (page 199). If I had the time (and a publisher who shared my passion), I'd gladly write an entire book about garlic and how to use it. Until that day, some general observations will have to suffice:

- Stay away from pre-peeled garlic. Those bottled masses of shiny, ready-to-chop cloves look tempting, but if there is such a creature as the Culinary Devil, these are surely his work. The machines that peel the cloves bruise the flesh and sometimes crush the precious garlic. If you want to simplify the peeling of garlic, make this the first thing you do when you come into the kitchen: Separate the cloves and get them soaking in some warm water. This will loosen up the skins and make them easier to peel when the time comes.

- To gain an appreciation of the potent and wonderful flavor of pure garlic, try this experiment: Next time you're grilling a steak, stick a clove of garlic on the end of a fork. Score the exposed side and brush the steak with the garlic on both sides as it's grilling. The flavor the clove transmits may shock you. It will definitely put a smile on your face. Keep this intensity in mind when working with garlic. The moral of the story is that a little garlic, properly harnessed, goes a very long way.

- When should you slice garlic? When sautéing garlic, usually at the beginning of a preparation, thinly slicing it is the best choice because the increased surface area will give off the most flavor, and by the time you're done cooking, the garlic itself will have melted away, leaving only its friendly ghost of flavor. (Another ideal use for thinly sliced garlic is with quickly sautéed greens, when the presence of the slivers in the finished dish is welcome.)

- When is it okay to crush garlic? When it's going to be left behind. When making, say, a sauce that will ultimately be strained, there's no need to spend time mincing garlic. Just bust it open to unlock the flavor and get it into the mix.

- When should garlic be minced? It's almost never necessary to go to the trouble of mincing a little clove of garlic. However, if the garlic won't be cooked much or at all—such as when it is going into a vinaigrette raw or will be added during the last seconds of a sauce's cooking—that's the time to really mince it well. The idea is to dissipate its qualities and intensity by distributing the actual herb because this won't be accomplished via heat.

- Roasted garlic is a category unto itself. It lends a sweet body to so many things, especially sauces. And a whole head of roasted garlic can be a wonderful accompaniment to meats and poultry. Keep it in mind when looking to add another dramatic dimension to a meal that seems somehow bland. It can make even the most commonplace dinner seem rustically romantic.

ROASTED GARLIC PUREE

Makes 3–4 tablespoons

The sweet, mellow flavor of roasted garlic adds a distinct accent and depth to sauces and soups. As with the Chopped Roasted Tomatoes (page 13), this recipe multiplies very well, so make and refrigerate (or freeze) as much as you can use.

1 head garlic, separated into cloves	Coarse salt
2 tablespoons olive oil	Freshly ground black pepper
2 tablespoons water	

Preheat the oven to 350°F.

Place the garlic cloves in a small baking dish just large enough to hold them.

Drizzle the cloves with the oil and water and season with salt and pepper.

Cover the dish and cook for 30–40 minutes, or until a paring knife slides easily into a clove.

Remove the baking dish from the oven, allow to cool, squeeze the soft garlic from the skins, and mash them with a fork.

❖ **IF MAKING IN ADVANCE,** the garlic may be covered and refrigerated for up to 3 days or frozen for up to 2 weeks.

CHOPPED ROASTED TOMATOES

Makes 3–4 tablespoons

These intensely flavored tomatoes are used throughout the book to add periodic bursts of flavor to sauces, risottos, and other dishes. You'll find they have unlimited uses in your own cooking as well. The recipe multiplies well, so make as much as you can use.

1 tablespoon olive oil	Pinch sugar
Coarse salt	1 teaspoon fresh thyme leaves
Freshly ground black pepper	3 plum tomatoes, thickly sliced

Preheat the oven to 300°F.

Combine the oil, salt, pepper, sugar, and thyme in a small bowl and stir to combine.

Place the tomato slices in the bowl and gently toss with your fingers to coat with the oil.

Gently shake off the excess oil and transfer the tomatoes to a cookie sheet.

Roast for 25 minutes, then carefully flip with a spatula and cook an additional 5 minutes. (Keep a careful eye on the tomatoes; if your oven runs a bit hot, they may need to be flipped after 15–20 minutes. It's okay if they shrivel slightly, but don't let them blacken or dry out.)

Remove from the oven and set aside to cool. Roughly chop.

❖ **IF MAKING IN ADVANCE,** the tomatoes can be coated with a thin film of olive oil, covered, and refrigerated for up to 2 days or frozen for up to 2 weeks.

OPTIONS: There's really no substitute for these tomatoes, but in cases where it won't diminish the dish too much, I've also offered alternatives such as chopped reconstituted sun-dried tomatoes or high-quality canned plum tomatoes.

Controlling the Elements:

FIRE AND WATER

Fire

Have you ever wondered why recipes tell you to cook some things over high heat, some over medium, and some over low? Or why you are sometimes given license to make the call, choosing from "low to medium"?

When I've had the opportunity to interact with home cooks, I've noticed that recognizing the level of heat at which to cook is among the biggest mysteries to most of them. "What cuts of meat require high heat?" "Which require low heat?" "What's the right temperature for sautéing spinach?" "How hot should the pan be before I start cooking a piece of fish?"

All good questions. And the answers to all of them begin with this universal truth: Cooking is not just warming things. It's *changing* them—altering, transforming, and fusing them—with heat. In many ways it's scientific, so it's very important to know how to harness the heat of your stove and oven because unsuccessful cooking often starts with bad heat-level decisions.

There is an infinite number of heat choices one could make when cooking and several exceptions to every so-called rule. That said, here's some guidance on how to choose the right heat intensity in a given situation:

- When working with heat, any level of heat, the importance of good cooking equipment that conducts it evenly cannot be overstated. If you are using a tin-can-thin sauté pan, chances are you'll burn even the garlic and onions that form the base of so many dishes.

- When it comes to meat, fish, and fowl, many of the decisions about heat level have to do with fat content because fat acts as a basting element, melting as the meat cooks and keeping it from drying out. For example, a beautiful marbled steak should be cooked over high heat, while a lean brisket should be cooked slowly over low heat. The ultimate example may be duck, which can take a stunning amount of heat thanks to the massive fat content of its skin. (The same principle applies when we put butter or oil in a sauté pan to heat herbs and vegetables, but not when we cook bacon, which supplies its own fat when it starts to cook.)

- High heat is crucial when we want to achieve a heat-related effect quickly. For example, we sear sea scallops in a small quantity of butter and oil over high heat to seal the exterior, which provides a pleasing contrast in texture and locks in their juices.

- Two heat sources are often required to produce a contrast in the finished product. Much of my cooking involves starting something on the stovetop and cooking it through in the oven. For example, the Braised Lamb Shanks (page 225) are first seared over high heat to create a flavorful exterior and seal in the initial seasoning, and then slow-cooked in the oven where they absorb the flavor of the braising liquid and become tender.

- You may have wondered why we bring a pot of water, sauce, or stock to a boil over high heat and then lower the heat to let it simmer. The reason is simple: It takes a long time to reach even a simmer over low heat. The boiling itself has no benefit other than to speed the cooking process. The low heat is ultimately what we're after because it is a gentler way of cooking. If cooked over high heat, the water, sauces, and stocks will evaporate or reduce and thicken. In the case of soups that feature vegetables, fish, poultry, or meat, high heat can destroy those ingredients.

- Often a decision has to be made based specifically on the ingredient we are using. When sautéing mushrooms, for example, different types require a different approach. Chanterelles give off some liquid, so we want to sauté them over high heat in a small quantity of fat (oil or butter) to quickly sear them and retain their flavor and moisture. Morels, on the other hand, absorb liquid and therefore should be cooked over lower heat with just enough fat to keep them from scorching.

Pay attention to the instructions and notes about heat level in the recipes throughout this book. Wherever possible I explain why I have selected a particular level and try to provide a universal lesson.

Water

The most common mistake I have seen made in my years as a chef is in the tasting of liquids and sauces. Many people, including young cooks fresh out of school, taste on a fingertip or sample a teaspoonful. What they fail to consider is how the component they are sampling will register in the context of a finished plate. If they did, they might be inclined to "open up" the qualities of what is being tasted.

The best example I can offer is that of great single-malt Scotch. It smells great straight, and a small sip might be deeply satisfying, but if you're getting ready to sit down in front of a roaring fire with a snifterful, you need to add some water to unlock the nuances of what is hidden within. It's the same with liquids in the kitchen.

In my kitchen we have a squeeze bottle of water on every station, and we always encourage cooks to use it to open up a sauce that's too reduced in an effort to balance the dish better.

In many kitchens water is taken for granted. Even veteran home cooks use unpurified tap water in their cooking, thinking little of the decision. While this is usually fine, great water does make a difference. If you have ever had a cup of coffee made with fresh spring water, you know what I mean.

Of all the elements that come into play in cooking, water is the one that is probably undervalued the most. Some of the invaluable ways water proves useful are as follows:

- Binding broken emulsions. If an emulsification such as mayonnaise or hollandaise sauce begins to break, a few drops of very hot water will often bring the ingredients back together. The first few drops should remedy the situation. If they don't, transfer a few tablespoons of the broken mixture to another bowl, add some hot water to that, whisk to emulsify, and then slowly whisk in the rest of the broken mixture.

- Halting a "boil-over." We all know those uncomfortable moments when we have turned our back on a pot of cream or milk coming to a boil, and it starts to rise over the top of the pot. A few drops of cold water splashed into that pot will stop the impending disaster instantly.

- For better sauce, just add water. If a sauce becomes too reduced and loses its nuance, adding some water can bring it back to life.

- Cooking greens. Here is a simple rule of thumb: If it's green—asparagus, haricots verts, peas, and so forth—use a lot of rolling, boiling water to cook it. You want to cook these vegetables at a high temperature to seal in flavor, vitamins, and crunch. And after you cook them, you want to shock them in . . . guess what? Ice *water*.

- Ice water can be a handy ally. For example, you can quicken the cooling process of just about anything by setting it in a bowl within a bowl of ice water. If you are making ice cream and just can't wait for the custard to chill before plopping it in the machine, now you know how to speed things up. You can even stop caramel from overcooking and becoming bitter by immersing the bottom half of the pot in ice water.

- When to use bottled water. If making something like a granite or sorbet or even a stock, use the best purified water. This is not as important if you are just blanching something. The more water present in the final product, the more important the water quality.

- As silly as it may sound, all bottled waters are not created equal. If you do a comparison, you may find that you have become a water snob. Some waters have a mineral quality while others seem just as pure as can be. This doesn't necessarily pertain to cooking but is a great way to acquaint yourself with the sensitivity of your own palate.

- Deglazing. When deglazing something after you have sautéed a piece of meat or fowl, a lot of recipes call for deglazing with white wine, red wine, vermouth, and so forth. For most of the recipes in this book, deglazing with water is fine as well because we are finishing with a complex stock base.

- Preserving color. Tossing a few ice cubes in the food processor when pureeing herbs or vegetables is often essential to keeping the blade from getting too hot and cooking the delicate leaves, which would ruin their flavor and color. (This is the same principle as shocking vegetables in ice water; essentially, you're shocking as you chop.)

- A vehicle for starch. When cooking pasta, the water takes on some of the pasta's starch, and that cooking liquid is often used to bind the sauce together. (See page 115 for more on this.)

- Cooking with water. Let's not forget cooking methods that actually use water to conduct heat. Steaming and poaching are among the most gentle, underappreciated ways to cook a piece of fish or poultry. If you don't believe me, try the recipes on pages 38 and 202. Double boilers, which harness the heat of water indirectly, are also wonderfully useful. Think about how hard it would be to make purees ahead of time or to melt a couple of ounces of chocolate if we didn't have the double boiler.

Seasoning

Seasoning is easily the most important aspect of cooking next to the quality of the actual ingredients. And seasoning all components of a dish to the best of your ability is worth the extra time and attention because flavor isn't just about the big things. Every time you cook something, you are changing its character, and seasoning is how you control that transformation. Cook some green beans in unsalted water, mildly salted water, and heavily salted water, and you'll see how true this is in even the most basic situations.

As for when to season, I believe strongly in seasoning as you go, building a depth of flavor, and getting as much out of each ingredient as possible. Take soups, stocks, and sauces, for example. I season a sauce as I add elements to the pot because I have a tendency not to reduce them. Therefore, I need to sense a roundness of flavor in each step because I don't leave myself much wiggle room at the end.

Another burning question is whether to salt fish, meats, and poultry before or after cooking. In my humble opinion, you should always season them before cooking in order to generate as much flavor as possible through the interaction of the seasoning, the item being cooked, and the heat.

Salt, Pepper, and Sugar

That's right . . . *and sugar*. For a long time sugar was, I thought, my little secret. Even though I was the executive chef at a respectable New York restaurant, I would prominently perch salt and pepper on my workstation and keep a hidden supply of sugar in a small container under the table where nobody could see it.

I don't know when I first happened upon this little trick, but I always found sugar useful in obtaining a certain roundness of flavor. I use so much acid in my cooking (see page 7) that my food cries out for a balancing element, something sweet to offset the vinegary edge. So I began using sugar. Then sometime in the mid-nineties I had the good fortune to spend a few days with a four-star chef I had long admired. We were going to be featured in an article for *New York* magazine in which we went fishing together and then cooked up our respective catches. When it came time to do the cooking, we got into some shop talk about seasoning, and he mentioned that he had salt, pepper, and sugar *at every station in his kitchen*.

This was a big moment for me because it taught me to be a bit less shy about things that I know by simple trial and error to be true. And the sugar thing just makes good sense. Here's why: There is quite a bit of natural sugar in many fruits and vegetables, but the level of sweetness changes during the year due to seasonality and other factors. Sugar is simply a way to pump up the sweetness, elevating one aspect of an ingredient just as salt and pepper ratchet up others. Although most cooks don't think of sugar as a seasoning element in savory dishes, there's nothing wrong with using some sugar to make an ingredient sweeter. That's why it was put on Earth, after all. (I should mention that this isn't a way to salvage horribly out-of-season ingredients but rather a way to punch up those that are just slightly below peak.)

Which brings me to another fine use for sugar: to quicken and enhance caramelization. What is caramelization? It's the conversion of sugar to a darker, sweeter state. When you caramelize onions, you are bringing out all of their natural sweetness. I often add a pinch of sugar to the pan to both accelerate and intensify this effect.

Salt

The most important thing about salt is to understand the different types. Iodized table salt is vastly different from kosher salt (which is what I use almost exclusively), which is different from sea salt. I favor Diamond Crystal Kosher Salt because it's pure, unadulterated salt.

Let me tell you a story about how important these distinctions are. I had a disaster once while working at Cascabel restaurant. My supplier ran out of kosher salt and sent us a different brand that contained prussiate of soda, an anti-caking agent, though none of us knew this at the time. Well, the prussiate of soda kept the salt from dissolving properly, so the flavor didn't register right away. The end result was that we were all overseasoning our food.

The bottom line is that, outside of desserts, where fine salt rules, it is hard to go wrong with kosher salt. But you should certainly experiment and taste the different varieties on the market. There are some fabulous options that offer great effects, such as sea salt and the exquisite French *fleur de sel*. Just be aware every time you give a new one a chance that it will behave differently from the one you are used to.

Pepper

If salt amplifies and focuses individual flavors, then pepper is more of a backdrop. (In fact, you sense salt on the front of the tongue and pepper on the back.)

If the four main taste sensations are hot, sour, salty, and sweet, then pepper is the everyday way to achieve heat. It completes the flavor profile of just about everything. Interestingly, while you tend to notice salt itself only when there is too much of it, you sense pepper both if there is too much and if there is too little. Whereas salt brings out the qualities of the item being salted, pepper is there to be sensed in all its individual glory. Accordingly, I always season with salt first, and only after I can sense all the flavors I'm looking for do I go ahead and start adding pepper.

Stocks and Other Bases

Just about all good cookbooks include a pep talk about how important stocks are. But there's a little secret out there—many home cooks use canned broth instead of fresh stock made from scratch. The reason is simple: It can be a hassle to make stock, and when nobody is looking and you just want to get dinner on the table, how much difference can it really make?

Quite a bit, actually. A store-bought chicken stock is quite high in sodium, which robs you of control over your own cooking. Over the years I have developed a few tricks to stock-making, some of which quicken the process (or make long cooking optional) and let you get on to the business of cooking with as little delay as possible. (If you are really pressed for time and are turning to canned broth, select a low-sodium or organic variety, which is less likely to overwhelm the palate.)

In this chapter you will find some of my favorite stocks and bases. A few of them, such as the Chicken Stock (page 23), Basic Vegetable Stock (page 24), and Clam Broth (page 28), employ fairly traditional recipes, though I don't feel the need to let them simmer for that long; by using the amount of liquid indicated, the infusion happens pretty fast.

Then there are those recipes in which I throw the rule book right out the window. One of the more distinctive recipes in this chapter is my basic formula for Dark Stocks (page 32), which I devised when I was a young impatient cook (as opposed to the middle-aged impatient cook I am today). My technique puts sweet, saline, and acidic elements right into the stock, giving it great utility. You can use these dark stocks as braising liquids and sauces with almost no extra work because they have tremendous flavor and complexity built in.

I have also included some very specific and simple stocks that save time in recipes by enhancing a particular flavor. These include Mushroom Stock (page 26), Onion Stock (page 34), Roasted Garlic Jus (page 31), and Tomato Broth (page 27). The most intense and personal entry here is Smoked Pork Jus (page 25), a soupy ode to the wonders of pork. Its flavor will haunt your taste buds for a good long while, and you may find that it becomes your own favorite ingredient in recipes for soups and stews as well.

FOOD FOR THOUGHT—SPANISH ONIONS: I use Spanish onions in my stock-making and in most of my cooking. To me they are the most dependable onions with the most consistent flavor and degree of freshness.

CHICKEN STOCK

❧

Makes about 1 quart

Most stock recipes insist that you cook the broth for several hours or even overnight, which makes it seem like a big production. I am convinced that one of the reasons most home cooks turn to canned broth is that this just seems like too much trouble. Well, guess what: If you cook this stock for just one hour, you'll get a perfectly respectable result, certainly something far superior to what you can buy in a can.

5 pounds chicken bones (or parts, ideally thighs; wings and/or necks may be substituted)	1 small Spanish onion, cut into large dice
1 rib celery, cut on the bias into thirds	1 teaspoon dried thyme
1 large carrot, cut on the bias into thirds	1 tablespoon black peppercorns
	3 cloves garlic, crushed
3 bay leaves	10 cups water, or enough just to cover all ingredients

Place all ingredients in a stockpot. Bring to a boil over high heat, then lower the heat and simmer, uncovered, for 1 hour.

Using a fine-mesh strainer or wand, skim off any impurities that rise to the surface. Strain the contents of the pot through the fine-mesh strainer and discard the solids.

After the stock has cooled, remove any fat that has risen to the surface.

❖ **IF MAKING IN ADVANCE**, this stock can be kept in an airtight container in the refrigerator for up to 3 days or in the freezer for up to 2 months.

FOOD FOR THOUGHT—REMOVING FAT FROM STOCK: To help the fat separate, throw a few ice cubes into the finished stock as it cools. You can also refrigerate it, let the fat rise to the top, and simply scrape it off after it has congealed.

Basic Vegetable Stock

Makes about 1 quart

This is a very flexible recipe that may be adapted to include whatever appropriate ingredients you have on hand. If you have mushroom stems remaining from a recipe, by all means use them. If not, go ahead and make this stock without them. Similarly, use whatever fresh herbs are available. The key thing here is the vegetables themselves, so use fresh ones and don't stress out over the rest of it.

2 ribs celery, cut on the bias into thirds	Handful of mushroom stems (optional)
1/2 Spanish onion, cut into 1-inch dice	5 herb sprigs, such as thyme, bay,
5 cloves garlic, smashed	oregano, and/or parsley
1 tomato, halved, seeds squeezed out	1 tablespoon black peppercorns
and discarded	1 tablespoon coarse salt
1 medium leek, white part and about 1	
inch of green part, cut into 1-inch	
pieces	

Place all the ingredients in a stockpot and add enough water just to cover. Place the pot over high heat and bring the water to a boil. Lower the heat to a simmer and continue to simmer for 1 hour.

Strain the stock through a fine-mesh strainer and discard the solids.

❖ **IF MAKING IN ADVANCE,** this stock can be kept in an airtight container in the refrigerator for up to 3 days or in the freezer for up to 2 months.

SMOKED PORK JUS

❧

Makes about 1 quart

This intensely flavored jus forms the base of many of my favorite dishes. It has almost endless applications in soups and sauce bases.

2 ribs celery, cut on the bias into thirds	2 tablespoons black peppercorns
1 large carrot, cut on the bias into thirds	6 tablespoons tomato paste
1 small Spanish onion, cut into large dice	1 cup dry white wine
2 tablespoons olive oil	2 tablespoons white vinegar
3 cloves garlic, crushed	Pinch sugar
3 sprigs thyme	2 pounds smoked ham hocks
2 bay leaves	5–6 cups water
	1 1/2 teaspoons coarse salt

In a stockpot, cook the celery, carrot, and onion in the oil over medium heat until lightly caramelized, 6–7 minutes.

Add the garlic, thyme, bay leaves, and peppercorns and cook another 3–4 minutes.

Add the tomato paste and stir to coat the other ingredients with the paste. Cook 5–6 minutes, stirring often to prevent scorching.

Add the wine and vinegar, and season with sugar.

Add the ham hocks, 5 cups water, and salt.

Raise the heat to high, bring to a boil, then lower the heat and let simmer for 1 hour and 15 minutes. Taste. If the stock seems too intense, add another cup or so of water. Continue to simmer another 45 minutes. Strain, discard the solids, and reserve.

If desired, you can pick the meat from the hocks for use in pastas or soups.

❖ **IF MAKING IN ADVANCE,** this stock can be held in an airtight container in the refrigerator for up to 3 days or in the freezer for up to 2 months.

MUSHROOM STOCK

Makes 2 cups

If cooking a mushroom dish, it is worth the extra effort to make this stock. It will add a woodsy flavor throughout, especially if you bring out the big guns and include the optional dry porcini.

NOTE: To double the volume, simply double all the ingredients.

2 tablespoons canola, vegetable, or soy oil	1/3 cup dry white wine
2 ribs celery, coarsely chopped	1 tablespoon white vinegar
1 large Spanish onion, coarsely chopped	1 pound button mushrooms
1 large carrot, coarsely chopped	1 teaspoon coarse salt
2 cloves garlic, smashed	3–4 pieces dried porcini mushrooms (optional)
2 sprigs thyme	1 1/3 cups cold water
1 bay leaf	
1 tablespoon black peppercorns	

Heat the oil in a pot over medium heat.

Add the celery, onion, and carrot to the pot and cook for 1 minute.

Add the garlic, thyme, bay leaf, and peppercorns and cook for 2 minutes.

Add the wine, vinegar, and button mushrooms and stir. Add the salt and dried porcini mushrooms (if using). Cook, stirring occasionally, for 8–10 minutes, or until the mushrooms give off their liquid.

Add the water to the pot. Raise the heat to high, bring to a boil, then lower the heat and let the liquid simmer for 25–30 minutes. Taste and adjust the seasoning if necessary. Strain and discard the solids.

❖ **IF MAKING IN ADVANCE,** this stock can be kept in an airtight container in the refrigerator for up to 3 days or in the freezer for up to 2 months.

TOMATO BROTH

❧

Makes 3/4 cup

This tomato broth—really just a thinned and seasoned juice—is useful for dressings, quick soup bases, and (with clarification) a fast consommé.

20 ounces tomato juice diluted with 3/4 cup water 2 bay leaves 1 clove garlic, crushed 4 sprigs thyme	1 sprig tarragon Coarse salt Freshly ground black pepper 2 teaspoons sugar 1 tablespoon white vinegar

Place all the ingredients in a small saucepan and warm together over low heat for 10 minutes to allow the flavors to infuse the juice.

Strain, discard the solids, allow to cool, and reserve.

❖ **IF MAKING IN ADVANCE,** this stock can be kept in an airtight container in the refrigerator for up to 3 days or in the freezer for up to 2 months.

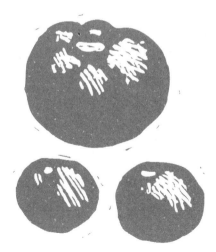

CLAM BROTH

Makes about 1 quart

I love using clam broth to perk up soups, vinaigrettes, and other dressings and sauces.

6 chowder clams	4 cloves garlic, smashed
1 cup dry white wine	

Put all the ingredients in a pot and add just enough water to cover the clams.

Cover the pot and place over high heat. Cook until the clams pop open, 7–8 minutes.

Strain the contents over a bowl. The liquid is your broth. Discard the clams or chop and freeze them for another use.

❖ IF MAKING IN ADVANCE, this stock can be kept in an airtight container in the refrigerator for up to 3 days or in the freezer for up to 2 months. (See Food for Thought.)

FOOD FOR THOUGHT—USE IT AS YOU NEED IT: A little of this broth goes a long way, so I freeze it in ice cube trays and pop 1 or 2 out to add an extra dimension to recipes at the last minute.

LOBSTER STOCK

❧

Makes 2¹/₂–3 cups

The unmistakable flavor of lobster is captured here and punched up with such complementary flavors as tarragon, tomato, and thyme. This is a perfect base for any lobster dish that calls for stock, and it also makes a sensational "Sauce Américaine" (see Option).

3 tablespoons olive oil	2 sprigs thyme
4 lobster bodies, tomalley and roe removed and reserved (see Food for Thought)	2 cloves garlic, thinly sliced
	¹/₃ cup dry white wine
	¹/₈ cup white vinegar
4 tablespoons tomato paste	Pinch sugar
2 plum tomatoes, coarsely chopped	1 tablespoon coarse salt
2 sprigs tarragon	1 tablespoon black peppercorns
2 sprigs flat-leaf parsley	

Heat the oil in a stockpot over high heat. Add the lobster bodies to the pot. (Be careful, they will spit.) Cook for 2–3 minutes.

Reduce the heat to low. Add the tomato paste and stir to coat the lobster with the paste. Cook for another 2–3 minutes.

In a small bowl, combine the reserved roe and tomalley with the tomatoes, tarragon, parsley, thyme, and garlic.

With the lobster still in the pot, add the white wine and vinegar. Add the tomato-herb mixture, the sugar, enough water to cover, and the salt and peppercorns.

Raise the heat to high and bring the liquid to a boil. Boil approximately 2 minutes, then lower to a simmer. Cook for 15 minutes. Taste. If the lobster flavor has not yet infused the broth, cook for another 5 minutes. (Pay special attention here. If overcooked, lobster stock can take on an unpleasant, murky flavor. As soon as you can taste the lobster, stop cooking.)

Strain over a bowl, discard the solids, and reserve.

❖ **IF MAKING IN ADVANCE,** this stock can be kept in an airtight container in the refrigerator for up to 3 days or in the freezer for up to 2 months.

FOOD FOR THOUGHT—LOBSTER BODIES: The recipe calls for lobster bodies, which refers to the portion remaining after the tail and claws have been removed from a cooked lobster. (Think of them as lobster "torsos," the section to which the legs are attached.) Many fish markets that sell lobster tails will sell you lobster bodies. If you are cooking your own lobster at home, this is a fine way to utilize all of its components. In either case, be sure to remove the outer shell (with the head attached) before beginning this recipe.

OPTION—LOBSTER SAUCE: To make Sauce Américaine, use the same recipe, replacing the water with heavy cream. I recommend this as a wonderful way to sauce a lobster you have just cooked. Simply remove the meat, cut it into 1-inch cubes, and reserve in a small bowl. Make Sauce Américaine and reheat the lobster meat in the sauce just before serving. Serve over egg noodles, couscous, rice, or Potato Puree (page 268).

ROASTED GARLIC JUS

This jus is rich enough to be used as a sauce and is especially delicious with a great many roast chicken recipes.

6 heads roasted garlic, cloves still in their skins (follow recipe on page 12, omitting the mashing step)	6 cups Basic Vegetable Stock (page 24) or water

Place the garlic and stock in a pot and bring to a boil over high heat. Lower the heat and let simmer for 35 minutes. Strain and reserve.

❖ **IF MAKING IN ADVANCE,** this stock can be kept in an airtight container in the refrigerator for up to 3 days or in the freezer for up to 2 months.

Dark Stocks

Yields $1^1/_2$–2 quarts

This is my basic recipe for dark stock bases. Follow the appropriate instructions to make veal, dark chicken, fish, and duck stock. (See Food for Thought for notes on where and how to obtain and cook the various bones called for in the different recipes.)

- 2 tablespoons olive oil
- 4 ribs celery, roughly chopped
- 1 Spanish onion, roughly chopped
- 3 medium to large carrots, roughly chopped (replace with leeks, white part only, for fish stock)
- 1 6-ounce can tomato paste (leave out if making fish stock)
- 1 teaspoon sugar
- 1 tablespoon black peppercorns
- 6 cloves garlic, smashed
- 3 sprigs thyme
- 1 bay leaf
- 2/3 cup white vinegar
- 2/3 bottle wine (red for veal and duck, red or white for chicken, white for fish)
- 1/2 teaspoon salt

Warm the oil in a stockpot over medium heat. Add the celery, onion, and carrots to the pot and cook for 6–7 minutes.

Add the tomato paste, sugar, peppercorns, garlic, thyme, bay leaf, vinegar, wine, and salt.

Raise the heat to high, bring to a boil, then lower the heat and let simmer for 10–15 minutes.

FOR VEAL STOCK

Add 5 pounds roasted veal bones to the pot. Add enough water to cover by 1 inch. Simmer for 3–4 hours. Strain.

FOR DUCK STOCK

Increase the wine to 1 1/2 bottles. Add 6 pounds duck necks to the pot. Add enough water to cover by 1 inch. Simmer for 3–4 hours. Strain.

FOR DARK CHICKEN STOCK

Add 6 pounds roasted chicken bones to the pot. Add enough water to cover by 1 inch. Simmer for 3–4 hours. Strain.

FOR FISH STOCK

Choose 5 pounds fish bones from non-fatty fish such as sole, bass, or halibut. (Be sure to avoid salmon bones in particular.) I don't use the head in stock-making, but if you would like to, be sure to remove the gills.

Soak the bones in cold water for 20 minutes, then add to the stockpot. Add enough water to cover by 1 inch and simmer for 1 hour, skimming impurities as they rise to the surface. Strain.

FOOD FOR THOUGHT: Veal, duck, and chicken bones are available from many butcher shops, and fish bones are sold by most mongers. Call ahead if possible and ask them to save the bones for you. Bones should be roasted in a 325°F oven until golden brown; chicken bones should be roasted until all the skin (if any) is rendered and crisp, 40–50 minutes. (Fish bones are almost never roasted.) I recommend heating the pan for 5 minutes before adding the bones. This will quicken the cooking and keep the bones from sticking and burning. It is also a good idea to stir with a wooden spoon every 5 minutes to help them cook evenly. One burned bone will tarnish an entire stock, so if one or two happen to turn, discard them. All stocks should be skimmed of fat and impurities that rise to the surface.

ONION STOCK

Makes 3 1/2 cups

The mighty, sweet flavor of caramelized onions makes this stock perfect for soup bases.

1 tablespoon unsalted butter	1 quart Basic Vegetable Stock
3 large Spanish onions, halved and thinly sliced	(page 24)

Warm the oil in a sauté pan over medium-high heat. Add the onions and cook over low heat until nicely browned and caramelized, 35–40 minutes.

Transfer the onions to a cutting board and roughly chop. Transfer to a pot and add the vegetable stock.

Bring to a boil over high heat, lower to a simmer, and cook for 30 minutes.

Strain the contents of the pot over a bowl, discard the solids, and reserve.

❖ **IF MAKING IN ADVANCE,** this stock can be kept in an airtight container in the refrigerator for up to 3 days or in the freezer for up to 2 months.

Starters and Salads

When I plan a menu, starters and salads play a very specific and challenging role—to both quell and pique one's hunger, satisfying the palate but leaving it and the appetite wanting more. For this reason my appetizers tend to be on the light side, comprising several small components such as bits of lobster, slivers of potatoes, or discs of fried pork. Often they are built on a base of greens to add some volume and texture without becoming too heavy.

What my starters and salads lack in bulk they make up for with an intensity and depth of flavor. In main-course compositions I usually separate the components to allow the diner to combine them according to taste. But in appetizers I believe that each bite should contain bits of everything for a memorable combination. For example, the Potato, Portobello, and Goat Cheese Timbale (page 40), the Roasted Beet Salad with Horseradish Cream and Balsamic Vinaigrette (page 51), and the Ragout of Mussels with White Beans and Wild Mushrooms (page 58) are best enjoyed when all ingredients are present in each bite.

Other Applications

Over the years the definition of what constitutes a salad or starter has changed dramatically. Because of the variety in this category today, many dishes that now serve this purpose can be adapted to other uses as well. So while this chapter offers close to twenty recipes intended primarily as the opening course of a meal, I encourage you to let your own flexibility guide you in determining how to best utilize them. With a little creativity you'll find that many of them can play roles other than as first courses. They can be reduced (or cut) into a smaller format for hors d'oeuvres (a good example is the Gravlax on a Chickpea Pancake with Caviar and Mustard Oil on page 69). Others can be expanded into hearty lunch dishes in their own right, such as the Pork Confit with Bitter Greens and Pickled Onions (page 42).

Choosing the Right Starter or Salad

If cooking a multicourse dinner, use appetizers to buy time. When guests arrive at your home, you don't want to leave them alone in the living room while you tend to the first course in the kitchen. Choose something simple to begin and have it ready to go before the first visitor shows up. Dishes such as Poached Mackerel with Crème Fraîche (page 38), Vegetable "Tart" (page 48), and Charred Lamb Salad with Lentils and Lemon-Cayenne Aioli (page 72) are prime examples of first courses that can be prepared well in advance.

One last thought in this vein: When serving a multicourse meal, soup is your friend—an option that can be made ahead of time, served hot or cold, and something that will bring variety to the meal. If you flip ahead two chapters, you will find about ten of them.

Salad Greens

Call me old-fashioned, but I still love an iceberg lettuce salad with lots of vinegar, olive oil, tomatoes, and onions. I am also crazy for any number of greens that are available in such great quantities today.

When mesclun mix showed up a few years ago, it was a wonderful development, but in most cases I now find the assortment a far inferior choice to a single, strategically selected green that adds to its context.

Familiarize yourself with the attributes of individual greens and make decisions based on what will surround and dress them in a salad. The salads in this chapter present an assortment of greens that run the gamut from the softest (Bibb lettuce and butter lettuce) to the most assertive (frisée and dandelion greens) and everything in between. Pay attention to the choice of greens in these recipes and apply the lessons learned there the next time you find yourself composing a salad of your own creation.

Poached Mackerel with Crème Fraîche

Serves 4

This is a perfect recipe for entertaining because it is best prepared a day in advance, and it takes only a few minutes. By pouring a hot and aromatic liquid over mackerel, the fish is poached ever so slightly. It is then refrigerated overnight, when it chills and takes on a lightly pickled flavor from the poaching liquid. As with a *nage* (a classic French preparation in which fish is gently poached in a cooking liquid to which aromatics and vegetables are added), the garnish is organically produced by the process as the vegetables, too, become pickled.

I came up with this recipe when I wanted something similar to pickled herring, which I love. The poaching base conjures up a vinegary sweetness with less work than pickling, and the mackerel's firm flesh and pronounced flavor lend themselves well to the acidic counterpoint.

Be sure to purchase super-fresh fish because it will be served cold the next day. Even with the best fish, however, this starter should be served and eaten the day after you make it. Don't save leftovers beyond this time.

4 4-ounce super-fresh mackerel fillets with the skin on (see Options)	1 teaspoon sugar
Coarse salt	1 small carrot, cut crosswise into 1/8-inch pieces
Freshly ground black pepper	2 shallots, thinly sliced
2 cups dry white wine such as sauvignon blanc, diluted with 3 cups cold water	1 tablespoon mustard seeds
	12 leaves flat-leaf parsley
2/3 cup white wine vinegar	1/4 cup crème fraîche
1 heaping tablespoon black peppercorns	

Score the mackerel's skin at 1-inch intervals. (See page 156 for tips on scoring fish.)

Season the fish on the skinless side with salt and pepper. Place the fillets skin side up in a small baking dish.

Pour the diluted wine into a pot and add the vinegar, 1 teaspoon salt, peppercorns, sugar, carrot, shallots, mustard seeds, and parsley. Bring to a boil over high heat.

Remove the pot from the heat and allow the boiling to stop.

Slowly pour the liquid over the fish.

Cover the baking dish tightly with plastic wrap, allow to cool, and refrigerate for at least 4 hours or preferably overnight.

WHEN READY TO PROCEED, remove the mackerel from the baking dish and divide among 4 chilled salad plates. (See Food for Thought.) Remove the carrot pieces and shallots from the baking dish and sprinkle around the fish. Top with a dollop of crème fraîche. Serve immediately while still very cold.

FOOD FOR THOUGHT—CHILLING PLATES: I rarely suggest going to the trouble of chilling or warming plates at home, but do yourself a favor and try it with this recipe. Having the plates very cold will help keep the mackerel at the ideal temperature when it reaches the table.

OPTIONS: If you want to make this more opulent, top each serving with an ounce of Sevruga caviar. Just about any firm-fleshed white fish, such as bluefish and halibut, can be substituted for the mackerel.

BEER AND WINE: Serve this with a Weissbier or a crisp pilsner, well chilled. A Chablis, pinot blanc, fumé blanc, or sauvignon blanc would also be a good accompaniment.

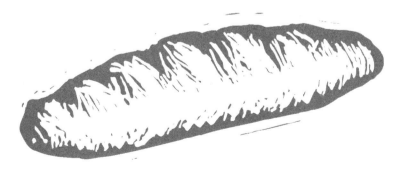

POTATO, PORTOBELLO, AND GOAT CHEESE TIMBALE

🌿

Serves 4

This appetizer, which can also be an effective side dish, brings together three enormously popular ingredients: potato, mushrooms, and cheese. Using a ring mold here isn't just for show; it offers a way to keep the ingredients together without a distracting element like puff pastry.

When making this recipe, take care to season and taste at every point along the way so that each component makes the greatest impact possible. Also be extra careful not to overcook the potatoes in the boiling water; you want them to hold their shape when cubed. Bear in mind that they will be warmed through in the oven and err on the side of undercooking them in the water.

SERVE THIS WITH roasted beets, cut into dice and tossed with Red Wine Vinaigrette (page 277). The combination makes for a satisfying starter.

Coarse salt

4 medium Yukon Gold potatoes
  (see Food for Thought)

1/2 cup plus 3 tablespoons extra-virgin
  olive oil

2 cloves garlic, smashed

1 teaspoon chopped fresh thyme leaves
  plus 4–8 sprigs for garnish
  (optional)

Freshly ground black pepper

2 large portobello mushroom caps,
  stems removed

1 tablespoon minced flat-leaf parsley
  (optional)

1 tablespoon minced chives (optional)

4 ounces good-quality fresh goat
  cheese, softened at room
  temperature

Preheat the oven to 375°F.

Bring a medium-sized pot of salted water to a boil over high heat.

Add the potatoes to the boiling water and cook until a sharp, thin-bladed knife is easily inserted in their centers, 10–12 minutes.

While the potatoes are cooking, make a seasoned oil: Pour 1/2 cup oil into a wide bowl. Add the garlic and chopped thyme leaves and season with salt and pepper.

Dip both sides of the mushroom caps in the seasoned oil. Gently shake off any excess oil and lay the mushrooms on a cookie sheet, rib side down.

Cook the mushrooms in the preheated oven until tender, 8–10 minutes.

Drain the potatoes and let them cool on a clean towel.

When the mushrooms are done, remove them from the oven, allow to cool, then cut into 1/2-inch cubes. Season to taste with salt and pepper.

When the potatoes are cool enough to handle, remove their skins (they should slip off easily with the aid of a paring knife) and cut into 1/2-inch dice.

Transfer the potatoes to a mixing bowl, dress with 3 tablespoons oil, sprinkle with the parsley and chives (if using), and season to taste with salt and pepper. Reserve.

Set four 3-inch ring molds on a cookie sheet. Spoon a 1/4-inch to 1/2-inch layer of potato dice into each mold. Make sure this layer is firmly packed, mashing the potatoes a bit if necessary.

Add a layer of mushrooms on top of the potatoes. Repeat with alternating layers until the timbale is about 11/2 inches high.

Top each timbale with 1 ounce of goat cheese and smooth it across the top using a metal spatula.

❖ IF MAKING IN ADVANCE, the timbales can be covered with plastic wrap and kept in the refrigerator for up to 24 hours. WHEN READY TO PROCEED, return the oven to 375°F and allow the timbales to come to room temperature.

Place the cookie sheet in the preheated oven and bake for 8–10 minutes.

Carefully transfer each timbale to the center of a small plate and remove the ring mold. Garnish with thyme sprigs if desired.

FOOD FOR THOUGHT—YUKON GOLD POTATOES: I love Yukon Gold potatoes because they have a firm yellow flesh and almost sweet flavor. For this reason they lend themselves to cold preparations (such as potato salad and potato chips). Though it may seem strange to do so, storing any kind of potato in soil, in a dark, cool basement or garage, helps preserve their natural flavor and character by approximating the conditions in which they were grown.

PORK CONFIT WITH BITTER GREENS AND PICKLED ONIONS

❧

Serves 4

The idea for this dish came from my love of Cuban sandwiches made with slow-roasted pork, *queso blanco* (sharp white cheese), and pickles. For my money that combination of flavors, textures, and temperatures (the pickles stay cold in the center of the sandwich) is sheer perfection. But, sadly, sandwiches are too casual for the dinner menu in the two- and three-star establishments where I've worked, and I have never had the pleasure of serving lunch. So I decided to do an end run and capture all the charms of a Cuban sandwich in an appetizer. This recipe takes a bit of work, but if you store it properly, the pork component will last up to five days. During that time you can use it in a variety of guises, such as salads and sandwiches.

By the way, sandwiches are *not* too casual for this book. There is a whole chapter of them coming up, and my recipe for an actual Cubano is featured on page 86.

Be sure to handle the pork discs very carefully when making this recipe because the heat will loosen their gelatinous quality and leave them quite fragile. Also, don't skimp on the cornichons and pickled onion—you want to be sure to have their sharp contrast in every bite. Finally, if you have the time, chill the pork *torchon* overnight to allow it to set as well as possible. (And see Food for Thought for more about the *torchon.*)

PORK BRAISING LIQUID

2 tablespoons canola oil

1/2 large Spanish onion, coarsely chopped

3 ribs celery, coarsely chopped

2 small carrots, coarsely chopped

2/3 cup tomato paste

1/2 bottle dry white wine

1/4 cup white wine vinegar

2 tablespoons black peppercorns

1 head garlic, halved

2 bay leaves, preferably fresh

5 sprigs thyme

2 1/2 cups Veal Stock (page 32) or canned low-sodium beef broth

Coarse salt

1/2 teaspoon sugar, or more to taste

Warm the oil in a medium-sized ovenproof pot over medium-high heat. (Be sure you have a cover for the pot.)

Add the onion, celery, and carrots to the pot and sweat them until they begin to caramelize, 8–10 minutes. Lower the heat and add the tomato paste. Stir to coat the vegetables with the paste and cook over low heat for 5–6 minutes, stirring frequently. Add the wine, vinegar, peppercorns, garlic, bay leaves, and thyme. Raise the heat to high, bring to a boil, and cook for 1 minute. Add the stock, bring to a boil, and season to taste with salt and, if it tastes bitter, sugar. Lower the heat to bring the liquid to a simmer.

❖ **IF MAKING IN ADVANCE,** the pork braising liquid can be cooled, tightly covered, and stored in the refrigerator for up to 3 days. (Do not freeze it because the vegetables won't survive well.) **WHEN READY TO PROCEED,** bring to a simmer in a medium-sized ovenproof pot.

PORK AND CHEESE *TORCHON*	Garlic powder
1 rack baby-back ribs (about	2 ounces aged white cheddar or
3 1/2 pounds)	Parmesan cheese, coarsely grated
Coarse salt	(about 1/2 cup)
Freshly ground black pepper	3 teaspoons powdered gelatin

Preheat the oven to 325°F.

Season the ribs generously with salt, pepper, and a sprinkling of garlic powder.

Place the ribs on a cookie sheet and cook in the preheated oven for 10 minutes, just to take the rawness out of them.

Remove the ribs from the oven and transfer to the simmering braising liquid. (Do not turn off the oven.) Cover the pot, transfer it to the oven, and cook for 2 hours, or until the meat is falling off the bones.

Carefully remove the ribs from the braising liquid. Reserve them and any meat that has fallen off the bones.

Strain the braising liquid through a fine-mesh strainer set over a bowl. Discard the solids and reserve the liquid. Allow the ribs to cool until they can be handled.

Using your fingers, separate the meat from the bones, discarding the bones as you work and accumulating the meat in a large stainless steel bowl.

Sprinkle the meat with the cheese.

In a small stainless steel bowl, dissolve the powdered gelatin in 1/2 cup strained braising liquid.

Pour the gelatin mixture over the meat and cheese. Stir to incorporate thoroughly, and adjust the seasoning if necessary. (Be careful here. After you taste it, you may be tempted to wolf down the whole thing.) Save any remaining braising liquid for another use such as short ribs or lamb shanks. Refrigerate for up to 3 days or freeze for up to 1 month.

Prepare a bowl of ice water and set it aside.

On a clean surface, lay a 10-inch length of plastic wrap, the shorter edge facing you.

Place a tight cylinder of pork about 6 inches long and about the same diameter as a broomstick about 1 inch from the front of the plastic wrap. Rolling away from you, encase the meat tightly and cut off the excess plastic wrap on either end of the pork.

Lay out another 10-inch sheet of plastic wrap, again with the short edge facing you. Lay the wrapped pork cylinder about 1 inch from the front and roll away from you to encase it tightly. This time don't trim the ends but twist them over and over until they seem incapable of coming undone.

Repeat the 2 preceding steps with the remaining pork.

Immerse the pork "sausages" in the ice water to cool through, then remove and transfer to the refrigerator. Allow to chill at least 4 hours or preferably overnight. They can be refrigerated for as long as 5 days.

POTATOES AND ASSEMBLY

4 small (4–5 ounces each)
    Yukon Gold potatoes
Coarse salt
1/4 cup dry bread crumbs
2 tablespoons Dijon mustard
1 tablespoon olive oil

4 cups loosely packed sturdy greens,
    such as frisée or dandelion greens
1/4 cup Creamy Mustard Vinaigrette
    (page 277)
12 cornichons, or more to taste, thinly
    sliced lengthwise

Remove the pork "sausages" from the refrigerator and cut them into 1-inch-thick discs.

Place the potatoes in a pot of salted water and bring to a boil over high heat. Cook until the potatoes are tender when pierced with the tip of a sharp, thin-bladed knife, about 15 minutes.

Drain the potatoes and, when cool enough to handle, cut into 1/2-inch-thick rounds (4 rounds per potato).

Spread the bread crumbs on a plate.

Cover 1 side of each pork disc with Dijon mustard and press that side into the bread crumbs to coat.

Pour the oil into an 8- to 10-inch nonstick pan and warm over high heat about 30 seconds.

Gently place the pork discs in the pan, bread crumb side down, with some space between discs to allow for even heating. Cook gently, moving the pan from side to side ever so slightly, for 20–30 seconds, until the bread crumbs are golden brown.

In a small mixing bowl, toss the greens and vinaigrette.

In the center of each of 4 salad plates, mound one-fourth of the greens. Place 4 potato rounds at equal intervals around the greens and top each round with a warmed pork disc. Scatter the cornichons around the plate.

FOOD FOR THOUGHT—WHAT IS A *TORCHON*? The word refers to a French technique in which foie gras, forcemeats, and other items are wrapped in cheesecloth in a cylindrical form and poached. I use plastic wrap, which is less porous than cheesecloth, to encase a product that has already been cooked. In the original, the cheesecloth allows fat to drain from the foie gras. Here, the plastic wrap keeps everything in. The technique is used in this recipe to maintain a desired shape.

OPTIONS: Go back to the roots of this recipe and use the pork *torchon* in a sandwich.

Salad of Roasted Mushrooms, Parmesan Cheese, and Roasted Garlic Vinaigrette

Serves 4

This recipe is presented here as a starter, but it makes for a very satisfying small meal as well. It is open-ended enough that you can expand on it with full-flavored accompaniments such as Roasted Garlic Puree (page 12), toasted sourdough croutons, smoked chicken, or duck confit. To create the greatest contrast of flavors, let the mushrooms roast in the oven until they are nicely done and crispy around the edges.

ROASTED WILD MUSHROOMS	
1/2 cup olive oil	Freshly ground black pepper
1 clove garlic, smashed	12 ounces assorted wild mushrooms,
2 sprigs thyme	such as oysters, chanterelles,
Coarse salt	or shiitakes, stems trimmed

Preheat the oven to 350°F.

Place the oil, garlic, and thyme in a small mixing bowl and season with salt and pepper. Dip the mushrooms in the oil, shake off any excess, and place on a cookie sheet. Roast in the preheated oven until golden brown and starting to crisp around the edges, 15–18 minutes. Remove from the oven, cover with foil to keep warm, and set aside.

ROASTED GARLIC VINAIGRETTE	
4 tablespoons Roasted Garlic	1 tablespoon fresh lemon juice
Mayonnaise (page 280) thinned	2 tablespoons grated Parmesan cheese
with 2 tablespoons warm water	Coarse salt
	Freshly ground black pepper

Place the mayonnaise, lemon juice, and cheese in a small mixing bowl. Stir to blend. Season with salt and pepper.

ASSEMBLY	**Freshly ground black pepper**
4 cups water	**4 eggs**
1 tablespoon white vinegar	**16 Parmigiano-Reggiano cheese shards,**
Coarse salt	**cut with a vegetable slicer**
1 head frisée lettuce	

Bring the water, vinegar, and a pinch of salt to a gentle simmer in a pot set over high heat.

In a mixing bowl, toss the frisee lettuce with all but 4 tablespoons of the vinaigrette. Season with salt and pepper.

Form a nest of dressed frisee in the center of each of 4 salad plates.

Crack the eggs, 1 at a time, onto a small plate and carefully slide them into the simmering water. Once the eggs are firm and white, 2–3 minutes, gently remove with a slotted spoon, allowing excess water to drain.

Place a poached egg on top of each frisée nest, and distribute the mushrooms evenly around the perimeter of each plate. Drizzle the remaining vinaigrette over the mushrooms and lean 4 cheese shards against each frisee nest.

OPTION: You can leave out the poached eggs, and this salad will still be delicious.

WINE: This is a very rich salad that I love serving with an inexpensive Chianti, though it would be even more delicious with a Barolo or Barbaresco.

FOOD FOR THOUGHT—PARMESAN CHEESE RINDS: Use these rinds to add flavor to soups; or save them in the refrigerator, wrapped tightly in plastic, and make a Parmesan stock by placing in the bottom of a pot 1/2 Spanish onion and 2 ribs of celery (all coarsely chopped), along with 2 smashed garlic cloves. Place 1 pound of cheese rinds (from 5 or 6 rinds) on top of the vegetables (to keep them from sticking to the bottom). Cover by 2 inches with a mixture of Chicken Stock (page 23) and water. Simmer for 1 hour, then strain. Use this as a base in soup recipes or as a simple broth to accompany ravioli and other filled pastas.

VEGETABLE "TART"

The vegetables in this recipe flourish in the late summer, but the long, slow cooking method will bring out the best in them any time of year. Caramelized vegetables are practically fused together for an intense flavor. The preparation of each layer is important, so take great care to slice each vegetable evenly and to season them uniformly.

Although this may be eaten the day you prepare it, it is worth planning ahead and enjoying it the day after, when the flavors are more intense and concentrated.

SERVE THIS as an accompaniment to grilled leg of lamb or grilled chicken.

---

1 tablespoon unsalted butter
3 Spanish onions, halved and thinly
 sliced
Pinch sugar
1 medium eggplant, peeled and very
 thinly sliced
1 teaspoon coarse salt, or more to taste
1/2 cup olive oil
5 cloves garlic, thinly sliced

1 teaspoon fresh thyme leaves
Freshly ground black pepper
2 medium zucchini, ends removed and
 sliced thinly lengthwise
3–4 large, very ripe beefsteak tomatoes,
 thinly sliced, placed in a bowl and
 tossed with 1 teaspoon coarse salt
 and 1/2 teaspoon sugar

Place the butter and onions in a sauté pan over medium-high heat. Add the sugar to the pan and cook, stirring often, until the onions are deeply caramelized and sweet, 35–40 minutes.

Meanwhile, sprinkle the eggplant slices with the salt and set in a colander in the sink for 30 minutes to extract as much moisture as possible.

Pour the oil into a saucepan. Add the garlic and thyme, and cook over low heat until the garlic is tender, 8–10 minutes. Remove from the heat and reserve.

Rinse the eggplant slices quickly with cold water, pat dry, and reserve.

Preheat the oven to 300°F.

When cool enough to handle, transfer the onions to a clean, dry cutting board and chop them coarsely.

Place the chopped onions on the bottom of a 9-inch ovenproof glass pie dish and press down to form an even layer about 1/4 inch deep.

Lay the eggplant slices over the onions, forming as even a layer as possible. The best way to do this is to form a circle of slightly overlapping slices around the perimeter of the dish and then lay 1 or 2 slices in the center to completely cover the onions.

Season the eggplant slices lightly but evenly with salt and pepper, and drizzle about 1 tablespoon garlic-thyme oil over them.

Repeat with a layer of zucchini slices on top of the eggplant.

PESTO

Makes about 1/2 cup

This is a classic pesto recipe that can be used on sandwiches or to top dishes such as this Vegetable "Tart."

2 cups tightly packed fresh basil
    leaves
1/2 cup pine nuts, toasted and cooled
1/4 cup grated Parmesan cheese

1 large clove garlic, cut into
    thick slices
1/2 cup olive oil
Coarse salt
Freshly ground black pepper

Place all the ingredients in a blender and puree until a thick paste is formed. If necessary, scrape down the sides and blend again to ensure a consistent texture. Season with salt and pepper, and blend a final time.

❖ **IF MAKING IN ADVANCE**, pesto will last up to 1 week in the refrigerator. Transfer to a glass or plastic container with a firm-fitting lid, cover with 1/8 inch of olive oil to help preserve color, and refrigerate. You can also freeze it for up to 3 weeks, but be sure to use a plastic container, not glass.

MOUSSELINE OF GOAT CHEESE

✿

Makes about 1/2 cup

3 ounces fresh imported goat cheese,
   at room temperature
1 ounce cream cheese, at room
   temperature
1/2 clove garlic, finely minced

1 teaspoon fresh thyme leaves
Few grinds of fresh black pepper
2 tablespoons excellent quality
   extra-virgin olive oil
3 tablespoons heavy cream

Place all the ingredients in the bowl of a standing mixer and whip until fluffy, 1–2 minutes.

❖ **IF MAKING IN ADVANCE,** the mousseline can be refrigerated for up to 2 days. **WHEN READY TO PROCEED,** allow to come to room temperature before using.

Using a slotted spoon, transfer the tomatoes to a cutting board. Chop them roughly, drain off any liquid, and form them into a layer over the zucchini. Pat down the tomatoes around the edge of the pie dish.

Place the pie dish in the preheated oven and cook for 4 hours. If the tomatoes begin to color, lower the temperature by 25 degrees. Remove the pie dish from the oven and let cool.

You can serve this dish immediately after it has cooled, but it is better to cover the cooled tart with plastic wrap, place some cans or other weights on top, and refrigerate overnight. The next day, allow to come to room temperature, drain off any liquid, and reheat in a 300° oven for 12–15 minutes or in a microwave on high for 2–3 minutes.

Cut into wedges and serve (see Food for Thought).

FOOD FOR THOUGHT—CUTTING TARTS: To keep the layers from pulling apart, use a very sharp chef's knife (rather than, say, a serrated knife) to cut this tart into portions.

OPTION: Top this tart with Pesto or a Mousseline of Goat Cheese (see sidebars).

ROASTED BEET SALAD WITH HORSERADISH CREAM AND BALSAMIC VINAIGRETTE

Serves 4

This is a visually arresting first course that is deceptively simple to prepare, yet makes quite an impact at the table.

BALSAMIC VINAIGRETTE
3 tablespoons balsamic vinegar
  (see Food for Thought)
3 shallots, minced

1 tablespoon minced flat-leaf parsley
1/2 cup olive oil
Coarse salt
Freshly ground black pepper

In a mixing bowl, whisk together the vinegar, shallots, parsley, and oil. Season with salt and pepper.

ROASTED BEETS
4 large red beets, well washed and
  root end trimmed

4 tablespoons extra-virgin olive oil
4 sprigs thyme
4 sprigs rosemary

Preheat the oven to 350°F.

Rub the beets with the oil.

Cut 4 pieces (about 8 × 8 inches) of aluminum foil and place 1 sprig thyme and 1 sprig rosemary in the center of each one.

Place 1 beet on top of the herbs in the center of each piece of foil, gather up the edges, and encase the beets. (The beets give off a lot of liquid when cooked, and this is a much easier and safer way to handle them than sealing them in 1 large package.)

Place the beets in the oven and roast until tender but still somewhat resilient, 35–40 minutes. (Poke a metal skewer or paring knife right through the foil to test.)

Remove the beets from the oven, unwrap them, and set aside to cool.

When the beets are cool enough to handle, remove the skins using kitchen gloves or paper towels to keep from staining your hands.

Cut 1/2 inch off the root end of each beet so the beet can stand on its end. Lay the beet on its side and hold it in place at the top and bottom with the thumb and forefinger of one hand. Use a sharp knife to cut it crosswise into 1/2-inch slices, keeping the slices pressed together as you work. As you finish slicing each beet, stand it up on its end.

Carefully transfer the beets to a baking dish and fan each one out so that its slices overlap. Drizzle with the balsamic vinaigrette and let marinate for 30 minutes.

HORSERADISH CRÈME FRAÎCHE	1/2 cup crème fraîche
2 tablespoons freshly grated white or	Coarse salt
red horseradish	Freshly ground black pepper

In a mixing bowl, gently stir the horseradish and crème fraîche together. Season with salt and pepper.

ASSEMBLY	Coarse salt
2 bunches baby arugula	Freshly ground black pepper
2 tablespoons extra-virgin olive oil	

"Reassemble" 1 beet, standing it up on its end, in the center of each of 4 salad plates. (You'll be surprised at how easy this is; the texture of the beets and the moisture of the vinaigrette will hold them together.)

In a mixing bowl, dress the arugula with the oil and season with salt and pepper.

To serve, on each of 4 salad plates lay some arugula around 1 beet in a tight concentric circle. Drizzle with the horseradish crème fraîche and spoon any remaining vinaigrette around the plate.

FOOD FOR THOUGHT—BALSAMIC VINEGAR: For this recipe an inexpensive balsamic vinegar will work well. To replicate the sweet viscous quality of more expensive balsamic vinegar, combine 1 cup balsamic vinegar and 1 tablespoon honey in a small pot, stir to incorporate thoroughly, and over medium-high heat reduce by one-half to two-thirds (depending on the thickness and intensity of flavor you desire).

SALMON "CONFIT" WITH CRÈME FRAÎCHE

🌿

Serves 6

In this recipe, salmon is seasoned with salt, pepper, garlic powder, and dill, and cooked in lukewarm oil. This technique helps the flavor of the spices penetrate the fish and yields a silky texture unlike any salmon preparation you've ever experienced.

Although it is often possible to avoid using a thermometer to control the heat of cooking oil (see page 102 for an example), you should use one here to avoid frying the fish.

1 12-ounce piece and 1 1-ounce piece sushi-grade (best and freshest available) skinless, boneless salmon, at room temperature	4 tablespoons coarsely chopped fresh dill
	4 cups canola oil
Coarse salt	1 bunch arugula, stems discarded
Freshly ground black pepper	2 tablespoons fresh lemon juice
Garlic powder	3 tablespoons crème fraîche, seasoned lightly with salt and pepper

Lightly coat the salmon on both sides with salt, pepper, and garlic powder, then sprinkle the dill on both sides. Press the seasoning into the fish with your fingers.

Warm the oil in a small pot set over medium heat to a temperature of 95°F.

Remove the pot from the heat and set it on a heatproof surface. Let rest for 1 minute.

Dip the 1-ounce piece of salmon into the oil to ensure that it doesn't color, then gently lower the 12-ounce piece into the pot. (If the test piece does color, wait another minute before lowering the larger piece.)

Cook the salmon for 30–35 minutes, or until the fish begins to flake when touched gently with a spatula.

Remove the salmon from the oil very carefully using a spatula or, if necessary, 2 spatulas to keep it intact. Set the salmon gently on a clean, dry cutting board and separate it into 6 pieces. (It will flake apart easily, without the aid of a knife.)

In a mixing bowl, toss the arugula with the lemon juice and season with pepper.

Pile some arugula in the center of each of 6 appetizer plates. Place a salmon portion on top of the arugula. Drizzle some crème fraîche over each piece of salmon. Serve warm.

OPTION: Boiled Yukon Gold or Red Bliss potatoes, with the skin on, make an ideal foil for the rich quality of the salmon. Use a fork to mash a few potatoes in the center of each plate and serve the salmon confit and arugula on top.

FOOD FOR THOUGHT—CONFIT: If you're wondering why the word *confit* is surrounded by quotation marks in the name of this recipe, it is because this isn't a classic application of the technique. Confit refers to the cooking method by which a meat (usually duck or goose legs) is marinated overnight in a mixture of salt, peppercorns, garlic, and herbs, then cooked slowly in its own fat. The confit meat is then stored in the fat, often for many months. The technique was a way to preserve foods in the olden days and is still used today for the intensity of the result.

WINE: To cut the fattiness of the salmon, serve this with a crisp fumé blanc or a nice oaky chardonnay.

PANZANELLA

❧

Serves 6

O ne of my favorite things about *panzanella* is that it makes day-old bread a prized possession because the crustiness keeps it from getting too soggy when drenched with dressing. Another thing I love about it is how much flavor can be had with so few ingredients. (It is a powerful tribute to the wonders of vinegar.) Let the tomatoes marinate in the vinaigrette for the full thirty minutes to really perk up the flavors.

---

3 medium tomatoes (red, yellow, or a combination), cut into 1-inch dice

1 cup Red Wine Vinaigrette (page 277) or less, to taste

Coarse salt

Freshly ground black pepper

1/2 Spanish onion, cut into 1/4-inch dice

1 clove garlic, minced

1/2 loaf Italian or French-style bread, 1 to 3 days old, cut into 1-inch cubes (if using fresh bread, toast it and let it cool)

In a mixing bowl, toss the tomatoes with about half of the vinaigrette. Season with salt and pepper and set aside for 30 minutes to allow the flavors to meld.

Add the onion, garlic, and bread cubes, and toss well. Taste and adjust the seasoning, and if necessary, add more vinaigrette. Let sit for 15–20 minutes to develop the flavors but do not refrigerate.

Serve at room temperature.

OPTION: For a more formal presentation and more complex taste sensation, divide the bread salad among ring molds (3 inches wide and 2 inches deep) in the center of 6 chilled salad plates. Press down to ensure it holds the shape when the molds are removed. Use your index finger to create a small well in the center of the molded bread salad and insert a few leaves of salad greens (such as arugula or chicory) so they stand up. Carefully unmold. Top with shaved or grated aged goat cheese. Drizzle any remaining vinaigrette around the plates.

LOBSTER SALAD WITH BUTTER LETTUCE, HARICOTS VERTS, AND CREAMY MUSTARD VINAIGRETTE

Serves 4

This is a simple salad that depends on the contrast between the creamy vinaigrette and the lobster. When preparing the vinaigrette, taste some on a piece of cooked, cooled lobster to be sure you are creating the effect you desire. If you double the ingredients, this becomes a substantial main-course affair.

BOILED LOBSTERS	1 lobster (1 pound)
Coarse salt	

Have an ice water bath ready.

Bring a large pot of salted water to a boil.

Carefully drop the lobster in the pot, cover, and cook over full heat for 5 minutes.

Turn off the heat and let the lobster sit in the covered pot for an additional minute. (See Food for Thought.)

Remove the lobster from the pot and submerge it in the ice water until chilled completely.

Remove the lobster meat from the body and claws and cut into 1-inch dice. Reserve.

❖ **IF MAKING IN ADVANCE,** the diced lobster meat may be covered tightly with plastic wrap and refrigerated for up to 24 hours. **WHEN READY TO PROCEED,** allow to come to room temperature.

HARICOTS VERTS	5–6 ounces haricots verts or fresh green
Coarse salt	beans, trimmed

Have an ice water bath ready.

Bring a small pot of salted water to a boil over high heat.

Add the haricots verts to the pot and blanch for 30–45 seconds.

Transfer the beans to the ice water to cool and set the color.

Drain the beans and cut into 1-inch pieces.

❖ **IF MAKING IN ADVANCE,** the beans may be covered and refrigerated for up to 24 hours. **WHEN READY TO PROCEED,** use the beans when they are cold and crisp, right from the refrigerator.

ASSEMBLY	1/2 tablespoon fresh lemon juice
1/3 cup Creamy Mustard Vinaigrette	Coarse salt
(page 277), plus more to taste	Freshly ground black pepper
1 tablespoon olive oil	1 head butter lettuce, leaves separated

In a small mixing bowl, toss the lobster pieces with the vinaigrette. Taste, and add more vinaigrette if desired. Reserve.

In another mixing bowl, toss the haricots verts with the oil and lemon, and season with salt and pepper.

To serve, lay a bed of butter lettuce on each of 4 salad plates. Spoon some dressed lobster over each one and scatter the haricots verts on top.

FOOD FOR THOUGHT—COOKING LOBSTERS: I let lobsters finish cooking off the heat to ensure thorough cooking while preventing the meat from toughening.

Before cracking a lobster claw to remove the meat, hold the claw with the points upward and open and close it a few times (like a pump). The excess juice will drain off. This will make removing the meat a much neater affair.

OPTION: If using female lobsters, puree some of the roe in the vinaigrette.

RAGOUT OF MUSSELS WITH WHITE BEANS
AND WILD MUSHROOMS

❧

Serves 6

This recipe embellishes the flavor of the ingredients by making a sauce that combines mushroom stock and the mussels' cooking liquid. The method for preparing the white beans may seem slow, but long cooking keeps them from rupturing and ensures that they cook evenly. When reheating shellfish (oysters, lobster, shrimp, mussels), it is important to keep the sauce from boiling, which would toughen the fish.

❖ **IF MAKING IN ADVANCE,** the white beans, mushrooms, and mussels can be cooled and refrigerated overnight in separate airtight containers.

GETTING ORGANIZED: If making this dish from scratch, just before serving sauté the mushrooms and steam the mussels while the beans are cooking.

WHITE BEANS

2/3 cup dry white beans

5 cups Chicken Stock (page 23)
  or water, or a combination

1 small carrot, cut on the bias into
  thirds

1 small Spanish onion, coarsely
  chopped

1 rib celery, cut on the bias into
  thirds

1 bay leaf

2 sprigs fresh thyme

1 tablespoon coarse salt

Freshly ground black pepper

Soak the beans in cold water overnight.

Drain the beans and transfer them to a small pot. Pour the chicken stock over the beans. Add the carrot, onion, celery, bay leaf, and thyme.

Bring the stock to a boil over medium-high heat, then lower the heat and allow the liquid to simmer until the beans are tender but still hold their shape, 1 1/2–2 hours. Add the salt and pepper in the final 10–15 minutes of cooking.

Remove the beans from the heat and strain.

When the beans are cool enough to touch, remove and discard the herbs and vegetables. Reserve.

MUSHROOMS	3 ounces oyster or shiitake mushrooms,
1¹/₂ tablespoons unsalted butter	quartered
³/₄ tablespoon olive oil	Coarse salt
¹/₂ clove garlic, minced	Freshly ground black pepper

Heat the butter, oil, and garlic in a sauté pan over medium-high heat.

Add the mushrooms to the pan, toss, and season with salt and pepper. Cook for about 30 seconds. Season again with salt and pepper. Remove from the heat and reserve.

MUSSELS	2 pounds mussels, scrubbed
¹/₂ cup dry white wine	and debearded
2 cloves garlic, smashed	(see Food for Thought)
¹/₂ small Spanish onion, coarsely	
chopped	

In a large pot over high heat, place the wine, garlic, onion, and mussels.

Cover and cook until the mussels open, about 5 minutes. Discard any mussels that do not open.

Strain the mussels through a fine-mesh strainer set over a bowl, and reserve the liquid. Remove the mussels from their shells.

❖ IF MAKING IN ADVANCE, store the mussels in their cooking liquid.

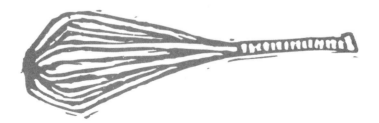

SAUCE AND ASSEMBLY
$^{1}/_{2}$ cup Mushroom Stock (page 26)
$^{1}/_{2}$ cup reserved mussel liquid
8 tablespoons (1 stick) unsalted butter,
    at room temperature, cut into
    8 pieces

Coarse salt
Freshly ground black pepper
2 tablespoons minced chives

In a small sauté pan, bring the stock and mussel liquid to a boil over high heat.

Lower the heat and whisk in the butter, 1 piece at a time, until all the butter is absorbed. Season with salt and pepper. Reserve.

❖ **IF MAKING IN ADVANCE**, this sauce can be kept covered and warm for up to 2 hours.

To assemble, gently reheat the sauce, stirring occasionally.

Add the beans and mushrooms to the sauce and heat through.

Add the mussels to the sauce last, cooking them just long enough to warm them, about 2 minutes. Taste and adjust the seasoning.

Using a slotted spoon, divide the mussels and vegetables among 6 bowls, then spoon the sauce over and around them. Sprinkle with the chives, season with a few grinds of black pepper, and serve immediately.

FOOD FOR THOUGHT—MUSSELS: Cultivated mussels are easier to clean and less gritty than their wild counterparts, but I find them less flavorful and so prefer to do the extra cleaning.

TOMATO SALAD WITH BLACK FOREST HAM
AND ROBIOLA CHEESE

Serves 4

This is a dish meant for late summer, when tomatoes are in all their glory. I have called it a starter here, but it could also be a main course at lunch. The key to this recipe's success is the Robiola, a sweet, creamy white cheese. You may need to visit a gourmet cheese shop to find Robiola. Just be careful not to buy Robiola Lombardia, which is a Taleggio-like cheese that won't work in this recipe. You want one of the cheeses that falls under the umbrella category of Robiola Piemonte from northern Italy.

8 ounces tomatoes, preferably Green
   Grape; leave small ones whole, and
   cut larger ones into small pieces
1/4 cup Sherry Vinaigrette (page 278)
8 ounces Robiola cheese
4 slices excellent-quality Black Forest
   ham, cut as thin as possible

3 ounces salad greens (about 2 cups
   loosely packed)
2 tablespoons minced shallot
2 tablespoons minced flat-leaf parsley

Place the tomatoes in a bowl and dress with the vinaigrette. Toss to coat and let marinate for 30 minutes. (See Food for Thought.)

Mound one-quarter of the cheese in the center of each of 4 salad plates.

Fold each ham slice lengthwise into thirds. Wrap 1 slice around the cheese in the center of each plate. Steady the ham as you place greens on top of the cheese.

Spoon some tomatoes around the outside of the ham collar. Drizzle with vinaigrette from the tomato bowl. Scatter the minced shallot and parsley around the plate.

OPTION: For a nice temperature contrast, grill the ham slices over high heat for 20–30 seconds just before making the salad.

FOOD FOR THOUGHT—WORKING WITH TOMATOES: Don't refrigerate the tomatoes after preparing them; it will mute the flavors.

Endive and Roquefort Salad with Lardons

Serves 4

This is a classic bistro dish that offers perfect contrasts of temperatures and textures. One of its charms is that it can be adapted to suit different tastes or what is available in your refrigerator and pantry. Some of my favorite variations include adding toasted walnuts warm from the oven (about a handful will accommodate four servings), thin slices of Granny Smith apple, or shaved red radish.

3 ounces bacon, cut into lardons (approximately 3/4 cup)	1 cup Sherry Vinaigrette (page 278)
4 large Belgian endives	2 tablespoons minced chives
4 ounces Roquefort cheese, crumbled (about 1 cup) (Stilton or Maytag Blue may be substituted)	2 tablespoons minced flat-leaf parsley
	Freshly ground black pepper

Cook the lardons in a sauté pan over medium-high heat until well done, about 6 minutes.

As the lardons are cooking, cut the endives in half lengthwise, and with the cut side down, slice into thin strips a bit wider than julienne.

On each of 4 plates create a square plank of endive slices. Sprinkle some cheese over each plank, then drizzle on some vinaigrette, chives, and parsley, using about half of each. Season generously with pepper. Lay another plank perpendicular to the first on top.

Place the lardons on a plate lined with paper towels to drain.

Distribute the lardons on top of each salad. Drizzle with the remaining vinaigrette, chives, and parsley. Season with pepper and serve.

FOOD FOR THOUGHT—BELGIAN ENDIVE: This herb preserves its white color because it is grown under a canvas cover, protecting it from the rays of the sun, which prevents photosynthesis.

GRILLED OCTOPUS WITH ROAST TOMATO COULIS AND GARLIC TOASTS

Serves 4

Octopus has a distinct taste that I love. Although it was once confined almost exclusively to Greek restaurants, today a great many Americans have come to adore it as much as I do. Here, braised octopus is marinated in an acidulated red wine solution that helps to further tenderize it before grilling.

Although most of the recipes in this book don't require much experience, this one does. It takes a bit of instinct to know when the octopus is done (cooking times can vary by as much as 30 minutes due to such factors as whether they are fresh or frozen and have thick or thin tentacles). If you like octopus and know your way around a grill, this is a sensational summer recipe.

MARINATED OCTOPUS
2 tablespoons olive oil
1 medium carrot, coarsely chopped
1 small Spanish onion, coarsely chopped
2 ribs celery, coarsely chopped
2 cups red wine
2/3 cup white vinegar
2 cups water
2 tablespoons coarse salt
1 teaspoon sugar

10 black peppercorns
1 bay leaf
3 sprigs thyme (optional)
1 fresh whole octopus (about 2 pounds), head removed
1/2 cup extra-virgin olive oil
1 tablespoon red wine vinegar
3 heaping tablespoons Chopped Roasted Tomatoes (page 13)
2 shallots, minced
1 tablespoon chopped flat-leaf parsley

Pour the olive oil into a pot. Add the carrot, onion, and celery, and sweat over medium-high heat for 2–3 minutes.

Add the wine and white vinegar to the pot and deglaze.

Add the water, salt, sugar, peppercorns, bay leaf, thyme (if using), and octopus to the pot. Raise the heat to high, bring to a boil, lower to a simmer, and cook for 1 1/2 hours.

Prepare a bowl of ice water and get a pair of tongs. To test for doneness, pull the octopus out of the cooking liquid and with a cold hand pinch the base of a tentacle. If it is tender enough for your fingers to meet, it is done.

Plunge the octopus into the ice bath.

Strain and reserve the braising liquid.

Once cooled, cut up the octopus. The center of the octopus (closest to the beak) is the most delicious part, so cut between the legs all the way up to the middle of the beak to make sure you waste none of it.

❖ **IF MAKING IN ADVANCE,** the octopus can be cooled, stored in an airtight container, and refrigerated for up to 3 days.

Create a marinade of 1 cup strained braising liquid, extra-virgin olive oil, red wine vinegar, roasted tomatoes, shallots, and parsley. Add the octopus to the bowl and marinate for 1–12 hours.

ROASTED TOMATO COULIS AND ASSEMBLY

6 tablespoons Chopped Roasted Tomatoes (page 13)
2 tablespoons tomato paste
2 tablespoons red wine vinegar
1 teaspoon red pepper flakes
Pinch sugar
1 teaspoon fresh thyme leaves
2/3 cup olive oil
1/3 cup hot tap water
Coarse salt

Place the tomatoes, tomato paste, vinegar, red pepper flakes, sugar, and thyme leaves in a blender.

Puree slowly, adding the oil in a thin stream to form an emulsion.

With the motor still running, add the water. Taste and season with salt if necessary. Reserve.

GARLIC TOASTS AND ASSEMBLY

1 French baguette, cut on the bias into 1-inch-thick slices
1 clove garlic, cut in half
4 cups loosely packed firm greens such as chicory
1/4 cup olive oil
Freshly ground black pepper

Rub the baguette slices on 1 side with the garlic. (See Food for Thought.) Preferably on the grill, toast with the garlic-rubbed side up, until crisp. Reserve.

Build a fire in an outdoor grill, letting the coals burn until covered with white ash. Remove the octopus from the marinade and grill for 15–20 seconds on each side, just to warm through. If you like it charred, leave it on the grill a bit longer.

In a small mixing bowl, toss the greens with the oil and season with pepper.

In the center of each of 4 plates, place a small nest of dressed greens. Pile a few octopus tentacles on top and spoon tomato coulis around. Set some garlic toasts around the perimeter. Serve immediately.

FOOD FOR THOUGHT—WORKING WITH GARLIC: A fork is a handy tool when scoring something as small as a garlic clove. Place a peeled clove on a fork and hold it up to score it with the tip of a paring knife. Then use the fork to manipulate the garlic.

FOOD FOR THOUGHT—TENTACLES: If you find them unappetizing, you can remove the skin and "suction cups" from the octopus's tentacles by pulling them off the cooked, cooled octopus under cold running water. But you'll be missing out on the impressive flavor they unleash when grilled, so I recommend keeping them.

FOOD FOR THOUGHT—THE POWER OF A CORK: Throwing a cork (such as one from a wine bottle) into the octopus's cooking liquid while it is braising is said to have tenderizing properties.

OPTION: When I serve this in a restaurant, I cut long slices of a baguette on the bias, rub them with a scored garlic clove, drizzle them with olive oil, toast them in the oven until golden, and then serve them as an accompaniment. Here you can grill the bread.

WINE: Enjoy this with a spicy Rioja.

Mussel Salad with Mâche, Artichokes, and Haricots Verts

Serves 6

In this salad the mussels' cooking liquid adds flavor to a homemade mayonnaise. Mâche, a delicate chicory with tongue-shaped leaves, provides a perfect nest in which to set the shelled mussels. Be careful not to overdress the mâche and take care when tossing it not to bruise the leaves.

HARICOTS VERTS	6 ounces haricots verts or fresh green
Coarse salt	beans, trimmed to uniform length

Prepare an ice water bath.

Bring a small pot of salted water to a boil over high heat. Add the haricots verts and blanch for 30 seconds.

Transfer the haricots verts to the ice water to stop the cooking and preserve their verdant color.

Drain the haricots verts, cut into thirds, and reserve.

❖ **IF MAKING IN ADVANCE**, the haricots verts may be covered and kept in the refrigerator for up to 24 hours. **WHEN READY TO PROCEED**, use them cool and crisp from the refrigerator.

ARTICHOKES	1 tablespoon all-purpose flour
Juice of 1 lemon plus 1/2 lemon	3 tablespoons coarse salt
6 artichokes	2 tablespoons extra-virgin olive oil

Put the juice of 1 lemon in a small bowl of water.

Trim the artichokes: Pull off the tough outer leaves. Use a heavy knife to remove the stem, if any, and then cut the choke just above the heart, about 1 1/2 inches from the stem end. Use a paring knife to trim away the excess until you get down to the yellow part, which is where the heart begins. Place the heart in the lemon water. Repeat with the other artichokes.

Place a quart of water in a pot and whisk in the flour and salt. Place the pot over medium-high heat and bring to a simmer.

Transfer the artichokes to the pot and cook at a simmer for 15–20 minutes, until a small knife goes right in.

Remove the artichokes and plunge them into the ice water. Remove the choke with a tablespoon or soup spoon.

Turn the hearts over and cut into 6 slivers. Drizzle with the oil and a squeeze of lemon.

STEAMED MUSSELS

1 cup dry white wine

4 cloves garlic, smashed

5 pounds mussels, scrubbed and debearded

In a large pot over high heat, place the wine, garlic, and mussels. Cover the pot and cook until the mussels open, about 5 minutes. Discard any mussels that do not open.

When cool enough to handle, remove the mussels from their shells and reserve. Strain and reserve the cooking liquid.

MUSSEL MAYONNAISE

2/3 cup Basic Mayonnaise (page 280)

2 tablespoons reserved mussel
   cooking liquid

1 heaping tablespoon Dijon mustard

Juice of 1/2 lemon

Pinch cayenne pepper

2 tablespoons minced shallot

Coarse salt

Freshly ground black pepper

In a small mixing bowl, whisk together the mayonnaise and mussel cooking liquid.

Taste and add a bit more liquid if necessary to really taste the mussel flavor.

Add the mustard, lemon juice, cayenne, and shallot. Season with salt and pepper.

ASSEMBLY	Freshly ground black pepper
6 bunches mâche	16 shards Parmesan cheese cut with
3 tablespoons extra-virgin olive oil	a vegetable peeler
Coarse salt	

In a small bowl, gently toss the mâche and haricots verts with the oil and season with salt and pepper.

To serve: Create a circle of artichoke slivers in the center of each of 6 salad plates. Place the mussels in the center. Spoon some dressed mâche and haricots verts on top of the mussels. Drizzle the mussel mayonnaise over the mâche and around the plate. Garnish with the Parmesan shards.

Gravlax on a Chickpea Pancake with Caviar and Mustard Oil

When a *New York Times* reporter visited my kitchen at Butterfield 81 to interview me for a gravlax story, he asked why I wasn't putting the usual amount of salt and sugar on the salmon. It is the same response I always get, and it points out how little we question tradition. The original method was used to preserve salmon, and far greater quantities of these ingredients were required. Today we need only as much as the desired flavor calls for.

This is a perfect make-ahead appetizer, and the unique method of tenderizing the salmon produces a luxurious silken texture with very little effort.

The chickpea pancake is based on the French technique for making *panisse,* a cake made from chickpea puree or cornmeal, which many people cut into batons and deep-fry.

GRAVLAX

1 2-pound fillet of salmon, pin bones removed

2 tablespoons vodka or aquavit

1/2 cup coarse salt

1/4 cup sugar

2 bay leaves, chopped

2 bunches dill, stems and all, minced

3 shallots, thinly sliced

1 tablespoon cracked black pepper

1 tablespoon caraway seeds, lightly toasted

1 tablespoon minced fresh tarragon

1 1/2 tablespoons green peppercorns

Place the salmon, skin side down, on a large sheet of plastic wrap and sprinkle it with the vodka or aquavit.

In a small bowl, combine the salt and sugar; sprinkle onto the flesh side of the salmon.

In the same small bowl, mix together the bay leaves, dill, shallots, pepper, caraway seeds, tarragon, and peppercorns. Cover the flesh side of the salmon with this mixture, making sure to coat it completely.

Cover the fish well with plastic wrap and sandwich it between two cookie sheets covered with plastic wrap (to prevent contamination). Place two 1-pound objects, such as canned tomatoes, on the top cookie sheet. Refrigerate with the weights in place for about 48 hours. (The weights are to quicken the penetration of salt and sugar and to compact the salmon, making it easier to slice.)

Unwrap the salmon and rinse off the coating. Dry it with paper towels.

❖ **IF MAKING IN ADVANCE,** the gravlax may be refrigerated for up to 3 days. **WHEN READY TO PROCEED,** slice the salmon as thin as possible on the bias. (See Food for Thought.) This recipe calls for 18 slices.

CHICKPEA PANCAKE

3 1/3 cups milk (low-fat, if preferred)

1/2 tablespoon unsalted butter, plus extra for greasing cookie sheet

1 small clove garlic, peeled and minced

4 ounces chickpea flour (available at Middle Eastern groceries and many health food stores)

2 ears corn, shucked and kernels cut off, or 2 cups frozen corn, defrosted

3 scallions, coarsely chopped

Coarse salt

Freshly ground black pepper

Combine the milk, butter, and garlic in a saucepan. Bring the mixture to a boil over high heat, then immediately lower the heat to a simmer.

Using a whisk, incorporate the chickpea flour into the mixture, taking care to eliminate all lumps. Once incorporated, stir the mixture vigorously and continuously using a rubber spatula until it attains a thick consistency, about 3–4 minutes. (The mixture scorches easily, so don't stop stirring.)

To finish, fold in the corn and scallions, and season to taste with salt and pepper.

Remove the pot from the heat and, using a spatula, transfer the mixture to a large cookie sheet.

Use the spatula to spread the mixture evenly over the surface of the cookie sheet to a thickness of 1/3 inch.

To achieve an even thickness, firmly press on the top with another cookie sheet of the same size that has been lightly greased on the bottom. (You're doing this so that the pancakes will brown evenly when heated later.)

Chill, covered with waxed or parchment paper, for 2–3 hours.

❖ **IF MAKING IN ADVANCE,** this can be prepared up to 2 days ahead of time and kept in the refrigerator, covered tightly with plastic wrap. **WHEN READY TO PROCEED,** take it directly from the refrigerator to the fryer.

MUSTARD OIL, CAVIAR, AND ASSEMBLY	3 ounces caviar (American sturgeon roe, salmon roe, or a combination)
1/4 cup mustard oil (available at most Middle Eastern groceries)	1 tablespoon chopped chives
1/2 cup extra-virgin olive oil	Canola oil, for frying
	8 tablespoons crème fraîche

In a mixing bowl, gently stir the mustard oil, olive oil, caviar, and chives together.

Fill a 1- or 2-quart pot with canola oil, 1-inch deep, and heat to 350°F.

Cut circular shapes 3 inches in diameter from the chickpea batter using a biscuit cutter—or use a knife to cut 3 by 3-inch squares.

Fry the circles in the preheated oil until golden, about 1 minute.

Remove the circles from the oil with a slotted spatula and pat dry on towels.

To serve: On each of 6 plates, top a chickpea pancake with 3 slices of gravlax and spoon the mustard oil–caviar sauce around the plate. Accompany with crème fraîche.

FOOD FOR THOUGHT—SLICING SALMON: If you find it difficult to slice the salmon on the bias, you can stand it up on your work surface and cut straight down on its side. It will be a slightly thicker cut but will still taste delicious.

OPTIONS: You may, of course, serve gravlax on its own, perhaps with some Creamy Mustard Vinaigrette (page 277) on the side. The chickpea pancakes also make wonderful serving vehicles for the Smoked Sturgeon (page 75).

CHARRED LAMB SALAD WITH LENTILS AND LEMON-CAYENNE AIOLI

Serves 4

This dish borrows the basic form of an Italian carpaccio, but the meat is well seasoned in a distinctly Moroccan way. The French-inspired lentil salad and lemon-cayenne aioli round out this multiethnic motif. If you have a squeeze bottle, put the mayonnaise in it to distribute perfect quantities and keep the dish nice and neat.

LENTIL SALAD

1 ounce bacon, cut into fine dice (about 1/4 cup) (place in freezer for 10 minutes before slicing to allow the bacon to firm up)

1/2 small Spanish onion, cut into small dice

1 small carrot, cut into small dice

1 rib celery, cut into small dice

1 tablespoon olive oil

1 cup French green lentils

2 1/4 cups Chicken Stock (page 23) (if using canned, use half water and half chicken stock)

1/2 tablespoon minced garlic

1/2 tablespoon chopped fresh thyme

1/2 tablespoon coarse salt, or more to taste

Freshly ground black pepper

3 tablespoons extra-virgin olive oil

2 tablespoons minced shallots

1 tablespoon minced flat-leaf parsley

In a heavy-bottomed pot, cook the bacon over medium heat until browned and some fat has rendered, about 5 minutes.

Add the onion, carrot, and celery to the pot and cook until tender, 3–4 minutes.

Add the olive oil and lentils, and stir to coat all ingredients evenly.

Raise the heat to high and add the stock, garlic, thyme, and salt. (If using homemade stock, you may want to increase the amount of salt slightly.) Season with pepper. Bring to a boil, lower to a simmer, and allow to simmer for about 1 hour, or until the lentils are tender.

Drain the lentils in a colander, then spread them out on a cookie sheet to cool. When the lentils are cool, transfer them to a mixing bowl and toss with the extra-virgin olive oil, shallots, and parsley. Adjust the seasoning and reserve.

CHARRED LAMB

2 tablespoons ground cumin

2 tablespoons ground coriander

4 tablespoons paprika

4 tablespoons garlic powder

1 tablespoon cayenne pepper

3 tablespoons coarse salt

1 tablespoon finely ground black pepper

1 tablespoon sugar

$1/2$ cup neutral oil, such as canola

1 boneless loin of lamb (about 1 pound), cut in half crosswise

2 cups loosely packed greens, such as arugula or mustard greens

2 tablespoons Red Wine Vinaigrette (page 277)

$1/2$ cup Lemon-Cayenne Aioli (page 282)

In a mixing bowl, combine the cumin, coriander, paprika, garlic powder, cayenne, salt, pepper, and sugar, and stir well. Add the oil and stir to make a paste.

Roll the lamb pieces in this mixture to coat them, then leave them in the bowl and let marinate in the refrigerator for at least 2 hours or preferably overnight.

The next several steps involve a very hot cast iron pan. Don't use any other type of pan for this recipe and be sure to wear a heavy oven mitt when working with it. Also allow the pan ample time (at least 45 minutes) to cool before attempting to clean it. Work on the back burner of your stove to keep a safe distance between you and the pan. (See Food for Thought.)

Heat a heavy-bottomed cast iron skillet over high heat for 5–6 minutes. (That is not a typo. Leave the pan on the flame for a long time to get it hot enough to blacken the lamb. The pan itself may begin to smoke. That's okay.)

Remove the lamb pieces from the marinade and shake off the excess.

With a pair of kitchen tongs, carefully place the lamb pieces in the pan. It will start throwing smoke immediately. Cook until each side is blackened, about 5–10 seconds per side. As each side is cooking, force the lamb against the pan a bit to really fuse the spices to the meat.

Set the lamb aside and allow to cool thoroughly.

Cover the lamb with plastic wrap and refrigerate until well chilled and firm.

❖ **IF MAKING IN ADVANCE,** the blackened lamb can be kept in the refrigerator for up to 2 days or frozen for up to 3 weeks, provided you use the *torchon* technique: On a clean, dry surface, lay out a 10-inch length of plastic wrap with the shorter edge facing you. Place the lamb loin section about 1 inch from the front of the plastic wrap. Rolling away from you, encase the meat in a tight roll, squeezing it into a sausage shape, and cut off the excess plastic wrap on either side of the lamb. Lay out another 10-inch sheet of plastic wrap, again with the short edge facing you. Lay the wrapped lamb cylinder about 1 inch from the end closest to you and roll away from you to encase it tightly. This time don't trim the ends but twist them over and over until they seem incapable of coming undone. **WHEN READY TO PROCEED,** allow to come to room temperature and slice by hand as thin as possible.

In a mixing bowl, dress the greens with the Red Wine Vinaigrette.

To serve: Mound some lentils in the center of each of 4 salad plates. Overlap slices of lamb around the perimeter of the lentils to form a circle. Place some dressed greens on top of the lentils and drizzle the lamb with the Lemon-Cayenne Aioli.

FOOD FOR THOUGHT—WHERE THERE'S SMOKE: If you have a smoke detector in or near your kitchen, turn it off before making this recipe and be sure to turn it back on when you're done.

SMOKED STURGEON WITH FRISÉE, LARDONS, AND POACHED EGG

Serves 4

This is one of my favorite signature dishes. The smokiness of the sturgeon and the comfort of the poached egg against the cool crunch of the greens with their vibrant mustard dressing makes this a complex, yet quick and easy-to-prepare starter. It is also a great lunch or brunch item.

This dish's success depends on temperature contrast. Have your ingredients well organized and work as quickly as possible to ensure that the components are ready at about the same time.

6 ounces excellent-quality double-smoked bacon, cut into 1/2-inch lardons (about 1 1/2 cups)

4 slices white bread

4 teaspoons Roasted Garlic Mayonnaise (page 281)

2 heads California frisée (very tender, small, yellow heads)

4 tablespoons Creamy Mustard Vinaigrette (page 277)

4 cups water

1 tablespoon white vinegar

Pinch coarse salt

4 eggs

6 ounces smoked sturgeon, thinly sliced (see Food for Thought)

Freshly ground black pepper

In a sauté pan over medium-high heat, cook the bacon until nicely browned and crisp, about 5 minutes.

Transfer the bacon to paper towels to drain, then return to the hot pan and cover to keep warm.

Using a 3-inch biscuit cutter, cut a round out of each slice of bread and toast the rounds in the toaster. Spread each with the garlic mayonnaise.

While the bread is toasting, in a mixing bowl, dress the frisée with the mustard vinaigrette.

Bring the water, vinegar, and salt to a gentle simmer in a pot set over high heat.

Crack the eggs, 1 at a time, onto a small plate and carefully slide them into the water.

Once the eggs are firm and white, 2–3 minutes, gently remove with a slotted spoon, allowing excess water to drain.

To serve: Place a crouton in the center of each of 4 salad plates and top with a poached egg. Drape slices of sturgeon over the warm eggs. Place the frisée on top of the sturgeon. Sprinkle lardons all around. Finish with a few grinds of pepper.

FOOD FOR THOUGHT—SMOKING YOUR OWN STURGEON: If you happen to own a cold smoker (a smoking device in which the heat source is away from the actual smoking vessel to prevent the heat from cooking the item being smoked), you can smoke your own sturgeon. Here is the recipe:

1 cup light brown sugar

1 cup soy sauce

Juice of 3 lemons

24 cracked black peppercorns

3 shallots, thinly sliced

2 cups coarse salt

1 pound very fresh skinless,
    boneless sturgeon fillet

Mix all the ingredients except the sturgeon in a bowl. Pour half of the mixture into a nonreactive (such as glass) vessel just large enough to hold the sturgeon. Lay the sturgeon in the vessel and pour the remaining mixture over it. Allow to marinate for 12–15 hours. Remove from the marinade, shake off the excess, and discard the marinade. Place the sturgeon in a cold smoker and smoke for 2$1/2$–3 hours, or until the sturgeon is very firm to the touch. Remove and cool on a rack, then transfer the rack to the refrigerator and chill. Once thoroughly chilled, wrap the sturgeon and keep refrigerated. This will keep for up to 2 weeks.

To serve, cut long, thin or $1/4$-inch pieces.

OYSTER STEW

❦

Serves 4

This recipe was inspired by the famous oyster pan roast at Grand Central Station's Oyster Bar, which I've always loved. What I have tried to do here is re-create the qualities of that dish in a different context. For this recipe it is worth splurging on beautiful fresh oysters such as Bluepoint or Wellfleet, and be very careful not to overcook them.

---

1 Idaho potato, cut into 1/2-inch dice
3/4 cup Chicken Stock (page 23)
   or water
1 clove garlic, crushed
Coarse salt
Freshly ground black pepper
4 slices white bread, toasted
1 1/2 tablespoons Curry Oil (page 247)
6 ounces bacon, finely diced
   (about 1 1/2 cups)
1/2 cup dry white wine

12 shucked oysters reserved in their
   own juice (ask your fishmonger to
   do this; see Food for Thought)
2/3 cup milk
2/3 cup heavy cream
1 tablespoon unsalted butter
Juice of 1/2 lemon, or more to taste
3 tablespoons Chopped Roasted
   Tomatoes (page 13)
3–4 ounces black trumpet mushrooms,
   cooked (optional; see Food for
   Thought)
2 tablespoons minced chives

Place the potatoes in a sauté pan and cover with stock.

Add the garlic to the pan and season with salt and pepper.

Bring the stock to a simmer over moderate heat and cook until the potatoes are tender, 6–7 minutes.

Strain the potatoes and spread them out on a clean, dry surface to cool.

Using a biscuit cutter or the rim of a small bowl, cut 3-inch rounds out of the bread. Toast the rounds and spread with the Curry Oil. Reserve.

Cook the bacon in a sauté pan over low heat.

Remove the bacon with a slotted spoon and transfer to paper towels to drain.

Remove all the fat from the bacon pan, then deglaze with the wine. Add the liquid from the shucked oysters to the pan and scrape up any particles from the bottom of the pan with a wooden spoon.

Raise the heat to high, add the milk and cream, and bring to a boil. Swirl in the butter and season with salt and pepper to taste.

Strain the liquid into a small saucepan. Add the lemon and taste. If you can't discern its distinct flavor, add a bit more until you can.

Add the bacon, potatoes, tomatoes, and mushrooms (if using), and warm over medium heat. Add the oysters and swirl them in the sauce until just warmed through. Do not allow to boil at any point.

Place a curried crouton in the center of each of 4 bowls. Using a slotted spoon, remove the oysters from the stew and pile 3 oysters on top of each crouton. Spoon the stew around the oysters.

FOOD FOR THOUGHT—BLACK TRUMPET MUSHROOMS: If using black trumpet mushrooms in this dish, prepare them in the following manner: Clean them well, snipping off part of the stem and agitating in cold water if necessary. Sauté in 1 tablespoon butter plus 1 teaspoon olive oil and 1/2 clove garlic, minced, for 1–2 minutes. Season well with salt and pepper. They will give off a lot of liquid even in this brief time. Remove them with a slotted spoon and set aside.

FOOD FOR THOUGHT—CHOOSING OYSTERS: When selecting oysters, each one should feel heavy in your hand. If you tap two of them together, they should produce a very dull thud. If they sound hollow, pass them by; this is an indication that they may not be at the peak of freshness.

MARINATED SEAFOOD SALAD

❧

Serves 4

I'm an avid fisherman and seafood lover, and this recipe features all of my favorites—scallops, shrimp, and squid—enlivened by a citrus dressing that derives some real heat from the jalapeño pepper. But don't be bound by my personal taste; feel free to adapt this salad to include your own favorites such as lobster, octopus, or mussels.

POACHED SEAFOOD

4 ounces fresh large sea scallops
  (see Food for Thought)
4 ounces fresh squid, cleaned and cut
  into 1/2-inch rings
4 ounces medium shrimp, shelled and
  deveined

Coarse salt
Freshly ground black pepper
1 1/2 cups dry white wine, such as
  sauvignon blanc
2 cloves garlic, peeled and crushed

Season the seafood with salt and pepper, and set aside.

Combine the wine and garlic in a medium sauté pan. Bring to a boil over medium-high heat and cook until reduced by one-third, about 6–7 minutes. Lower the heat to medium and poach the shellfish as follows:

- First poach the shrimp. Lower them into the mixture and cook for 3–4 minutes, or until bright pink and firm to the touch. Remove with a slotted spoon and set aside to cool but leave the liquid over the heat.

- In the same liquid, poach the scallops for 3 minutes. (If they are not completely submerged, flip after 1 1/2 minutes.) Remove with a slotted spoon and set aside to cool with the shrimp.

- Place the squid in the liquid and remove as soon as the pieces turn opaque, about 30–40 seconds. Test the squid (or any of the shellfish) for doneness by taking a bite as you're cooking.

❖ **IF MAKING IN ADVANCE,** you may refrigerate the seafood for up to 24 hours in a well-sealed container, but be sure to allow them to cool completely before covering and refrigerating. **WHEN READY TO PROCEED,** allow to come to room temperature.

JALAPEÑO-LIME VINAIGRETTE	1/4 jalapeño pepper, seeds removed
Juice of 2 limes	and finely minced
1/3 cup extra-virgin olive oil	Coarse salt
1 clove garlic, minced	Freshly ground black pepper

Stir all the ingredients together in a mixing bowl.

❖ **IF MAKING IN ADVANCE,** this vinaigrette can be refrigerated in an airtight container for up to 72 hours.

ASSEMBLY	2 ripe avocados
6 ounces tender young greens, such as Lolla Rosa, Tango, or mizuna (about 4 cups)	

Slice and decoratively arrange 1/2 avocado on each of 4 salad plates, either fanning the slices out or creating your own shapes. Dress the seafood with the vinaigrette.

In a separate bowl, dress the greens judiciously, being careful not to overdress them.

Distribute the greens in the center of or on top of the avocado slices and place the seafood on the greens. Drizzle any remaining vinaigrette around the plate.

FOOD FOR THOUGHT—SHOPPING FOR SCALLOPS: While all seafood should be purchased with a discerning eye (and nose), I have found that you need to be particularly careful when selecting scallops. For this dish it is best to use diver scallops, although fresh bay scallops will also be delicious. (Note that the smaller bay scallops will cook in a fraction of the time, about 45–50 seconds.) Scallops are often shipped in a preserving solution that doesn't represent the fish very well. Ask your fishmonger if the scallops arrive in a preservative. You can use scallops stored in this way, but because they absorb the liquid, they won't taste as good.

OPTION: You can omit the avocado if they are out of season.

Sandwiches

I have never had the opportunity to serve sandwiches in a restaurant setting, largely because I've never been the executive chef in a restaurant that is open for lunch. But sandwiches are one of my favorite things to eat at home. When you're looking for some quick sustenance or to turn a fridge raid into something memorable, sandwiches are one of the surest ways to go.

But as easy as it is, sandwich-making shouldn't be a mindless act. Instead, you should take advantage of its simplicity to focus on the details that will take a sandwich from good to great. Here are some of my favorites:

- After completing a sandwich, press it together gently between your palms to combine the flavors and shrink the ratio of bread to filling. This little-known technique will make any sandwich better.

- Even if you are the most sophisticated home cook, don't try to get fancy when it isn't necessary or appropriate. For example, as far as I'm concerned, the best hamburger buns you can choose are those little eight-to-a-package mass-produced numbers you see in supermarkets. Similarly, there are times when some basic white, whole wheat, or rye is what you really want. So show some restraint with the focaccia and ciabatta.

- Pay attention to the order in which you lay the ingredients on the bread. For example, there is a recipe in this chapter for a Smoked Salmon, Mozzarella, Roasted Peppers, and Pesto sandwich (page 83) in which I encourage you to put the peppers on the bread first. This is important because the bread will soak up the pepper juice and become more flavorful. If you were to put the peppers in the middle of the sandwich, the juice would run off the sides and mess up the salmon. Similarly, in the Cubano sandwich (page 86), the pickles are placed in the middle of the filling to keep them protected and crisp by insulating them from the heat when the sandwich goes in the oven. These are good examples of how you might think about constructing sandwiches of your own design.

- Textural contrasts are great in sandwiches. One of the best things you can use to achieve this is a sturdy green, anything from iceberg lettuce to bok choy. (By the way, though I don't use it here, bok choy is a great ingredient if you're making a sandwich in advance; it holds up well without making the ingredients around it soggy.)

Many people focus on the ratio of bread to filling in a sandwich, but my decision-making criteria are a bit different. In my kind of sandwich there is a lot of weight and wetness, and my bread selection is based on what bread will hold up best. For example, there is a Grilled Vegetable and Goat Cheese Sandwich (page 84) that uses peasant loaf or boule for the bread's weight and a Sautéed Spinach Sandwich (page 89) that simply has to go on something sturdy like a baguette. When in doubt, toast the bread to give it extra strength.

SMOKED SALMON,
MOZZARELLA, ROASTED PEPPERS, AND PESTO

❧

Makes 4 sandwiches

I created this sandwich as an outlet for my love of smoked salmon. While you are certainly welcome to grill the peppers on an outdoor barbecue, because they are the only cooked ingredient in this sandwich it's hardly worth the trouble. I have provided a perfectly acceptable method for cooking them over a gas burner in the kitchen.

When making the sandwich, don't just lay the ingredients on the bread in any order. By placing the roasted peppers down first, the bread will absorb some of their tasty juice, leaving you with a neat and flavorful sandwich.

2 tablespoons olive oil	4–6 ounces fresh mozzarella, sliced into
2 large red bell peppers	1/4-inch-thick rounds
4 heaping tablespoons Pesto (page 49)	6–8 ounces smoked salmon, nova, or
8 thin slices dense peasant or	gravlax (whichever you prefer),
sourdough bread, lightly toasted	thinly sliced

Lightly oil the peppers and place them over the medium flame of a gas burner until the skin starts to blacken, 3–4 minutes per side.

As soon as the skin begins to separate from the flesh, transfer the peppers to a stainless steel bowl and place plastic wrap tightly over the top. Let the peppers steam in their own contained heat until the skin loosens up significantly, 10–12 minutes.

Remove the peppers, cut off the tops, seed them, and cut into 4 "panels."

Spread 1/2 tablespoon pesto on 1 side of each slice of bread. Arrange in front of you half of the bread slices, pesto side up.

Build the sandwiches by laying down the roasted peppers, mozzarella, and then the salmon. Top with the remaining slices of bread and press down firmly on each sandwich to meld the flavors. Cut each sandwich in half and serve.

GRILLED VEGETABLE
AND GOAT CHEESE SANDWICH

✣

Makes 4 sandwiches

This is a great summer recipe that can be cooked on an outdoor grill, although I've provided an indoor version here. This sandwich can break apart, so be sure to select a sturdy bread and cut it as thickly as described.

---

2 cloves garlic, thinly sliced
Juice of 2 lemons
1 cup olive oil
1 tablespoon coarse salt
Freshly ground black pepper
1 teaspoon fresh thyme or oregano,
    or a combination
1 medium zucchini, sliced lengthwise
    into 1/2-inch-thick slices
1 yellow squash, sliced lengthwise into
    1/2-inch-thick slices

2 portobello mushrooms, stems
    removed, ribs removed with a knife,
    and sliced on the bias into
    1/2-inch slices
1 medium head radicchio, quartered
3 bell peppers (red, yellow, green, or a
    combination), cored, stem removed,
    seeded, and cut into thirds
1 small Spanish onion, cut into
    1/2-inch-thick slices (about 8)
8 1-inch slices peasant loaf or boule
4–8 ounces goat cheese, at room
    temperature

Preheat the oven to 350°F.

In a bowl large enough to hold the vegetables, make a marinade of the garlic, lemon juice, oil, salt, pepper, and thyme.

Add the zucchini, yellow squash, mushrooms, radicchio, peppers, and onion, and allow to marinate for 15 minutes.

Remove the vegetables from the marinade, shaking off any excess, and transfer them to a cookie sheet. Reserve any leftover marinade.

Roast the vegetables in the oven until tender, about 20 minutes. When cool enough to handle, remove the radicchio core and separate each quarter into leaves.

Lay 4 slices of bread in front of you.

Divide half of the goat cheese among the 4 slices, spreading it with a knife and taking care not to neglect the edges.

Neatly and evenly pile the vegetables on the bread slices.

Crumble the remaining goat cheese and sprinkle it over the top of the sandwiches, then drizzle the sandwiches with some of the remaining marinade.

Top the sandwiches with the remaining slices of bread and press down gently to meld the flavors. Cut each sandwich in half and serve.

CUBANO

🌿

The classic Cubano sandwich is one of my all-time favorites, comprising ham, queso blanco, roast pork, and pickles. It is a perfect blend of temperatures, textures, and flavors. One of the most charming things about ordering a Cubano in an authentic Cuban restaurant is watching the cook warm the finished sandwich on a press. In this recipe there is a makeshift technique for making a Cubano that creates the same texture as the press by placing a hot skillet on top of the sandwich in the oven.

---

4 individual ciabatta, cut in half across the center (potato roll or hamburger bun may be substituted)

6 tablespoons Dijon mustard, or to taste

4 ounces sliced ham (boiled, Virginia, or Black Forest, whichever you prefer)

8 ounces leftover Braised Pork Shoulder (page 227), pork chop meat, or store-bought porchetta (Italian pork loin encased in pork fat and herbs)

4 ounces white cheese (queso blanco or good-quality white American), thinly sliced

Sliced dill pickles to taste

2 tablespoons unsalted butter

Preheat the oven to 350°F.

Open each bun and spread both sides with the mustard.

Place 1 or 2 ham slices on 1 side of the buns and 1 or 2 pork slices on the other.

Lay a slice of cheese on top of both the ham and the pork, then line some pickles lengthwise along the center of one half. Close the sandwiches, pressing down.

In a nonstick pan large enough to hold all the sandwiches, melt the butter over medium heat. Swirl it around to coat the pan, then lay the sandwiches in the pan.

Place a cast iron skillet on top of the sandwiches and carefully place in the oven, making sure that the skillet doesn't topple. Cook until the bread on the top and bottom of the sandwiches is crisped and the contents of the sandwiches are warm, 7–8 minutes.

VEGETABLE SALAD SANDWICH

Makes 4 sandwiches

This is a perfect summertime sandwich for those days when you crave something rich but don't want to feel too full when you jump back in the pool. If you don't have any Lemon-Cayenne Aioli on hand and don't feel like making it, you can dress up a store-bought mayonnaise with some lemon juice and cayenne, or simply use plain mayonnaise.

---

12 slices of your favorite whole wheat or multigrain bread, lightly toasted

4 heaping tablespoons Lemon-Cayenne Aioli (page 282)

2 ripe California avocados, halved and cut into 1/4-inch slices

3 ounces Gruyère or Swiss cheese, coarsely grated (1/3 cup)

1 cup loosely packed arugula leaves

1 seedless cucumber, peeled, cut in half crosswise, and cut into 1/4-inch-thick strips

2 cups loosely packed alfafa sprouts or bean sprouts

Lay 3 slices of bread in front of you. Spread the aioli on the upward-facing side of all 3 slices. Place one-fourth of the avocado slices on 1 slice and sprinkle them with some cheese.

Flip over the second slice and place it, aioli side down, on top of the avocado and cheese. Spread more aioli on the upward-facing side of that slice.

Place one-fourth of the arugula on this slice and top it with some cucumber slices and sprouts. Flip the last slice on top, aioli side down. Press down to merge the flavors.

Repeat all the steps to make the other 3 sandwiches.

GRILLED HAM AND CHEESE

Makes 4 sandwiches

As simple as this sandwich is, you can turn it into a make-ahead recipe by preparing it a day in advance, perhaps the day before a summer gathering. Just cover the sandwiches snugly with plastic wrap and refrigerate overnight.

2/3 cup Basic Mayonnaise (page 280)	12 ounces Black Forest ham
2 tablespoons coarsely chopped cornichons	8 thin slices Swiss, Gruyère, or Emmentaler cheese
1 tablespoon ketchup, or more to taste	1 red onion, thinly sliced
8 slices good-quality rye bread	2 tablespoons unsalted butter

In a mixing bowl, stir together the mayonnaise, cornichons, and ketchup.

Lay 4 slices of bread in front of you.

Divide half of the mayonnaise among the slices, spreading it out evenly and taking care not to neglect the edges.

Build the sandwiches by laying down the ham, cheese, and onion.

Spread the remaining mayonnaise over the other 4 slices of bread and place on the sandwiches, pressing down gently.

Melt the butter in a nonstick pan over medium-high heat.

Place the sandwiches in the pan and grill for 3–4 minutes per side. If you like, you may work in batches, but be sure to keep the finished sandwiches on a cookie sheet in a low (200°F) oven until the last one is cooked.

Serve the sandwiches from a platter or on individual plates.

SAUTÉED SPINACH SANDWICH

❧

Makes 4 sandwiches

When I was a kid, my grandmother encouraged me to eat greens by sautéing spinach, kale, escarole, or arugula and sandwiching it between great slices of bread. As the years went by, the ratio of greens to bread grew greater, and eventually I was eating the healthy stuff on its own. But I still love this sandwich and often make it for myself as a quick lunch when I'm working.

1 pound spinach (see Food for Thought)	Coarse salt
3 tablespoons olive oil	Freshly ground black pepper
2 small cloves garlic, thinly sliced	4 6-inch baguette sections, cut in half down the center and lightly toasted

Wash the spinach and shake off the excess water, but leave it a little damp because the lingering moisture produces the perfect amount of steam when cooked.

Warm the oil and garlic in a sauté pan over medium-high heat.

When the garlic begins to sizzle, add the spinach and cook, stirring continuously, until it softens and steams. Season with salt and pepper.

Once the spinach is completely cooked, about 1 minute, transfer to a cookie sheet and allow to cool. Check the seasoning. Divide the spinach among the 4 baguette sections, sprinkle with salt, close to form sandwiches, and serve.

FOOD FOR THOUGH—CHOOSING SPINACH: Whenever possible choose a bunch of flat-leaf spinach. It has the most pleasing texture and flavor.

OPTIONS: I have been known to add goat cheese, Roquefort cheese, feta cheese, and Chopped Roasted Tomatoes (page 13) to this sandwich. You should feel free to do the same or to incorporate your own little touches.

SHORT RIB SANDWICH WITH GRILLED ONIONS AND HORSERADISH

🌿

Makes 4 sandwiches

I find that a well-done piece of meat, cooked on the grill, has incredible flavor and texture contrasts, which led me to create this sandwich. It is so delicious that after you've had it, you may be tempted to make up a batch of short ribs for the sandwiches alone. If you do, plan ahead and refrigerate the cooked short ribs overnight. This is best made with meat that has had a good twenty-four hours to develop its flavor and chill in preparation for the grill.

1 pound leftover Braised Short Ribs (page 241), cut into 1/2-inch-thick slices

1 large Spanish or Vidalia onion, cut into 8 1/4-inch-thick slices

8 tablespoons favorite mayonnaise mixed with 2 tablespoons prepared grated horseradish that has been squeezed of its liquid

4 kaiser rolls

If freshly cooked, allow the short ribs to cool, then slice into 1-inch-thick slices.

Prepare an outdoor grill, letting the coals burn until covered with white ash.

Oil the grill grate and place the onion slices on the grill. Cook until golden and tender, about 20 minutes.

Set the onions aside to keep warm on the side of the grill.

Place the short rib slices on the hottest part of the grill, probably the center. Cook until the meat is caramelized, about 30–45 seconds per side. Transfer them to the side of the grill over indirect heat to warm through for 2 minutes.

Spread the dressing on the insides of the 4 rolls.

Divide the short rib slices evenly among the 4 rolls, top with the onion, close the sandwiches, and serve.

FRIED OYSTER SANDWICH

🌿

Makes 4 sandwiches

Although I have never experienced one in New Orleans, this is my version of a po'boy, inspired by countless New York renditions.

12 shucked oysters in liquid (be sure to ask the fishmonger to store them in liquid to maintain their freshness)	Coarse salt
	Freshly ground black pepper
	8 tablespoons Remoulade Sauce
2 cups all-purpose flour	(page 157), or more to taste
Milk	4 high-quality hamburger buns
2 cups dry bread crumbs or Japanese bread crumbs (panko)	8 slices iceberg lettuce
	4 slices beefsteak tomato
2 cups canola oil	

Remove the oysters from their liquid and pat dry with paper towels or a clean kitchen towel.

Spread the flour on a plate and dredge the oysters in the flour.

One by one, dip the oysters in the milk and shake dry.

Roll the oysters in the bread crumbs to coat them.

Pour the oil into a saucepan deep enough to prevent boiling over and bring to 350°F over medium-high heat.

Carefully lower the oysters into the oil, 3 or 4 at a time, and fry until golden, 1–2 minutes. Using a slotted spoon, transfer the oysters to paper towels to drain and season immediately with salt and pepper.

Build the sandwiches by spreading the Remoulade Sauce on both interior sides of each bun. Stack the oysters, lettuce, and tomato, in that order, on top of the bread. Gently close and serve.

OPTION: Soft-shell crabs are a great option for this.

Soups

I grew up thinking that soups were reserved for those nasty, wet, cold upstate New York winters when the sniffles or the flu set in. I remember being cordoned off from all the other delights in the fridge and relegated to soup and saltine crackers. I can almost conjure up the vision of those yellow "police line do not cross" banners wrapped around my grandmother's old rounded-edge refrigerator.

When those days arose, unless there just happened to be a chicken broth cooking on the stove, there was a quick reach for some canned thing with mushy noodles and those perfectly square little pieces of chicken that I envisioned coming from some mysterious square part of the bird. It wasn't until some years later that my travels opened my eyes to the possibilities of soup—the pistous, veloutés, and beautifully refined consommés of France, the seafood chowders of New England, the vegetable soups of Italy, the gazpachos of Spain.

Here are some tips:

- Make more than you need. Soups, like stews, have a unique property: Many of them actually get better after a day or so in the refrigerator. Accordingly, I highly recommend making a large quantity of soup and enjoying it over the course of several days, or freezing it in batches for later use. The recipes that follow all multiply very well.

- Shortcuts to creaminess. If you seek a creamier or thicker soup, try removing a portion and pureeing it, as opposed to adding cream. This works particularly well with vegetable soups, such as Lisa's Corn Chowder (page 111) and bean-based soups.

- When blending a soup, or any hot liquid, I encourage you to put the lid firmly on the blender, remove the small plastic insert from the lid to allow steam to escape, and cover it with a clean towel while pureeing to keep hot liquid from spraying out.

- Season with restraint. Soups, especially clear broths, are influenced by seasoning more than almost any other type of dish. This is especially true of thin soups, such as Tomato Consommé (page 96). So, contrary to what I say almost everywhere else in this book, you need to go easy here.

- If adding sliced meats or shellfish at the last minute, as in the Spicy Clam Chowder (page 94) and Smoky Lobster Minestrone (page 108), heat gently so as not to toughen them.

SPICY CLAM CHOWDER

Serves 4

This clam chowder recipe differs from the traditional one in two ways. First, it goes easy on the tomatoes, focusing more on the flavor of the clams by seasoning their cooking liquid and using it as a fresh and aromatic base. Second, in my constant search for a complete flavor profile, I add some red pepper flakes at the end. You can certainly leave them out, but they really provide a compelling undercurrent. Don't add an excessive amount of red pepper flakes. You want a gentle hint of heat without a lingering, burning sensation.

CLAMS AND COOKING LIQUID
1 cup dry white wine
2 cloves garlic, smashed
Coarse salt

Freshly ground black pepper
10 cherrystone clams (see Food
    for Thought)

Pour the wine into a large pot and add the garlic. Season with salt and pepper, and place the pot over high heat.

Add the clams to the pot and cook until they open, 8–10 minutes. Remove the pot from the heat and use tongs to gently remove the clams from the pot. Set aside to cool.

Strain and reserve the liquid. (You should have about 1/2 cup.)

When the clams are cool enough to handle, remove them from their shells and coarsely chop the meat. Reserve.

ASSEMBLY

1 teaspoon olive oil

6 ounces excellent-quality double-
smoked bacon, cut into fine dice
(about 1 1/2 cups)

3 small carrots, cut into fine dice

1 medium Spanish onion, cut into
fine dice

2 celery ribs, cut into fine dice

6 cloves garlic, thinly sliced

3 tablespoons tomato paste

3–4 plum tomatoes, cut into
1-inch cubes

1 teaspoon chopped fresh thyme leaves

1 bay leaf

1 medium or 2 small Yukon Gold
potatoes, peeled and cut into
1/2-inch cubes

3 cups Basic Vegetable Stock
(page 24), or 2 cups Chicken Stock
(page 23) thinned with
1 cup water

Coarse salt

Freshly ground black pepper

1 teaspoon red pepper flakes, or less
to taste

Put the oil and bacon in a soup pot and sauté the bacon over medium heat until tender, 4–5 minutes.

Add the carrots, onion, celery, and garlic to the pot. Cook, stirring occasionally, for 2–3 minutes.

Add the tomato paste and stir to coat the vegetables with the paste. Cook another 3–4 minutes.

Add the tomatoes, thyme, bay leaf, and potatoes, and cook for 3 minutes.

Pour the stock and reserved clam cooking liquid into the pot. Raise the heat to high and bring to a boil.

Lower the heat, taste, adjust the seasoning if necessary, and simmer for 15–20 minutes. Add the clams and red pepper flakes during the last 5 minutes of cooking, heating gently. Serve.

❖ **IF MAKING IN ADVANCE,** this soup can be stored in the refrigerator, tightly covered, for up to 2 days or frozen for up to 2 weeks.

FOOD FOR THOUGHT—CHOOSING CLAMS: When selecting clams, a good rule of thumb is that larger clams are tougher but also more flavorful than smaller ones.

Tomato Consommé

Makes 7 cups

Over the years, I have developed my own method of making consommé. I'm told I use more egg white than you're supposed to, but this makes the recipe very forgiving because it is the egg white that produces the clarification.

Tomato consommé is wonderfully versatile. Beautifully clean and pure on its own, when chilled it is also a perfect vehicle for cold seafood (perhaps the components of the Marinated Seafood Salad on page 79), diced tomatoes in season, or cubed avocado. Warmed, it is wonderful with Goat Cheese Ravioli (page 125).

This is one case where the final step isn't seasoning with salt and pepper. Because consommés are so delicately flavored, even these elements would be distracting. But use your judgment; if it tastes flat, season a little bit, leaving time for the salt to dissolve.

STOCK BASE	3 sprigs tarragon
2 tablespoons olive oil	2 sprigs thyme
3 small carrots, coarsely chopped	1 bay leaf
1/2 Spanish onion, coarsely chopped	1 tablespoon black peppercorns
2 ribs celery, cut into 1-inch pieces	6–8 ripe plum tomatoes, coarsely
1 6-ounce can tomato paste	chopped
2/3 cup dry white wine	1 tablespoon coarse salt
1/4 cup white vinegar	2 cups water
1 tablespoon sugar	1 cup tomato juice

In a large pan, warm the oil over medium heat. Add the carrots, onion, and celery, and sweat for 4–5 minutes, until they soften. (Do not allow them to color.) Reduce the heat to low. Add the tomato paste to the pot and cook the rawness out of the paste, 5–6 minutes, stirring occasionally and taking care not to burn the paste.

Add the wine and vinegar, and deglaze.

Add the sugar, tarragon, thyme, bay leaf, peppercorns, tomatoes, and salt. Stir well and let cook for 2–3 minutes.

Add the water and tomato juice. (Increase the water by 1 cup if the tomatoes aren't particularly juicy.)

Raise the heat to high, bring to a boil, and then lower the heat and let simmer. Allow to cook gently for 1 hour. (Don't overcook; you want to preserve the fresh flavor.)

Strain the liquid through a fine-mesh strainer, pushing on the solids to extract as much liquid as possible. Allow the mixture to cool. (If you are in a hurry, put it in the freezer to cool it faster. Just be sure to let it come to room temperature before proceeding.)

RAFT (SEE FOOD FOR THOUGHT)	**4 extra-large egg whites, plus shells**
4 ounces boneless, skinless chicken meat (dark meat okay) or ground chicken or turkey (beef or lamb may be substituted)	**1 small carrot, coarsely chopped**
	1 rib celery, coarsely chopped
	12 black peppercorns
	3 sprigs tarragon

Put all the ingredients in a food processor and pulse for 30–40 seconds. (The result will resemble a failed science experiment. Don't worry; that's the way it is supposed to look.)

Reheat the stock base in a heavy-bottomed saucepan over low heat.

Whisk the pureed raft ingredients vigorously into the stock.

Continue to stir for 5–6 seconds, then leave alone over low heat for 20–25 minutes.

A white raft will form on the surface of the pot. Once it has, allow to cook for another 90 minutes. In what will seem like a slow process, the center of the raft will develop a crust. Gently cut out and remove a circle from the top of the raft using a slotted spoon. Ladle the liquid into a fine-mesh sieve, preferably lined with cheesecloth, set over a bowl. The clarified product in the bowl is the consommé.

❖ **IF MAKING IN ADVANCE,** this consommé can be refrigerated for up to 1 week or frozen for up to 3 months. Make sure to thaw thoroughly before using.

FOOD FOR THOUGHT—WHAT IS A RAFT? It is the solidified egg white that rises to the surface when making a consommé, so named because it floats like a raft on the broth.

GARLIC SOUP WITH POACHED EGG, BLACK PEPPER, AND CHIVES

Serves 4

If you hear the words *garlic soup* and think of an overpowering brew that might best be used to ward off vampires, then you, my friend, have another thought coming. As aggressive as its name sounds, this recipe is actually a very pleasant reminder that garlic is an herb and is capable of herbaceous grace. Cooking garlic, particularly using this method, yields a subtle, almost sweet result.

This is a wonderful, hearty dish that is especially appropriate at the beginning of winter. I usually make it with cream but have provided an olive oil method that also yields a thick, satisfying result.

The poached egg here provides two effects: The white takes on the flavor of the soup, while the yolk adds to its creamy richness. After breaking the yolk, you should swirl it into the soup to distribute its flavor and texture throughout.

---

10 heads garlic, peeled (see Food for Thought)
1 quart Chicken Stock (page 23) or Basic Vegetable Stock (page 24)
Coarse salt

Freshly ground black pepper
Sugar
1/2 cup heavy cream or 1/4 cup excellent-quality extra-virgin olive oil

---

Place the garlic in a saucepan and add enough water to cover by 2 inches. Bring to a boil over high heat, then drain. (This takes the harsh rawness out of the garlic, softening its flavor without really cooking it.)

Repeat the boiling and draining twice more, then return the garlic to the pot.

Add the stock to the pot and season with salt, pepper, and a pinch of sugar. Bring the stock to a boil over high heat.

Lower the heat and simmer until the cloves are quite tender when pierced with the tip of a sharp, thin-bladed knife, about 15 minutes.

Remove the pot from the heat and allow the mixture to cool.

Transfer the mixture to a blender and puree until smooth.

Add the cream to the mixture and blend until thoroughly incorporated. Reserve.

❖ **IF MAKING IN ADVANCE,** cover and refrigerate up to 2 days. **WHEN READY TO PROCEED,** reheat gently in a soup pot set over low heat.

POACHED EGG AND ASSEMBLY	Pinch coarse salt
4 slices plain white bread	4 eggs
1 tablespoon unsalted butter	Freshly ground black pepper
4 cups water	2 tablespoons finely chopped chives
1 tablespoon white vinegar	

Using a 3-inch biscuit cutter, cut a round out of each slice of bread.

Melt the butter in a sauté pan over medium-high heat. Add the bread rounds to the pan and toast until crisp, 1–2 minutes per side. Reserve.

Bring the water, vinegar, and salt to a gentle simmer in a pot over high heat.

Crack the eggs, 1 at a time, onto a small plate and carefully slide them into the water. Once the eggs are firm and white, 2–3 minutes, gently remove with a slotted spoon, allowing excess water to drain.

Place each egg on top of a crouton and sprinkle with pepper.

Divide the soup among 4 bowls. Garnish with the chives and float a crouton in the center. Serve immediately.

FOOD FOR THOUGHT—PEELING GARLIC: Peeling 10 heads of garlic is, to put it mildly, a hassle. There is no easy way to do it, but 2 time-savers are to soak the separated garlic cloves in warm water to loosen the skin, or to use elephant garlic, which has fewer and larger cloves per head (3 or 4 heads of elephant garlic will do).

OPTION: Finish each serving with a drizzle of excellent-quality extra-virgin olive oil.

ONION SOUP WITH FRIED SHALLOTS AND PARMESAN CROUTONS

Serves 4

This is an intensely flavored dish that dresses up a classic French onion soup with a gourmet version of onion rings: fried shallots. To make it possible to float the shallots on the soup (keeping them crispy), the recipe calls for cheese croutons rather than the conventional layer of cheese. I use Parmesan rather than Gruyère because there is less of it here, and Parmesan's flavor makes more of an impact. If you prefer the traditional Gruyère coating, however, you can adapt this recipe by floating unadorned croutons in the soup, topping with enough grated or sliced Gruyère to completely cover the opening of the bowl, and melt under a broiler.

ONION SOUP

2 tablespoons unsalted butter

5 Spanish onions, cut in half and thinly sliced

1 teaspoon coarse salt, plus more to taste

1 tablespoon sugar, plus more to taste

1 teaspoon freshly ground black pepper, plus more to taste

2 cups dry sherry

1 cup Chicken Stock (page 23)

1 cup Veal Stock (page 32) or canned beef broth

1 cup water (optional)

Melt the butter in a large pot over medium heat and add the onions. (It is best to add them one-third at a time, adding another third when the first third has wilted, and so on.)

Once the onions start to become translucent, season with 1 teaspoon salt, 1 tablespoon sugar, and 1 teaspoon pepper. Cook, stirring frequently, until deeply caramelized, 35–40 minutes.

Add the sherry.

Raise the heat to high and bring to a boil. Cook for 3–4 minutes.

Add the chicken stock, veal stock, and water to the pot.

Reduce the heat to low-medium and cook for 20 minutes.

Taste and adjust the seasoning if necessary or dilute with more water if desired.

❖ **IF MAKING IN ADVANCE,** cover and refrigerate up to 5 days. (This soup happens to taste even better after a day or two.) **WHEN READY TO PROCEED,** reheat gently in a soup pot set over low heat.

PARMESAN CROUTONS	4 tablespoons grated Parmesan cheese
8 ½-inch-thick baguette rounds	(Gruyère may be substituted)
(2 per portion)	

Preheat the oven to 350°F.

Cover the baguette rounds with cheese, place on a cookie sheet, and bake until crisp and golden brown, about 8–10 minutes.

❖ **IF MAKING IN ADVANCE,** these can be wrapped in plastic and refrigerated overnight. **WHEN READY TO PROCEED,** allow to come to room temperature and, if desired, reheat briefly in a 200°F oven.

FRIED SHALLOTS AND ASSEMBLY	¼ cup all-purpose flour
3 tablespoons buttermilk	Coarse salt
2 shallots, sliced very thin and	Freshly ground black pepper
separated into rings	Canola oil for frying

Pour the buttermilk into a small mixing bowl. Add the shallots and let soak for 10 minutes.

Spread the flour on a plate and season with salt and pepper.

Remove the shallot rings from the buttermilk and shake off any excess milk.

Dredge the shallot rings in the seasoned flour.

Pour 1 inch of oil in a deep pot and over medium heat bring to a temperature of 325°F or test the oil by lowering a shallot ring into it. (See Food for Thought.) Fry the shallots until golden brown, about 10 seconds, then immediately remove with a slotted spoon and allow to drain on paper towels. (Be sure to get the shallots out of the oil as soon as they turn golden brown; they burn very quickly.)

Divide the soup among 4 bowls. Float 2 croutons in each bowl and place a few shallots on each crouton.

FOOD FOR THOUGHT—NO THERMOMETER? If you don't have a thermometer to check the temperature of the oil before frying the shallots, perform this test: Lower 1 shallot ring into the hot oil. If the oil around the shallot begins to bubble slowly, it is at the right temperature. If the bubbling is rapid, lower the heat. If it doesn't bubble at all, raise the heat a bit.

CURRIED CAULIFLOWER SOUP
WITH FRIED OYSTERS

❧

I think of the fried oysters in this recipe as party crashers. Cauliflower soup suggests, to me, great tradition and formality while fried oysters bring to mind the blissfully casual grub of a beachside clam shack. It turns out that, as with people, opposites attract; these two components seem made for each other. To punch up the soup I have added a bit of curry powder.

Because it will be pureed, let the cauliflower cook until it really softens up. You are interested in preserving and intensifying its flavor, not its texture.

1 large head cauliflower	1 teaspoon curry powder
2 tablespoons unsalted butter	1 small Spanish onion, cut into
4 cups Chicken Stock (page 23)	small dice
Coarse salt	4 cloves garlic, thinly sliced
Freshly ground black pepper	1 cup heavy cream
Sugar	

Preheat the oven to 350°F.

Break the cauliflower into equal-sized florets.

Melt 1 tablespoon butter in a deep-sided ovenproof sauté pan. Add the florets to the pan and sauté, stirring, until lightly browned, about 5 minutes.

Add the stock, season with salt, pepper, and a pinch of sugar, then add the curry powder.

Raise the heat to high and bring to a boil.

Transfer the pan to the preheated oven and cook until the florets are very tender and break apart very easily, 15–20 minutes.

Meanwhile, in a soup pot, melt the remaining 1 tablespoon butter over medium-high heat.

Add the onion and garlic and cook until tender, 4–5 minutes.

Transfer the cooked cauliflower to the pot with the onion and garlic, and continue to cook over medium-high heat for 2–3 minutes to allow the flavors to mingle.

Transfer the contents of the soup pot to a blender and puree, starting slowly, until emulsified and smooth, about 3 minutes. (You may need to work in batches.) See tip, page 93, regarding blending hot liquids.

❖ IF MAKING IN ADVANCE, this soup can be tightly covered and refrigerated in an airtight container for up to 2 days or frozen for up to 1 month. WHEN READY TO PROCEED, allow to come to room temperature, then reheat in a pot over low heat.

Stir the heavy cream into the soup, taste, and adjust the seasoning.

FRIED OYSTERS, CROUTONS, AND ASSEMBLY

4 slices plain white bread
1 tablespoon unsalted butter
1 cup milk
1 egg
12 shucked oysters in liquid (be sure to ask the fishmonger to store them in liquid to maintain the oysters' freshness)
2 cups all-purpose flour

2 cups dry bread crumbs or Japanese bread crumbs (panko)
2 cups canola oil
Coarse salt
Freshly ground black pepper
2 tablespoons minced chives

Using a 3-inch biscuit cutter, cut a round out of each slice of bread.

Melt the butter in a sauté pan over medium-high heat. Add the bread rounds to the pan and toast until crisp, 1–2 minutes per side. Reserve.

In a mixing bowl, whisk together the milk and egg.

Remove the oysters from their liquid and pat dry with paper towels or a clean kitchen towel.

Spread the flour on a plate and dredge the oysters in the flour.

One by one, dip the oysters in the milk and shake dry.

Roll the oysters in the bread crumbs to coat them.

Pour the oil into a saucepan deep enough to prevent boiling over and bring to 350°F over medium-high heat.

Carefully lower the oysters into the oil, 3 or 4 at a time, and fry until golden, 1–2 minutes.

Using a slotted spoon, transfer the oysters to paper towels to drain and season immediately with salt and pepper.

To serve: Ladle the soup into 4 bowls, season with pepper, and garnish with the minced chives. Float a crouton in the center of each bowl and carefully pile 3 fried oysters on top of each crouton. Serve immediately.

FOOD FOR THOUGHT—CURRY: From culture to culture, curries vary from mild to hot and are actually a combination of many spices such as cardamom, coriander, cumin, and turmeric.

OPTION: If you would like to omit the oysters and croutons, this soup will be delicious on its own.

WILD MUSHROOM SOUP

✣

This perfect autumn recipe celebrates roasted wild mushrooms in a creamy soup that acts as a backdrop for them. You make the call here, selecting whatever wild mushrooms you like to suit your own taste. Feel free to combine varieties or to focus on one to really emphasize it. My advice is not to overthink the decision; go with whatever you are in the mood for and do it as boldly as possible.

ROASTED WILD MUSHROOMS
1/4 cup extra-virgin olive oil
2 cloves garlic, smashed
Coarse salt
Freshly ground black pepper

8 ounces assorted wild mushrooms, such as shiitake, oyster, hen of the wood, chanterelle, black trumpet, cut into bite-sized pieces

Preheat the oven to 350°F.

Place the oil and garlic in a small mixing bowl and season with salt and pepper.

Dip the mushrooms in the seasoned oil, shake off any excess, and place on a cookie sheet. (Be sure to shake off as much excess oil as possible to avoid turning the soup greasy.)

Roast the mushrooms in the preheated oven until golden brown, 12–15 minutes.

Remove the mushrooms from the oven, cover with aluminum foil to keep warm, and set aside.

MUSHROOM SOUP	1/4 cup all-purpose flour
AND ASSEMBLY	1/2 cup dry white wine, such as
3 cups Chicken Stock (page 23) or	sauvignon blanc
Basic Vegetable Stock (page 24)	1 cup heavy cream (use up to 1/2 cup
2 tablespoons unsalted butter	less if you like by diluting it
3 cloves garlic, minced	with water)
12 ounces button mushrooms,	1 teaspoon minced fresh chervil leaves
thinly sliced	1 teaspoon minced fresh tarragon leaves
Coarse salt	1 teaspoon minced chives
Freshly ground black pepper	1 tablespoon sherry, or to taste

Pour the stock into a pot and bring to a simmer over medium heat.

Place the butter and garlic in another pot and cook over medium-high heat until the butter is melted.

Add the mushrooms to the butter and garlic, season with salt and pepper, and cook over medium-high heat until the mushrooms are tender but still white, 2–3 minutes.

Lower the heat and sprinkle the flour over the mushrooms, stirring as you do.

Cook the mushrooms for 5 minutes, scraping the pan and stirring every minute or so.

Raise the heat under the mushrooms to medium and add the wine to the pot.

Add the simmering stock to the mushrooms, 1 cup at a time, stirring to avoid lumps. Cook for 10 minutes.

❖ IF MAKING IN ADVANCE, allow to cool, then refrigerate in an airtight container for up to 2 days or freeze for up to 1 month, keeping the button and wild mushrooms separate. WHEN READY TO PROCEED, allow to come to room temperature and reheat in a pot over low heat.

Add the cream, adjust the seasoning, and add the reserved wild mushrooms. If necessary, thin with some hot water. Add the chervil, tarragon, and chives to the pot.

Divide the soup among 4 soup bowls and drizzle with the sherry.

OPTIONS: This is a great vehicle for grated fresh black truffles. If you choose to shave some over each serving, omit the herbs.

SMOKY LOBSTER MINESTRONE

Serves 4 as a main course

There are vast regional differences to minestrone. I grew up on minestrone with pasta and beans, while my wife remembers strictly vegetable versions in Italy. Like much Italian cooking, minestrone is open to interpretation. This version uses a number of my favorite ingredients such as lobster, Smoked Pork Jus, and basil puree. It takes a bit of work, but I think it's worth the effort.

BASIL PUREE
1 cup tightly packed fresh basil leaves
2/3 cup olive oil
1 clove garlic
1 tablespoon grated Parmigiano-
    Reggiano cheese

1 ice cube (see Food for Thought)
Coarse salt
Freshly ground black pepper

Place all the ingredients in a blender and puree until well incorporated.

❖ **IF MAKING IN ADVANCE,** this puree can be tightly covered and refrigerated up to 24 hours.

BOILED LOBSTERS
Coarse salt

4 1-pound lobsters

Have an ice water bath ready.

Bring a large pot of salted water to a boil.

Carefully lower the lobsters into the pot, cover, and cook over full heat for 5 minutes.

Turn off the heat and let the lobsters sit in the covered pot for an additional minute.

Remove the lobsters from the pot and submerge in ice water until chilled completely.

Remove the lobster meat from the body and claws and cut into 1-inch dice.

❖ IF MAKING IN ADVANCE, the cubed lobster meat can be covered tightly with plastic wrap and kept in the refrigerator for up to 24 hours.

WHITE BEANS
1/3 cup dry white beans
2 1/2 cups Chicken Stock (page 23) or water
1/2 small carrot, cut on the bias into thirds
1/2 small Spanish onion, coarsely chopped
1/2 rib celery, cut on the bias into thirds
1 bay leaf
1 sprig thyme
1/2 tablespoon coarse salt
1/2 teaspoon freshly ground black pepper

Soak the white beans in cold water overnight.

Pour the stock into a small pot and add the carrot, onion, celery, bay leaf, and thyme. Bring to a boil over high heat.

Drain the beans and add them to the pot.

Lower the heat and cook the beans at a simmer until they are tender but still hold their shape, 1 1/2–2 hours. Add the salt and pepper in the final 10–15 minutes of cooking.

Remove the beans from the heat and drain. When cool enough to handle, pick out the herb sprigs and vegetables, and discard.

❖ IF MAKING IN ADVANCE, the beans can be cooled, covered, and refrigerated for up to 24 hours.

VEGETABLES
Coarse salt
1 cup minced carrot (from 1 medium carrot)
1 cup minced onion (from 1 medium onion)
1 cup minced celery (from 2 ribs)

Have an ice water bath ready.

Bring a small pot of salted water to a boil over high heat. Add the carrot to the pot and cook for 1 minute. Remove with a slotted spoon to the ice water bath to shock.

Add the onion to the pot and cook for 1 minute. Remove with a slotted spoon to the same ice water bath as the carrot.

Add the celery to the pot and cook for 1 minute. Remove with a slotted spoon to the ice water bath. Drain and reserve the vegetables.

❖ **IF MAKING IN ADVANCE,** the vegetables can be covered and refrigerated overnight.

ASSEMBLY	1 cup dry tubetti pasta, cooked
1 quart Smoked Pork Jus (page 25)	and drained
3 tablespoons Chopped Roasted	
Tomatoes (page 13) or an equal	
quantity of canned plum tomatoes	

In a soup pot, heat the pork jus over medium-high heat.

Add the tomatoes, tubetti, white beans, and vegetables to the pot.

Simmer until the ingredients are heated through, about 10 minutes.

Lower the temperature and add the lobster in the last 30 seconds of cooking time.

Ladle the soup into 4 bowls and top each one with a tablespoon or so of basil puree.

OPTION: To make a shellfish stew, heat the pork jus with the chopped roasted tomatoes stirred into it. Add some clams and/or mussels to the pot and cook them in the jus. At the last second toss in diced cooked lobster or cooked shrimp or cod and let it warm through. Add a pinch of saffron and serve with baguette croutons and Roasted Garlic Mayonnaise (page 280) on the side.

FOOD FOR THOUGHT—WHY AN ICE CUBE? Adding an ice cube to the processor when pureeing delicate herbs (such as the basil in this recipe) keeps the heat of the rotating blade from "cooking" the herbs; this would dull their color and diminish their flavor.

LISA'S CORN CHOWDER

Serves 4

My assistant, Lisa Reilly, put this together some years ago, and it is just sheer perfection. Obviously, it is best made at the height of corn season in late summer.

3 tablespoons olive oil

1 large Spanish onion, cut into 1/4-inch
dice

6 medium carrots, cut into 1/4-inch dice

4 ribs celery, cut into 1/4-inch dice

9 cups corn kernels (from 9 ears), juice
from scraping cobs reserved
(defrosted frozen corn may be
substituted; see Food for Thought)

2 cups Chicken Stock (page 23)

Sugar (optional)

Coarse salt

Freshly ground black pepper

3 medium Idaho potatoes, diced
(about 3 cups)

2 cups heavy cream

Pour the oil into a soup pot and set over moderate heat. Add the onion, carrots, and celery to the pot and sweat until tender but do not allow to color, about 5 minutes.

Add 6 cups corn, two-thirds of the reserved corn juice, and the stock to the pot. Raise the heat to high and bring to a boil.

Lower the heat and allow the soup to simmer for 10 minutes. Taste. If the corn doesn't seem particularly sweet, add sugar. Season with salt and pepper.

Add the potatoes and simmer until tender, about 15 minutes.

Ladle two-thirds of the soup from the bottom of the pot (to include as many solids as possible) into a blender or processor and puree until thick but not liquefied. (See tip, page 93, regarding blending hot liquids.)

Return the pureed soup to the pot.

Add the remaining corn and juice and the cream. Simmer another 15 minutes. Taste and adjust the seasoning.

Ladle the soup into 4 bowls and serve.

FOOD FOR THOUGHT—CHOOSING CORN: When choosing corn, look for heavy cobs and a tight green husk.

OPTIONS: This soup is delicious hot or cold. If making it in advance, allow to cool and then cover tightly and store in the refrigerator for up to 2 days. Allow to come to room temperature before serving or gently reheating.

Additionally, feel free to puree as much or as little of the soup as you like to reach your own desired consistency.

Pasta and Risotto

The single best thing I ever ate was on a snowy Christmas Eve several years ago in New York City. I dropped in on my good friend David Burke, then of the River Cafe (now at Park Avenue Cafe), and he gave me a beautiful golf-ball-sized black truffle as an impromptu holiday present. I tucked it in my pocket, went home, popped open a box of DeCecco linguine, cooked it up, and finished it with butter and olive oil. Then I shaved the entire truffle over it and sat down to enjoy it with the most basic green salad, dressed

with nothing but olive oil, salt, and pepper. As simple as that sounds, it was something I remember more completely and fondly than any meal I've ever had.

You will have to forgive me for this public display of affection, but I adore pasta. Love it. Can't get enough of it. When my wife, Abigail, and I go out to eat, pasta is easily the choice 50 percent of the time. Much has been written about what a versatile medium pasta is because you can pair it with just about anything. But I happen to like the *flavor* of pasta itself. Give me a great pasta drizzled with some high-quality olive oil and seasoned with garlic, salt, and pepper, and I'm in heaven.

When cooking pasta, it is important to remember that, as simple as it seems, it is not a brainless exercise. Cooking great pasta requires a basic understanding of how it is cooked and the quantity of sauce that accompanies it (or, in some cases, the sauce that the pasta accompanies).

We have all experienced limp, watery, overcooked spaghetti, drowned in tomato sauce and pinned down by two gargantuan meatballs. To me that was never pasta. I grew up in an Italian-speaking home and was fortunate to have experienced and understood the real deal at an early age. When I was growing up, there was always a wedge of Parmigiano-Reggiano cheese on the table, with a knife embedded in it to facilitate loping off a chunk whenever the spirit moved you. We ate pasta tossed with a great tomato sauce and accompanied with a green salad and crusty bread.

Here are a few notes that will lead you down the road to successful pasta:

- Cooking liquid. You just fill a pot with water, add some salt, and start cooking, right? Well, not really. You have noticed how pasta grows in volume as it cooks, haven't you? Well, that's because the pasta is taking on some of the water. If that water is too salty, then the pasta itself will become irreversibly salty. So be careful. Salt the water enough to taste it but not so that it becomes like seawater. A good rule of thumb is 6 quarts of water and 2 tablespoons of salt per pound of pasta.

- Cooking liquid, part two. Just as the pasta takes on the quality of the water, the water takes on some of the quality of the pasta. Specifically, some of the starch from the pasta will be released into the water. For this reason it is often a good idea to reserve about 1/2 cup of the cooking liquid just before draining the pasta. That liquid can be used to bind the sauce and the pasta together. And that's another reason to watch out for the salt.

- *Al dente*. Aren't those great words? *Al dente*. They mean "to the tooth," and getting your pasta to come out toothsome every time takes some practice. There is no easy trick to it, but I have found that you'll usually get pretty close if you shave one minute off the recommended cooking time on the manufacturer's box. You should also taste a piece of pasta during the last minute or two of cooking. Truly *al dente* pasta, the kind they serve in Italy, may be more firm that what you're used to. Taste it as it cooks, and as soon as it no longer registers as raw or hard, it is ready to go. Drain it, sauce it, and serve it.

    Some people think that if pasta is piping hot, you don't need to heat the sauce that is going to dress it. Those people are wrong. You will get a better integration of pasta and sauce if they come together at equivalent temperatures. There are, of course, exceptions, such as a simple sauce of perfectly fresh chopped tomatoes with basil and olive oil that is left uncooked to preserve the delicate flavors of the herbs.

Risotto

Risotto is one of the most popular dishes in American restaurants today, but I usually find it a bit too monotonous for a stand-alone main course. I prefer it instead as a side dish or accompaniment (in fact, there are two fish dishes, on pages 178 and 189, that feature risotto as a component)—except for risotto with white truffles, in which case all bets are off.

Risotto is a subject that inspires great debate among chefs, many of whom swear by their particular techniques. Some advice I think we can all agree on includes the following:

- Stock is particularly important in making risotto. This is one area in which it really pays big dividends to make your own.

- Don't hurry risotto. Take the time to patiently stir until each addition of stock is absorbed, then add the next addition. Don't try to cheat the clock by adding more stock than you are supposed to or by raising the heat to quicken the absorption. You'll ruin the dish.

- A heavy-bottomed pot is key. You don't want the rice to scorch, and you want to cook it evenly. A stainless steel or copper pot with an aluminum core that distributes heat evenly is preferable.

- Take the time and care to chop the onions small and even. You don't want them to show in the finished dish.

- If adding wine, allow plenty of time to cook the wine so that it evaporates.

- If using the cook-ahead method featured with the following recipes, be sure to spread out the risotto very thinly on a cookie sheet and get it cooled and refrigerated as soon as possible.

- When you eat risotto, start from the outside and work your way in. This allows the dish to retain as much of its heat as possible for as long as possible.

FOOD FOR THOUGHT—MAKE-AHEAD TECHNIQUE: Contrary to popular belief, it is possible to make risotto a few hours in advance, which can be a great convenience when entertaining because it keeps you from having to disappear from your dining room for half an hour. Omit the final addition of stock and place the partially cooked risotto on a cookie sheet. Allow it to cool, then transfer it to an airtight container and refrigerate. When ready to serve, reheat the risotto and finish with the final addition of stock and whatever garnish you plan to add.

TUBETTI WITH CLAMS AND BACON

🌿

Serves 6 as an appetizer or 4 as a main course

This is one of my favorite dishes: small tubular pasta, clams, and a hearty red sauce. What are bacon and clams doing together here? I'm not sure, but I think I first got the idea from the recipe for clams casino.

SMOKED BACON AND TOMATO SAUCE

8 ounces very good quality smoked bacon, cut into 1/2-inch lardons (ask the butcher to cut a 1/2-inch-thick slab to facilitate this)

2 large carrots or 4 small carrots, cut into 1/4-inch dice

1 Spanish onion, cut into 1/4-inch dice

3 ribs celery, cut into 1/4-inch dice

3 heaping tablespoons tomato paste

Pinch sugar

2/3 cup dry white wine, such as sauvignon blanc

1/4 cup white wine vinegar

1/2 teaspoon red pepper flakes

5 fresh plum tomatoes, cut into 1-inch dice and sprinkled with salt, freshly ground black pepper, and a pinch of sugar, or one 32-ounce can excellent-quality plum tomatoes, such as San Marzano, drained of their liquid and crushed by hand

6 cloves garlic, very thinly sliced

1 bay leaf

1 teaspoon chopped fresh thyme leaves

1 teaspoon chopped fresh marjoram leaves

Coarse salt

Freshly ground black pepper

In a saucepan, render the bacon over moderate heat until it releases enough fat to coat the bottom of the pot, 3–5 minutes.

Add the carrots, onion, and celery to the pot and sweat them for 4–5 minutes.

Add the tomato paste and sugar, and stir to coat the vegetables with the paste. Cook until slightly caramelized, another 3–4 minutes.

Add the wine and vinegar, and deglaze, stirring to remove any crusty bits from the bottom of the pot.

Add the pepper flakes, tomatoes, garlic, and bay leaf. Cook, stirring occasionally, until the tomatoes are completely broken down and the sauce has thickened slightly, 25–30 minutes. In the final minutes of cooking, add the thyme and marjoram.

Season to taste with salt and black pepper, bearing in mind that the bacon and clams (which will be added shortly) are salty and that the red pepper flakes have already contributed some heat. In other words, season gradually and with care.

❖ **IF MAKING IN ADVANCE,** this sauce base can be made up to 4 days ahead of time and kept covered in the refrigerator. **WHEN READY TO PROCEED,** reheat gradually over low heat.

STEAMED CLAMS	2 pounds fresh, heavy clams, such as
1/2 cup dry white wine, such as	cherrystone or Manila, or New
sauvignon blanc	Zealand cockles
3 cloves garlic, smashed	

Heat a 10- or 12-inch sauté pan over medium-high heat. Add the wine and garlic to the pan and cook for 30 seconds.

Add the clams and cover with a lid or inverted sauté pan of the same size. Cook just until the clams have opened, 2–3 minutes, or longer for cherrystones. (See Food for Thought. If you like, you may work in batches, reserving the liquid from the first batch to cook the second.)

Drain the clams over a bowl and reserve the clams and liquid separately.

❖ **IF MAKING IN ADVANCE,** the clams can be prepared up to 24 hours ahead of time and kept covered in the refrigerator in their cooking liquid. **WHEN READY TO PROCEED,** drain and allow to come to room temperature.

PASTA AND ASSEMBLY	1 pound dry tubetti
Coarse salt	

Bring a large pot of salted water to a boil over high heat. Add the tubetti to the pot, return to a boil, and cook until *al dente* according to the package directions, probably about 9 minutes. Drain.

Add the clams and 3 tablespoons reserved clam cooking liquid to the smoked bacon and tomato sauce.

Add the pasta and toss to combine. Taste and add more reserved clam cooking liquid if desired. Serve immediately.

OPTIONS: If cooking this recipe just before serving, you may leave the clams in their shells for a more dramatic effect. Simply cook them a little longer. Once they pop, turn off the heat and allow them to sit, covered, for an additional minute or two.

Though one normally would not serve Parmesan cheese with a seafood dish, this one is so hearty that you can serve some grated Parmesan alongside it at the table.

Feel free to use another pasta shape, but stay with a tubular pasta, such as rigatoni, which will hold a lot of sauce.

FOOD FOR THOUGHT—COOKING CLAMS: When first cooking the clams, get them off the heat as soon as they have opened up. Because they will be added to a hot sauce, the only goal of steaming them here is to cause the shells to pop. If you continue to cook them at this stage, they will overcook and turn tough and rubbery in the finished dish.

BEER: Serve this with a high-quality Pilsner Urquell.

ORECCHIETTE WITH BROCCOLI RABE
AND SAUSAGE

❧

Serves 6 as an appetizer or 4 as a main course

Broccoli rabe and sausage is a classic combination. (In fact, our agent, Judith Weber, told us about a sausage she once enjoyed that had pieces of broccoli rabe mixed in with the pork.) I make my own sausage, but you don't have to. It happens to be a lot of fun and wonderfully simple, and telling someone that you've made your own sausage is like telling them you built your own car—it never fails to impress. If you want to get adventurous and make link-style sausage, it is a much bigger production that probably uses more equipment than you have at home. (I sure don't have the necessary production line at home.) This recipe can be used to stuff a sausage casing but is really best served in patty form or, in the case of this recipe, coarsely ground. A lot of older recipes call for saltpeter to preserve the color, but that is not necessary when making fresh sausage for immediate use.

FENNEL AND GARLIC SAUSAGE

2 tablespoons fennel seeds, lightly
   toasted
12 cloves garlic, peeled, smashed,
   and coarsely chopped
2 tablespoons coarse salt
3/4 tablespoon freshly ground
   black pepper

1/2 teaspoon sugar
3/4 teaspoon ground coriander
1 teaspoon red pepper flakes (optional)
2 pounds fatty coarse-ground pork butt
   or pork shoulder

Spread half of the fennel seeds, garlic, salt, pepper, sugar, coriander, and red pepper flakes (if using) on a cookie sheet, being careful to distribute each one evenly. (If you like, combine them in a small bowl before sprinkling.)

Crumble the ground pork over the seasoning, then sprinkle the rest of the seasoning over the top of the pork. (This technique ensures a more thorough blended flavor than simply adding the spices and herbs to a bowl of ground meat. It also preserves the texture of the meat by limiting the amount of time your warm hands are in contact with it.) Gather up the pork and knead it together briefly on a clean, dry surface.

At this point I strongly recommend that you brown a bit of sausage and adjust the seasoning to suit your taste. (See Food for Thought.)

Let the sausage cure for 1 hour in the refrigerator.

❖ **IF MAKING IN ADVANCE,** you can freeze this in patties for up to 2 weeks.

BROCCOLI RABE

Coarse salt

1 bunch broccoli rabe (about 1 pound),
    lower inch of stem cut off and
    discarded

2 tablespoons olive oil

2 cloves garlic, thinly sliced

1/2 teaspoon red pepper flakes

Have an ice water bath ready.

Bring a saucepan of salted water to a boil; the saucepan should be large enough to hold the broccoli rabe.

Blanch the broccoli rabe in the water for 1 minute.

Shock the broccoli rabe in the ice water to stop the cooking and preserve its color.

Drain and pat dry with paper towels.

Warm the oil in a sauté pan over medium-high heat. Add the broccoli rabe, garlic, and red pepper flakes, and cook until the broccoli is heated through and the flavors are incorporated, about 2 minutes. Toss lightly, cover to keep warm, and set aside.

PASTA AND ASSEMBLY

Coarse salt

1 pound dry orecchiette

2 1/2 cups Chicken Stock (page 23)
    or Basic Vegetable Stock (page 24)

1/2 cup grated Parmesan cheese, plus
    more for serving at the table

Freshly ground black pepper

Bring a large pot of salted water to a boil over high heat. Add the orecchiette, return to a boil, and cook, uncovered, until *al dente* according to the package directions, probably about 11 minutes.

Drain the pasta.

Warm a nonstick pan over high heat, allowing it to become very hot.

Crumble the sausage into the pan (with no butter or oil) and cook until you get a rich brown sear, about 1 minute. (If this doesn't seem like enough time, bear in mind that the sausage will cook further in the sauce.)

Remove the sausage from the heat and keep covered and warm.

Pour the stock into a pot and bring to a boil over high heat.

Whisk the cheese into the stock.

Reduce the heat to low and add the broccoli rabe and sausage to the pot. Allow the flavors to blend together and the sauce to infuse for 1–2 minutes. Season with salt and pepper.

Add the pasta and toss to combine. Transfer to a serving bowl or plates and serve immediately.

FOOD FOR THOUGHT—CREATE YOUR OWN HOUSE SAUSAGE: We all have different preferences when it comes to sausage. The ideal amount of garlic and the degree of spiciness or sweetness are very personal decisions. After following this recipe, brown some of the sausage in a pan. Taste it and adjust the rest of the sausage, adding more garlic or herbs to suit your taste. Write down the adjustment you've made and make that your house recipe for sausage.

OPTIONS: Use more or less stock to create a soupier or drier effect. Also feel free to increase the quantities of garlic and cheese to taste.

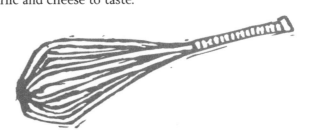

Ravioli "Ovo" with Mushroom Puree and Parmesan Cheese

Serves 4 as an appetizer

I didn't invent this dish, but I'm thrilled to be able to share my version of it with you because it exemplifies the sort of concentrated bursts of flavor that I strive for in my cooking. As complex as each bite is, the recipe could not be simpler. A large raviolo (one ravioli) is filled with a ring of pureed, sautéed mushrooms, a fresh egg yolk, shaved Parmesan cheese, and a drop of white truffle oil. The raviolo is sealed and cooked just until done. When you cut into this gargantuan raviolo, the egg runs out, adding an air of unrestrained decadence. The raviolo is sauced with a simple emulsion of cream and butter, and chives and a drop of truffle oil are added for good measure.

Be very gentle when constructing and handling the raviolo. You don't need or want the water to be in a rolling boil. Carry this caution all the way through to the end, removing each individual raviolo with a slotted spoon and gingerly placing it in its bowl. Have warmed bowls ready to go.

---

1 1/2 tablespoons extra-virgin olive oil

9 tablespoons unsalted butter

3/4 pound white button mushrooms or your favorite mushroom, thickly sliced

1 large clove garlic, finely minced

Coarse salt

Freshly ground black pepper

1/2 cup heavy cream

2 sheets *very thin* fresh pasta (approximately 10 × 12 inches), cut into 8 circles 3 inches in diameter; you may substitute 8 wonton (gyoza) skins but will get a much more refined and logical dish with fresh pasta

4 egg yolks, plus extra eggs in case you break a yolk

12 Parmesan shards, cut from a wedge with a vegetable peeler

1 teaspoon white truffle oil

2 tablespoons minced chives

Warm the olive oil and 1 tablespoon butter in a sauté pan over medium-high heat.

Add the mushrooms and garlic to the pan, season with salt and pepper, and cook until the mushrooms begin to give off their liquid, about 5 minutes.

Transfer the mushrooms to a food processor and puree until a thick paste forms.

Place the heavy cream in a saucepan set over moderate heat. Cook the cream until it is warmed through. Turn off the heat.

Add the remaining 8 tablespoons butter, 1 piece at a time, and blend with an immersion blender or in a traditional blender to form a thick, creamy sauce. (See tip on page 93 about blending hot liquids.) Season with salt and pepper.

Bring a pot of salted water to a gentle (not rolling) boil.

Using a teaspoon, lay a ring of mushrooms around the perimeter of half of the ravioli skins, starting about 1/8 inch from the outer edge and leaving room for an egg yolk in the center.

Carefully transfer an egg yolk to the center of each raviolo.

Place 3 Parmesan shards on top of the egg yolk.

Lay another raviolo skin on top and seal the edges by pressing down firmly.

Repeat with the remaining skins to form 4 large ravioli.

Gently lower the ravioli into the boiling water. Cook just until they float to the surface, about 2 minutes. (It is important to remove them right away because you don't want the egg to overcook.)

Remove the ravioli with a slotted spoon. Place in the center of 4 soup bowls and spoon some sauce around each one. Garnish with a drop of truffle oil and some minced chives.

OPTIONS: Go for broke and shave some white or black truffles over each serving instead of using truffle oil.

WINE: Serve with a white Burgundy.

Goat Cheese Ravioli with Tomato, Bacon, and Basil

❧

Serves 6 as an appetizer or 4 as a main course

My first view of goat cheese ravioli was from Alfred Portale. While I don't remember his exact preparation at the Gotham Bar and Grill, I do recall that it was tomato based and that it made me swoon. In my rendition the creamy goat cheese is offset by not just tomato but also smoky bacon and herbaceous basil. You should know going in that the tomato and bacon sauce is more of a concasse, a fine dice of ingredients with very concentrated flavor. For a lighter, wetter sauce, spoon some Tomato Consommé (page 96) around the ravioli instead.

Be sure that the goat cheese and cream cheese are at room temperature before attempting to blend. Since you are working by hand, you won't be able to work them together properly if they're cold.

GOAT CHEESE FILLING

10 ounces fresh imported goat cheese, at room temperature

4 ounces cream cheese, at room temperature

1 small clove garlic, finely minced

1 teaspoon fresh thyme leaves

Few grinds of fresh black pepper

2 tablespoons excellent-quality extra-virgin olive oil

Place all ingredients in a mixing bowl and blend by hand using a fork. Set aside.

❖ **IF MAKING IN ADVANCE,** this can be prepared 1 day ahead and stored, covered, in the refrigerator.

BACON AND TOMATO SAUCE
6 ounces excellent-quality smoked
   bacon, sliced very thin
   (ask your butcher to do this)
5 cloves garlic, minced
1 cup dry white wine
1 tablespoon white vinegar
3 tablespoons tomato paste

4 tablespoons Chopped Roasted
   Tomatoes (page 13)
1 tablespoon fresh thyme leaves
1 teaspoon coarse salt
1 teaspoon freshly ground black pepper
2/3 cup Chicken Stock (page 23)
6 leaves fresh basil, cut into chiffonade

Cut the bacon into fine dice. (If you freeze it for a few minutes, it will harden a bit and become easier to slice.) Place in a pot and set over medium heat.

Add half of the garlic to the pot and cook, stirring frequently, until the bacon renders a bit, 3–4 minutes.

Add the wine and vinegar, raise the heat to high, and bring to a boil. (The sauce will emulsify a bit because of the bacon fat and wine.)

Lower the heat and add the tomato paste, stirring to coat the bacon and garlic. Add the tomatoes, remaining garlic, thyme, salt, and pepper. Cook for 3–4 minutes.

❖ **IF MAKING IN ADVANCE,** cool and freeze at this point. It will last 2 months if frozen. **WHEN READY TO PROCEED,** let the sauce come to room temperature and reheat in a pot over medium heat.

Add the stock and cook until warmed through, about 2 minutes.

Add the basil just before spooning the sauce over the ravioli.

PASTA AND ASSEMBLY
2 fresh pasta sheets, about 12 × 18
   inches (page 153), or
18 wonton skins

1 egg yolk, whisked (only if using
   wonton skins)
Coarse salt

Lay 1 pasta sheet in front of you.

Place tablespoon portions of the goat cheese filling about 2 inches apart on the sheet, leaving a 1-inch border at the top, bottom, and sides.

Lay the other sheet on top and allow it to conform to the shape of the filling mounds.

Using a pizza cutter or very sharp knife, cut around the filling.

Using the tines of a fork, smooth the edges of each raviolo.

IF USING WONTON SKINS, brush the edges with egg yolk and spoon 1 tablespoon of filling on one half of the skin. Fold the skin over to form a rectangle (or choose a diagonal fold and make agnolotti).

For either pasta sheets or wonton skins, seal the edges with a fork or your fingers, leaving one corner unsealed.

One by one, place the ravioli in the palm of your hand and gently squeeze out any excess air, then seal the open corner.

❖ **IF MAKING IN ADVANCE,** freeze the ravioli on a cookie sheet, then transfer to a plastic bag. **WHEN READY TO PROCEED,** take the ravioli directly from the freezer to the pot.

Bring a pot of salted water to a gentle boil over high heat. Carefully lower the ravioli into the water and cook until they float to the surface, 1–2 minutes for fresh or 4–5 minutes for frozen.

Remove the ravioli to bowls, using a slotted spoon, and spoon some sauce over each serving.

WINE: Serve this with a pinot gris.

SWEET PEA AGNOLOTTI WITH PARMESAN BROTH

🌿

Serves 6 as an appetizer or 4 as a main course

I got the idea for this agnolotti from the Italian combination of fava beans and pecorino cheese, which is about as popular a dish as you will find in Tuscany. I find that peas are creamier than favas when pureed and that Parmesan cheese is more successfully grated than pecorino, which is a softer, less salty cheese. Like its Italian inspiration, this dish is best enjoyed in the spring when peas are in their prime. Be sure to grate the Parmesan cheese as finely as possible to aid its incorporation into the broth.

SWEET PEA FILLING

1 teaspoon coarse salt, or more to taste

10 ounces freshly shucked peas or high-quality frozen *petits pois* (about 3 cups)

1 teaspoon sugar (if using frozen *petits pois*)

2 tablespoons unsalted butter

1 small Spanish onion, cut into fine dice

3 cloves garlic, thinly sliced

1/2 cup Chicken Stock (page 23)

Few grinds of fresh pepper

Bring a pot of salted water to a boil.

While the water is coming to a boil, prepare an ice water bath.

If using fresh peas, add to the boiling water and cook for 1 minute, or until tender. If using frozen peas, blanch from the frozen state for 10 seconds in lightly salted and sugared water.

Remove the peas from the boiling water, shock in the ice water, drain well, and set aside.

Melt 1 tablespoon butter in a soup pot over medium heat.

Add the onion and garlic to the pot and cook until soft and translucent, about 4–5 minutes. Do not allow them to color.

Turn the heat to high, add the stock, and cook, stirring frequently, until the mixture is almost dry, 5–6 minutes. (If you want to be amazed, taste it at this point and see how much the flavor resembles peas.)

Put the cooked peas into the onion-garlic-stock mixture and toss. Add the pepper.

Transfer the contents of the pot to a food processor. Begin running the processor and add the remaining 1 tablespoon butter to help the mixture emulsify. Taste and adjust the seasoning.

Push the pea mixture through a mesh strainer to yield a satiny smooth result. (Feel free to skip this step if you are not that fussy. You'll be left with double the desired volume of pea mixture; freeze the leftover portion for another day.)

PARMESAN BROTH
2 cups Chicken Stock (page 23)

4 tablespoons grated Parmigiano-
Reggiano cheese, or more to taste

In a saucepan, bring the stock to a boil over high heat.

Stir in the cheese.

AGNOLOTTI AND ASSEMBLY
2 fresh pasta sheets, about 12 × 18
inches (page 153), or 18 wonton
skins
1 egg yolk, whisked (only if using
wonton skins)

Coarse salt
4 tablespoons grated Parmigiano-
Reggiano cheese, or more to taste
2 tablespoons extra-virgin olive oil
(see Food for Thought)

Use a ring mold or biscuit cutter to cut 3-inch circles from each sheet of pasta. (This step is unnecessary if you are using wonton skins.)

Place one pasta-circle or wonton skin in front of you. (If using wonton skin, brush the edges with egg yolk). Place a tablespoon of filling in the center of the dough and fold the dough over diagonally to form a half-moon shape. Using the tines of a fork, seal the edges, leaving one corner unsealed.

Repeat with the remaining pasta and ravioli. One by one place the agnolotti in the palm of your hand and gently squeeze out any excess air, then seal the open corner.

❖ **IF MAKING IN ADVANCE,** freeze the agnolotti on a cookie sheet, then transfer to a plastic bag. They will keep up to 2 weeks. **WHEN READY TO PROCEED,** take the agnolotti directly from the freezer to the pot.

Bring a pot of salted water to a gentle boil over high heat. Carefully lower the agnolotti into the water and cook until they float to the surface, 1–2 minutes for fresh or 4–5 minutes for frozen.

Remove the agnolotti to bowls, using a slotted spoon, and spoon some sauce over each serving.

Shave more cheese on the top. Finish with a drizzle of extra-virgin olive oil.

FOOD FOR THOUGHT—WHEN TO USE EXTRA-VIRGIN OLIVE OIL: Some recipes in this book call for olive oil, while others call for extra-virgin olive oil. If you have ever wondered what the difference is, plain old olive oil is usually used as a fat in cooking, just as butter or other oils are. Extra-virgin olive oil is more of a condiment—a more expensive and more delicious version that is almost never used for cooking but instead is drizzled over soups, pastas, salads, and other dishes. Olive oils are largely interchangeable, but extra-virgin olive oils possess their own personality; some, for example, are considerably more fruity than others. Find an extra-virgin olive oil that you like and use it to add a final flourish to a variety of dishes.

WINE: Serve this with a crisp gewürztraminer.

LINGUINE WITH TUNA AND PEPPERONCINI

🌿

Serves 6 as an appetizer or 4 as a main course

This is my variation of a dish I enjoy about once a week at Piccolo Paese, a road-side place on the way from New York City to my weekend home upstate. The proprietor, Chef Baco, makes a scrumptious pasta with tuna and pepperoncini—those little, pale green peppers you probably associate with salad bars. I have never asked him for the recipe, but I've done my level best to steal it here.

If you have enough time, let the sauce sit for a while to allow the flavor of the tuna to infuse it as thoroughly as possible.

---

4 tablespoons olive oil

3 cloves garlic, thinly sliced

1/2 cup dry white wine

3/4 cup Chicken Stock (page 23)

1 large, very ripe beefsteak tomato, seeds removed and cut into 1/4-inch dice

1 5 1/2-ounce can Italian tuna packed in oil (1/4 cup), drained

Coarse salt

1 pound dry linguine

2 tablespoons tiny capers, rinsed and drained

12 pitted black Kalamata olives, coarsely chopped

6 pepperoncini, or more to taste, stems removed and sliced crosswise into 1/4-inch rounds

1 teaspoon red pepper flakes (optional)

2 tablespoons roughly chopped flat-leaf parsley

Freshly ground black pepper

Warm the oil in a large sauté pan over medium-high heat. Add the garlic to the pan and cook until it begins to sizzle, about 1 minute.

Add the wine. (Be careful here; when the wine hits the oil, it will spit a bit.) Bring the wine to a boil and add the stock.

Cook until reduced by one-third, about 2 minutes, then add the tomato and tuna. Reduce the heat to low and allow to heat gently for 6–7 minutes.

❖ **IF MAKING IN ADVANCE**, you can prepare the sauce to this point, turn it off, and leave it, covered, for up to 20 minutes.

Meanwhile, bring a large pot of salted water to a boil and add the linguine. Cook according to the package directions, until *al dente*, about 9 minutes. Reserve a few tablespoons of cooking liquid and then drain.

Add the capers, olives, pepperoncini, red pepper flakes (if using), parsley, and pepper to the sauce. Taste and adjust the seasoning.

Add the pasta to the pan with the sauce. Add 1 or 2 tablespoons of reserved cooking liquid, toss well, and serve immediately.

WINE: Serve this with a Sangiovese.

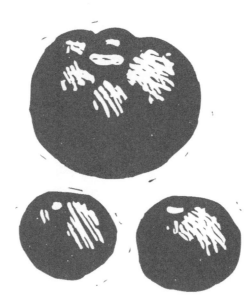

BRAISED DUCK LEGS WITH
EGG NOODLES

❧

Serves 6 as an appetizer or 4 as a main course

Braised duck sauce is one of those things, like *coq au vin*, best served with something simple that will soak up its juices without distracting from its flavor. In this case, egg noodles hit just the right note. Because they are the most delicate form of pasta, be careful not to overseason or overcook them.

4 duck legs	Pinch sugar
Coarse salt	4 plum tomatoes, cut into 1-inch dice
Freshly ground black pepper	2 cups red wine
1 tablespoon canola oil	1/4 cup white vinegar
1 large Spanish onion, cut crosswise and then into slices	6 cloves garlic, thinly sliced
	1 teaspoon chopped fresh rosemary
3 small carrots, cut on the bias into 1/2-inch pieces	1 pound egg noodles
	4 tablespoons mascarpone cheese
4 tablespoons tomato paste	(optional)

Season the duck legs liberally with salt and pepper.

Pour the oil into an ovenproof casserole and place the duck legs, skin side down, in the oil. Cook over medium heat until the skin is rendered and crisp, 10–12 minutes.

Turn over and cook an additional 2 minutes.

Preheat the oven to 300°F.

Remove the duck and all but 2 tablespoons duck fat from the casserole.

Return the casserole to the heat and add the onion and carrots. Cook for 3–4 minutes.

Add the tomato paste and cook another 3–4 minutes. Season with salt, pepper, and the sugar.

Add the tomatoes to the casserole and cook another 2–3 minutes.

Add the wine, vinegar, garlic, rosemary, and 1/2 cup water. Taste and adjust the seasoning.

Raise the heat to high and bring the mixture to a boil. Adjust the seasoning and return the legs to the casserole. (They should just be immersed.) Return to a boil.

Transfer the casserole to the preheated oven. Cook for 2 hours, or until the duck meat is practically falling off the bone.

Remove the casserole from the oven. Remove the legs from the liquid and allow to cool. Skim any residual fat from the sauce.

As soon as the duck legs are cool enough to handle, pick off any meat and return it to the sauce. (You may leave the skin on or strip it off before picking off the meat.)

Bring a pot of salted water to a boil. Add the noodles and cook until tender, about 3–5 minutes.

While the noodles are cooking, gently reheat the sauce over low heat.

Drain the noodles and divide them among 4–6 bowls. Top with the braised duck sauce and, if desired, a dollop of mascarpone.

WINE: Serve this bistro-style dish with a full-bodied red wine such as a zinfandel or a pinot noir.

FOIE GRAS RAVIOLI WITH CHICKPEAS, LEEKS, AND BASIL

By using a prepared foie gras mousse, this recipe gives the full impact of rich foie gras without the expense. The economy is furthered by cutting the foie gras mousse with chicken mousse, which helps maintain a silken texture when the ravioli filling is heated. This recipe produces a bit more chicken mousse than you need here because it is impossible to blend a smaller quantity with any consistency. It is also worth noting that although this produces the same number of ravioli as the other recipes in this book, it is recommended for six people because the foie gras is so rich.

FOIE GRAS AND CHICKEN MOUSSE

1 boneless, skinless, single chicken breast (about 3 ounces), ground or chopped
1 small clove garlic, minced
1 tablespoon fresh thyme leaves
Coarse salt
Freshly ground black pepper
1/2 egg white
1/3 cup heavy cream
8 ounces prepared foie gras mousse (available at specialty shops and gourmet markets, or by mail order from such companies as Dean and DeLuca and D'Artagnan)

Working in a bowl set over a bowl of ice, season the chicken with the garlic, thyme, salt, and pepper. (Do not taste the raw chicken for seasoning; just use your eyes to judge.)

Transfer the chicken to the bowl of a food processor. Add the egg white and process. Add the cream slowly in a thin stream until it is absorbed and the mixture is thick and smooth. You may want to stop the machine once to stir the mixture with a spatula to be sure the cream adheres.

Return the chicken mixture to the mixing bowl over ice to chill briefly.

Remove half of the chicken mixture to another bowl, add the foie gras mousse, and stir to incorporate. (Reserve the remaining mousse for another use, such as rounding out another filling or poaching balls of it for soup dumplings. If you are going to utilize it, do so right away; it spoils very quickly.)

To test for seasoning, cook a teaspoon of filling in simmering salted water and taste.

RAVIOLI	
2 fresh pasta sheets, about 12 × 18 inches (page 153), or 18 wonton skins	1 egg yolk, whisked (only if using wonton skins)
	Coarse salt

Lay 1 pasta sheet in front of you.

Place tablespoon portions of the foie gras filling about 2 inches apart on the sheet, leaving a 1-inch border at the top, bottom, and sides.

Lay the other sheet on top and allow it to conform to the shape of the filling mounds.

Using a pizza cutter or very sharp knife, cut around the filling.

Using the tines of a fork, smooth the edges of each raviolo.

IF USING WONTON SKINS, brush the edges with egg yolk and spoon 1 tablespoon of filling onto one half of the skin. Fold the skin over to form a rectangle (or choose a diagonal fold and make agnolotti).

For either pasta sheets or wonton skins, seal the edges with a fork or your fingers, leaving one corner unsealed.

One by one, place the ravioli in the palm of your hand and gently squeeze out any excess air, then seal the open corner.

❖ **IF MAKING IN ADVANCE,** freeze the ravioli on a cookie sheet, then transfer to a plastic bag. **WHEN READY TO PROCEED,** take the ravioli directly from the freezer to the pot.

SAUCE AND ASSEMBLY

3 large leeks, white part only, tough
    outer skin removed and sliced on
    the bias into 1-inch pieces
2 cups Chicken Stock (page 23)
9 tablespoons unsalted butter (1 stick
    plus 1 tablespoon), chilled and
    cut into 9 pieces

Coarse salt
Freshly ground black pepper
1 tablespoon soy sauce
1 tablespoon truffle oil
3/4 cup cooked chickpeas
4 tablespoons fesh basil chiffonade

Place the leeks in a small pot and add the stock and 1 tablespoon butter. Season with salt and pepper, and bring to a boil over high heat. Lower the heat to a simmer and braise for 10 minutes, or until tender. Strain the leeks over a bowl and reserve the leeks and stock separately.

Place the stock in a saucepan over moderate heat. Bring to a boil. Lower to a simmer.

Whisk in the remaining butter, 1 piece at a time, then blend with an immersion blender (or whisk intensely) to form a thick, creamy sauce.

Add the soy sauce and truffle oil to the sauce and season with salt and pepper.

Bring a pot of salted water to a gentle boil over high heat. Carefully add the ravioli and cook until they float on the surface, about 2–3 minutes for fresh or 4–5 minutes for frozen.

While the ravioli are cooking, add the leeks, chickpeas, and basil chiffonade to the sauce.

Transfer the ravioli to bowls using a slotted spoon. Spoon some sauce over each serving.

WINE: Serve this with a Riesling.

BUTTERNUT AGNOLOTTI WITH SMOKED DUCK, WILTED KALE, AND PARMESAN CHEESE

Serves 6 as an appetizer or 4 as a main course

The sublime pairing of butternut squash and sage makes this an ideal fall dish. The key to this recipe is making sure that the filling is intensely flavored and not at all watery. With squash that means a multistep process that concentrates the flavor and then removes the liquid created by doing so. Roasting and sautéing are the means to this end, whereas another method, such as boiling, would only add water and diminish the flavor. As focused as you need to be on extracting the liquid, make sure you don't burn the squash. Keep it from caking up in the pan by adding more butter as it cooks if necessary.

BUTTERNUT SQUASH FILLING

1 butternut squash (about 2 pounds)
2 1/2 tablespoons unsalted butter
Coarse salt
Freshly ground black pepper
Sugar
2 strips bacon

Preheat the oven to 400°F.

Cut the squash in half lengthwise and remove the seedbed.

Lay the squash halves, cut side up, on a cookie sheet and put a tablespoon of butter in each cavity.

Sprinkle each half very lightly with salt and pepper. If the squash appears particularly starchy or doesn't have a deep fiery orange color, sprinkle some sugar over each half as well.

Lay a strip of bacon lengthwise over each squash half.

Roast the squash halves in the preheated oven until tender, 35–40 minutes. (When done, I highly recommend snacking on the bacon because the only other alternative is to discard it.)

Drain the liquid from each squash half, then scoop the flesh into a food processor. Add the remaining 1/2 tablespoon butter to the bowl and puree until thick and creamy.

Transfer the puree to a large nonstick pan set over low heat. Cook, stirring with a rubber spatula every few minutes, until most of the moisture has evaporated, 10–15 minutes. Reserve.

AGNOLOTTI
2 fresh pasta sheets, about 18 × 20 inches (page 153), or 18 wonton skins

1 egg yolk, whisked (only if using wonton skins)
Coarse salt

Use a ring mold or biscuit cutter to cut 3-inch circles from each sheet of pasta. (This step is unnecessary if you are using wonton skins.)

Place one pasta circle or wonton skin in front of you. (If using wonton skin, brush the edges with egg yolk). Place a tablespoon of filling in the center of the dough and fold the dough over diagonally to form a half-moon shape. Using the tines of a fork, seal the edges, leaving one corner unsealed.

Repeat with the remaining pasta and ravioli. One by one place the agnolotti in the palm of your hand and gently squeeze out any excess air, then seal the open corner.

❖ **IF MAKING IN ADVANCE,** freeze the agnolotti on a cookie sheet, then transfer to a plastic bag and keep in the freezer for up to 2 weeks. **WHEN READY TO PROCEED,** take the agnolotti directly from the freezer to the pot.

SAUCE AND ASSEMBLY

1 tablespoon olive oil

1 clove garlic, thinly sliced

1 pound fresh green kale, stems and center stalks removed, well washed, and left a little damp

Coarse salt

Freshly ground black pepper

1/2 cup Chicken Stock (page 23)

12 tablespoons unsalted butter (1 1/2 sticks), at room temperature, cut into 12 pieces

1 tablespoon grated Parmesan cheese, plus 8 shards cut with a vegetable peeler

4 ounces store-bought smoked duck breast, cut into julienne strips (about 1 cup)

In a large saucepan, warm the oil over medium heat. Add the garlic to the pan and cook until it begins to sizzle, 2–3 minutes.

Add the slightly damp kale leaves. (It will kick and spit a bit, which is what you want.) Season with salt and pepper, then stir constantly until the kale is well wilted and tender, 5–6 minutes. Taste and adjust the seasoning if necessary.

Transfer the kale to a cookie sheet and spread it out to allow it to cool.

Pour the stock into a saucepan and bring to a boil over high heat.

Whisk in the butter, 1 tablespoon at a time.

Transfer to a blender and process on "frappe" or "chop" for about 3 seconds (or process in a food processor for the same amount of time), just to reinforce the emulsification. (See the tip on page 93 about blending hot liquids.)

Return the mixture to the pan over low heat. Season with salt, pepper, and the grated cheese. Add the wilted kale and duck. Keep over low heat to avoid overcooking the duck.

Bring a pot of salted water to a gentle boil over high heat. Carefully add the agnolotti and cook until they float on the surface, 1–2 minutes for fresh or 4–5 minutes for frozen.

Using a slotted spoon, divide the agnolotti among 4 bowls. Spoon some of the kale-duck mixture over each serving, season with pepper, and garnish with shards of Parmesan.

WINE: Serve this with an oaky chardonnay.

TRUFFLED POTATO RAVIOLI WITH ROAST SHIITAKES AND ROAST GARLIC BROTH

❦

Serves 6 as an appetizer or 4 as a main course

This ravioli may remind you of a pierogi because the potato filling is so hearty. Sauced with a heady garlic broth featuring roast shiitakes, this is dish is especially appropriate on cold winter days. Making it in advance is actually advantageous because it allows the truffle to permeate the potato.

RAVIOLI

2 fresh pasta sheets, about 18 × 20 inches (page 153), or 18 wonton skins

2 1/2 cups Potato Puree (page 268)

1 very small black truffle (1 ounce); white truffle or 1 tablespoon truffle oil may be substituted (see Food for Thought)

1 egg yolk, whisked (only if using wonton skins)

Coarse salt

Lay 1 pasta sheet in front of you.

Place tablespoon portions of the puree about 2 inches apart on the sheet, leaving a 1-inch border at the top, bottom, and sides.

Top each filling mound with a slice of truffle, or if using truffle oil, make a small indentation in each mound and place a drop of oil in the indentation.

Lay the other sheet on top and allow it to conform to the shape of the filling mounds.

Using a pizza cutter or very sharp knife, cut around the filling. Using the tines of a fork, smooth the edges of each raviolo.

IF USING WONTON SKINS, brush the edges with egg yolk and spoon 1 tablespoon of filling onto one half of the skin. Fold the skin over to form a rectangle.

For either pasta sheets or wonton skins, seal the edges with a fork or your fingers, leaving one corner unsealed. One by one, place the ravioli in the palm of your hand and gently squeeze out any excess air, then seal the open corner.

❖ **IF MAKING IN ADVANCE**, freeze the ravioli on a cookie sheet, then transfer to a plastic bag and keep in the freezer for up to 2 months. **WHEN READY TO PROCEED**, take the ravioli directly from the freezer to the pot.

ROAST GARLIC BROTH AND ASSEMBLY	1 cup Chicken Stock (page 23)
6 large shiitake mushrooms, stems removed	2 tablespoons Roasted Garlic Puree (page 12)
2 tablespoons olive oil	1 tablespoon finely grated Parmigiano-Reggiano cheese
Coarse salt	2 tablespoons finely chopped chives
Freshly ground black pepper	

Preheat the oven to 375°F.

Place the mushrooms in a small stainless steel bowl. Drizzle with the oil and season with salt and pepper.

Spread the mushrooms out on a cookie sheet and roast in the preheated oven for 4–5 minutes. Remove from the oven, allow to cool, and slice very thin.

Bring the stock to a simmer in a pot over medium-high heat. Whisk in the garlic puree and cheese.

Remove the stock from the heat, stir in the mushroom slices, and cover to keep warm.

Bring a pot of salted water to a boil over high heat.

Carefully add the ravioli to the water and cook until they float on the surface of the water, about 2–3 minutes for fresh or 4–5 minutes for frozen.

Transfer the ravioli to bowls using a slotted spoon. Spoon the mushrooms and broth over each serving and finish with the chopped chives.

FOOD FOR THOUGHT—TRUFFLES: Truffles can be dirty, so brush them gently and rinse and dry them quickly just before using them. If you don't have a truffle slicer, cut a sliver off one side to create a flat bottom and use a very sharp, thin-bladed knife to slice it as thin as possible.

OPTIONS: With the addition of some sliced poached or gently roasted chicken breast, pheasant, or guinea hen, and/or sautéed greens such as spinach, kale, or Swiss chard, this becomes a very substantial meal.

White Bean Ravioli with Rabbit "Stew"

🌿

Serves 4 as a main course

This is a dish that I conjured up for the awards reception when I was named one of the Top Ten Best New Chefs in America by *Food & Wine* magazine. Each of us was asked to prepare a dish for four hundred people, and this was ideal because it could be made in advance and frozen, and the sauce and meat could be held for several days. Also, the recipe can be multiplied beautifully.

Because of its lean nature, the rabbit should only be gently reheated. You don't want a stringy, cooked-to-death stew meat; rather, you are "moist-cooking" a very delicate meat.

BRAISED RABBIT AND SAUCE

4 rabbit fryer legs (see page 197)
Coarse salt
Freshly ground black pepper
3 tablespoons canola oil
1 tablespoon unsalted butter
1 large Spanish onion, cut crosswise
    and then into slices
3 small carrots, cut on the bias into
    1/2-inch pieces

2 tablespoons tomato paste
Pinch sugar
4 plum tomatoes, cut into 1-inch dice
2 cups dry white wine
1/4 cup white vinegar
2 cups Dark Chicken Stock (page 32)
6 cloves garlic, thinly sliced
1 teaspoon chopped fresh marjoram
1 teaspoon chopped fresh thyme
1 bay leaf, preferably fresh

Preheat the oven to 300°F.

Season the rabbit legs liberally with salt and pepper.

Put the oil and butter into a heavy-bottomed ovenproof casserole and heat over medium-high heat until the butter stops sizzling and is nicely browned.

Add the rabbit legs, skin side down, to the casserole and cook until nicely browned, about 2 minutes per side.

Remove the legs and all but 2 tablespoons melted butter and oil from the casserole.

Return the casserole to the heat and add the onion and carrots to the casserole. Cook for 3–4 minutes. Add the tomato paste and cook another 3–4 minutes. Season with salt, pepper, and the sugar.

Add the tomatoes to the casserole and cook another 2–3 minutes, then add the wine, vinegar, stock, garlic, marjoram, thyme, bay leaf, and 1/2 cup water. Taste and adjust the seasoning.

Raise the heat and bring the mixture to a boil. Adjust the seasoning again and return the legs to the casserole. Return to a boil.

Transfer the casserole to the preheated coven. Cook for 30 minutes, or until the meat is tender to the touch.

Remove the casserole from the oven. Remove the legs from the liquid and allow to cool. Skim any residual fat from the sauce. As soon as the legs are cool enough to handle, pick off all the meat.

❖ IF MAKING IN ADVANCE, the sauce and meat can be refrigerated separately for up to 3 days. WHEN READY TO PROCEED, reheat the sauce gently over moderate heat, then add the meat and heat through.

WHITE BEAN RAVIOLI AND ASSEMBLY	
2 fresh pasta sheets, about 12 × 18 inches (page 153), or 24 wonton skins	3 cups White Bean Puree (page 259) 1 egg yolk, whisked (only if using wonton skins) Coarse salt

Lay 1 pasta sheet in front of you.

Place tablespoon portions of the white bean puree about 2 inches apart on the sheet, leaving a 1-inch border at the top, bottom, and sides.

Lay the other sheet on top and allow it to conform to the shape of the filling mounds.

Using a pizza cutter or very sharp knife, cut around the mounds.

Using the tines of a fork, smooth the edges of each raviolo.

IF USING WONTON SKINS, simply spoon a tablespoon of filling onto 1 skin and cover with another skin. Brush the edge with egg yolk and lay another wonton skin on top.

For either pasta sheets or wonton skins, seal the edges with a fork or your fingers, leaving one corner unsealed. One by one, place the ravioli in the palm of your hand and gently squeeze out any excess air, then seal the open corner.

❖ **IF MAKING IN ADVANCE,** freeze the ravioli on a sheet pan, then transfer to a plastic bag. **WHEN READY TO PROCEED,** take it directly from the freezer to the pot.

Bring a pot of salted water to a boil over high heat. Carefully add the ravioli and cook until they float on the surface of the water, about 2–3 minutes for fresh or 4–5 minutes for frozen.

Transfer the ravioli to bowls using a slotted spoon. Spoon some sauce over each serving.

OPTIONS: This dish allows a lot of flexibility. If you want more textured ravioli, puree half the beans and leave the others whole. The rabbit sauce has a great affinity with Garlic Confit (page 199), assorted Roasted Wild Mushrooms (page 46), or a combination of both.

WINE: Serve this with a Sangiovese blend.

SPAGHETTI BOLOGNESE WITH
HERBED RICOTTA

🌿

I have always loved lasagna but never feel like waiting around while it bakes. This gives you the same combination of flavors with much less work.

BOLOGNESE SAUCE

2 small carrots, cut into 1/4-inch dice	1 tablespoon chopped fresh thyme
1 Spanish onion, cut into 1/4-inch dice	1 teaspoon chopped fresh oregano
3 ribs celery, cut into 1/4-inch dice	2 bay leaves
6 tablespoons olive oil	3 anchovy fillets
6 cloves garlic, thinly sliced	2 cups red wine
6 tablespoons tomato paste	1/2 cup white vinegar
6 plum tomatoes, coarsely chopped	1 cup Veal Stock (page 32) (optional)
Coarse salt	1 1/2 pounds coarsely ground meat
Freshly ground black pepper	(8 ounces each of beef, pork, and
1 tablespoon sugar	veal is ideal)

In a large saucepan, sweat the carrots, onion, and celery in 3 tablespoons oil over low to medium heat until tender, 6–7 minutes.

Reduce the heat to low and add the garlic and tomato paste. Cook for 3–4 minutes.

Add the tomatoes and season with salt, pepper, and half of the sugar. Cook for 2–3 minutes.

Add the thyme, oregano, bay leaves, anchovies, wine, vinegar, and veal stock. Raise the heat to high, bring to a boil, then lower the heat and let simmer.

Season the meat liberally with salt and pepper.

Heat 1 tablespoon oil in a large nonstick sauté pan set over high heat.

Add one-third of the meat to the pan and work it with a wooden spoon to ensure even cooking. Brown the meat on all sides, about 2–3 minutes, and transfer to the sauce. Repeat twice with the remaining oil and meat.

Let the sauce simmer for 90 minutes from the time you add the last portion of meat. Taste and adjust seasoning with salt, pepper, and remaining sugar, if needed.

❖ **IF MAKING IN ADVANCE,** this sauce can be refrigerated for up to 3 days and frozen for up to 1 month.

HERBED RICOTTA
2 cups finest-quality fresh ricotta cheese
3 tablespoons grated Parmigiano-
   Reggiano cheese
1 small clove garlic, finely minced
1 tablespoon chopped fresh basil
Pinch coarse salt
1 teaspoon freshly ground black pepper

In a mixing bowl, mix all the ingredients together with a rubber spatula until well incorporated.

PASTA AND ASSEMBLY
Coarse salt
1 pound dried spaghetti

Bring a large pot of salted water to a boil and add the spaghetti. Cook until *al dente*, about 9 minutes.

Drain the pasta and transfer to the pot with the hot sauce. Toss to coat. Divide among 4 large bowls. Top each serving with a healthy dollop of herbed ricotta.

OPTION: If you want to take this recipe one step further, cut some seeded plum tomatoes into dice, toss with extra-virgin olive oil, and spoon that over the ricotta.

WINE: Serve this with a Barolo.

TOMATO-THYME RISOTTO

🌿

Serves 4 as an accompaniment or side dish

This risotto is delicious on its own, but I recommend it as a versatile accompaniment to roast chicken, guinea hen, lobster, or scallops.

1 quart Chicken Stock (page 23)	1/4 cup dry white wine
2 tablespoons unsalted butter	4 heaping tablespoons Chopped
1 tablespoon olive oil	Roasted Tomatoes (page 13)
1 small Spanish onion, cut into	2 tablespoons Roasted Garlic Puree
1/4-inch dice	(page 12)
1 clove garlic, thinly sliced	1 teaspoon chopped fresh thyme
8 ounces (1 cup) arborio rice	

Pour the stock into a pot and bring to a simmer over high heat. Lower the heat and allow the stock to simmer.

In a large, heavy-bottomed pot, melt the butter and warm the oil over medium heat. Add the onion and garlic to the pot, and cook, stirring continuously, for 5 minutes.

Add the rice and stir to coat with the butter and oil. Stir constantly until the rice turns opaque in the center, 3–4 minutes. Add the wine and stir until it evaporates.

Add about 1 cup simmering stock and cook, stirring continuously, until the rice is almost dry. Continue to add stock by the cupful, stirring as you cook and adding more stock only as the previous addition has been absorbed. After about 15 minutes, begin adding the stock in smaller increments until you reach the desired consistency. The rice should be fully cooked, *al dente*, and have a pleasing, slightly creamy consistency.

❖ **IF MAKING IN ADVANCE,** omit the final addition of stock. Spread the risotto out on a cookie sheet and allow it to cool. Transfer to an airtight container and refrigerate. **WHEN READY TO PROCEED,** allow to come to room temperature, reheat in a pot over low-medium heat, and pour in the final addition of stock.

Gently stir the tomatoes, garlic puree, and thyme into the risotto.

HERB RISOTTO WITH LOBSTERS AND CHANTERELLES

❧

Serves 6 as an appetizer or 4 as a main course

As presented here, with lots of lobster, chanterelles, and a festive green herb puree, this luxurious recipe is perfect for special occasions. If you want to make something really outrageous, make a lobster stock using the shells from the cooked crustaceans (triple the recipe on page 29) or create a lobster butter to finish the dish (see sidebar). You might also increase the quantity of lobster, offering one per person, if that suits your budget and your guests' appetites.

GETTING ORGANIZED: This recipe *looks* complicated at first glance, but keep in mind that the individual processes for making the herb puree, lobster, and mushrooms are all very simple, and that any or all of them can be made up to a day ahead of time.

HERB PUREE	Coarse salt
24 sprigs very fresh flat-leaf parsley, tough stems discarded	1/2 clove garlic, sliced
2 sprigs tarragon	1 teaspoon cold water
1 bunch chives	1 tablespoon olive oil
	1 ice cube

Have an ice water bath ready.

Using a basket or very clean fine-mesh strainer, immerse the parsley, tarragon, and chives in boiling salted water for 5–6 seconds, until wilted but still bright green.

Remove the herbs from the water and, keeping them in the basket, immediately immerse in the ice water until completely cool.

Transfer the herbs to a cutting board, pat dry with paper towels, and chop coarsely by hand.

Place the herbs in a blender. (Don't use a food processor; you need the close quarters of a blender to ensure that the puree reaches the proper consistency.) Add the garlic, water, oil, and ice cube to the blender. (The ice cube will keep the blender blade from heating up and cooking the color out of the puree.) Pulse until the mixture becomes incorporated, then blend thoroughly for another 30–40 seconds. (You may need to stop the blender once or twice to scrape down the sides.)

Transfer the puree to a stainless steel bowl set in ice water to cool completely.

❖ **IF MAKING IN ADVANCE,** the puree can be stored in a tightly covered container in the refrigerator for up to 24 hours.

BOILED LOBSTERS	2 1-pound lobsters, or more if you're
Coarse salt	so inclined

Have a large ice water bath ready.

Bring a large pot of salted water to a boil. Carefully lower the lobsters into the pot, cover, and cook on high heat for 5 minutes.

Turn off the heat and let the lobsters sit in the covered pot for an additional minute.

Remove the lobsters from the pot and plunge into the ice water until chilled completely.

Remove the meat from the lobsters and cut into 1 1/2-inch dice. Reserve.

❖ **IF MAKING IN ADVANCE,** the lobster can be cooked, chilled, and diced up to 24 hours ahead of time. Wrap the pieces together in plastic wrap and refrigerate. **WHEN READY TO PROCEED,** allow to come to room temperature.

SAUTÉED CHANTERELLE MUSHROOMS	8 ounces chanterelle mushrooms, larger ones cut in half or quartered, smaller
1 tablespoon olive oil	ones left whole, and bottom tip of
1 tablespoon unsalted butter	stems trimmed (oyster mushrooms
2 cloves garlic, minced	can be substituted)
	Coarse salt
	Freshly ground black pepper

In a sauté pan, warm half of the oil, half of the butter, and half of the garlic over medium-high heat.

Add half of the mushrooms to the pan, season with salt and pepper, and cook until they begin to give off their liquid, about 3 minutes.

Drain the liquid from the pan and transfer the mushrooms to a cookie sheet, spreading them out to allow them to cool. (See Food for Thought.)

Repeat with the remaining ingredients.

❖ IF MAKING IN ADVANCE, the mushrooms may be chilled and stored in an airtight container in the refrigerator for up to 24 hours.

RISOTTO AND ASSEMBLY	1 large onion, cut into 1/4-inch dice
2 quarts Chicken Stock (page 23)	1 clove garlic, thinly sliced
2 tablespoons unsalted butter	1 pound (2 cups) Arborio rice
2 tablespoons olive oil	1/2 cup dry white wine

Pour the stock into a pot and bring to a simmer over high heat. Lower the heat and allow the stock to simmer.

In a large, heavy-bottomed pot, melt the butter and warm the oil over medium-high heat.

Add the onion and garlic to the pot, and cook, stirring continuously, for 5 minutes.

Add the rice and stir to coat with the butter and oil. Stir constantly until the rice turns opaque in the center, 3–4 minutes.

Add the wine and stir until it evaporates.

Add about 1 cup simmering stock and cook, stirring continuously, until the rice is almost dry. Continue to add stock by the cupful, stirring as you cook and adding more stock only when the previous addition has been absorbed. After about 15 minutes, begin adding the stock in smaller increments until you reach the desired consistency. The rice should be fully cooked, *al dente*, and have a pleasing, slightly creamy consistency.

❖ IF MAKING IN ADVANCE, leave out the final addition of stock. Spread the risotto out on a cookie sheet and allow it to cool. Transfer to an airtight container and refrigerate for up to 4 hours. WHEN READY TO PROCEED, allow to come to room temperature, reheat in a pot over low-medium heat, and pour in the final addition of stock.

Gently stir the mushrooms into the risotto, remove from the heat, and just before serving stir in the lobster meat and herb puree.

LOBSTER BUTTER

This adds an extra elegance to lobster dishes.

1/2 cup Lobster Stock (page 29)
Reserved roe from 1 or 2 female
   lobsters
8 tablespoons (1 stick) unsalted
   butter at room temperature

Pinch cayenne pepper
1/2 teaspoon chopped fresh tarragon
1/4 teaspoon tomato paste
Freshly ground black pepper

In a saucepot set over high heat, reduce the lobster stock to 1 tablespoon. Toward the end of the reduction, add the roe and blend with an immersion blender.

In a nonreactive mixing bowl, mix the butter with the reduced stock and roe, cayenne, tarragon, tomato paste, and pepper. Blend together well using a rubber spatula. Work into a log shape and cover tightly with plastic wrap. Refrigerate for up to 1 week or freeze for up to 2 months.

FOOD FOR THOUGHT—SPREADING HOT FOOD OUT TO COOL: After the mushrooms in this recipe are cooked, spread them out on a cookie sheet to allow them to cool, a technique I also use with cooked greens such as spinach and kale. Spreading these ingredients out on a cool surface prevents their contained heat from continuing to cook them.

OPTIONS: The herb puree may be used in other risottos or to finish soups. To create a wonderful sauce for simple roast chicken or broiled fish, stir some herb puree into the pan juices or cooking liquid and, if necessary, augment with some stock or butter.

PASTA DOUGH

❧

This recipe for basic pasta dough is provided for the ravioli recipes in this book. You can also cut the sheets to make spaghetti and other shapes, but I prefer dried pasta for those recipes because it can attain the proper *al dente* texture. If you have a pasta machine, by all means use it, but you'll have to make a greater quantity of more narrow sheets.

3 cups unbleached all-purpose or semolina flour	4 eggs, beaten Pinch coarse salt

Put the flour in a large mixing bowl and make an indentation in the center. Pour the egg into the indentation and add the salt. With a fork, gradually mix the flour and egg together. When the flour has been incorporated, turn the dough out onto a floured work surface. Work the dough, kneading it and flattening it out over and over, until it forms a smooth, elastic ball. This should take about 10 minutes. (If the dough doesn't hold together as you knead it, add a few drops of lukewarm water. If the dough feels sticky, sprinkle it lightly with flour.) Dust the dough with flour, cover with plastic wrap, and refrigerate for 30 minutes.

Keep in mind that climate and humidity will have an effect on the dough, so you may need to add some flour or water to arrive at the desired result.

Dust the dough with flour, cover with plastic wrap, and let rest in a cool place for 30 minutes before proceeding.

Separate the dough into 2 equal balls. Working on a floured surface and using a rolling pin, roll the dough into 2 sheets, each about 1/8 inch thick and roughly 18 × 20 inches. The sheets should have a slight elasticity to them; when pulled, they should give just a bit but return to their original shape. Be careful when rolling to ensure that you are creating a uniform thickness across the sheets.

Fish and Shellfish

When I was a kid in upstate New York, there was little access to fresh fish. As a matter of fact, there wasn't *any* access to it. In the early seventies, however, a friend of mine invited me to join him and his father on a smelting expedition in Ithaca, New York's, Fall Creek. We had a blast. You threw a net affixed to a long pole into the water and let the current pull it along. As the smelts moved upstream, they'd be caught, and just like that you'd pull a half-gallon basket of smelts out of the water. I took a bucket home with me, and when my grandmother caught sight of them, she insisted that they be eaten immediately. Before I had my coat off, she had set about gutting them, dredging them in flour, and frying them, and before I knew what had happened, I was wolfing down one of the first gourmet meals I had ever experienced. Forgive the pun, but I was hooked.

There is so much sushi-grade fish served as rare as can be these days that it is amusing to recall that not too long ago that quality of fish wasn't available. Even during my early years of cooking I didn't come across that much fresh fish. Then I went to France where we had daily deliveries that blew my mind—things like cases of just-caught sea bass or langoustines that were still alive and twitching around in the basket. When we cooked them, they were like nothing I had ever tasted.

As was the case with a lot of my peers, I returned to New York eager to cook fish in the same rare fashion that we did over there. Although a few people were doing it here (most notably the late great Gilbert Le Coze of Le Bernardin), there wasn't the supply or—more significant—the demand for it. As years went by, it became fashionable, of course. When fish is the highest quality, I love it simple, with just some lemon and parsley, although I also enjoy it with more assertive accompaniments such as the ones that follow.

Here are a few strong opinions that I've developed over the past two decades of cooking fish and seafood:

- There are a few things that every single cookbook ever published says about shopping for fish, so I'm going to dispense with them in record time. When shopping for fish, stay flexible and be prepared to use the freshest catch available on any given day. Look for the signs of freshness: clear eyes, bright red gills, and, above all, that the fish doesn't smell fishy. Here is a shortcut to having to pay too much attention to all that stuff—identify a first-rate fishmonger whom you trust. That person will have the most popular fish available all the time and wouldn't think of selling you an inferior product. He'll also cut things the way you need them for recipes and do a better job of it than you or I ever could.

- With filleted fish, wherever applicable, leave the skin on. It adds a nice protective element to tender flesh and also supplies a crisp contrast when cooked. To keep it from curling in the pan when it cooks, score the skin with a razor blade at 1-inch intervals. This will lend it an extra flexibility, and those score marks will add a nice presentational element.

- Like meat and poultry, fish tastes better on the bone. But since most home cooks don't know how to fillet a fish, the recipes in this chapter are geared toward fillets. If you can, though, I encourage you to cook your fish on the bone and experience the difference for yourself.

- I use the phrase "tuna mignon" to refer to a cut from the tuna's loin that approximates the size and shape of a filet mignon. I happen to think that the meatiness of this cut is ideal for most preparations. However, if you prefer a 1-inch-thick steak, by all means use that instead; just be sure to eliminate the broiler step in the recipes and cook it about 20–30 seconds on each side if you like your fish rare.

- When grilling fish, make sure the grill is extremely hot and be careful to brush away any old ash before laying a new fish on the grate. It is also advantageous to oil the fish very lightly and give the grill a quick rub of oil just before placing the fish on it. A trick that many chefs use is to ball up an old but clean rag and tie it up with butcher's twine. Use tongs to dip the rag in a shallow container of oil and then rub the grill grate with it just before laying the fish on top.

- The single biggest problem with shellfish is overcooking. My personal rule of thumb is to shave one minute off the cooking time and let that final minute pass off the heat. The contained heat of the water will finish the cooking more gently. By the same token, when reheating shelled shellfish in broth or sauce, do it gently and never let the sauce or soup boil when the meat is in it.

- Buy it and use it. Buy fish the day you're going to use it or the night before at the earliest.

GRILLED SALMON WITH YUKON GOLD POTATOES, BRAISED CELERY, AND REMOULADE SAUCE

❧

Serves 4

The remoulade sauce in this dish provides a wonderful contrast to the smoky grilled fish, and when combined with the Yukon Gold potatoes, the result brings to mind a warm, sophisticated version of a potato salad. If you don't want to go to the trouble of smoking the salmon, simply grill a fresh fillet, although you'll be sacrificing one layer of flavor.

GETTING ORGANIZED: Although you need to be rather organized to have this come out right, some components, such as the lettuce leaves, can actually be served cold and the potatoes can drop down to lukewarm without losing anything.

REMOULADE SAUCE
3 egg yolks
1 clove garlic, minced
Juice of 2 lemons, plus more to taste
1 1/2 cups extra-virgin olive oil
2/3 cup coarsely chopped cornichons
2 tablespoons capers, rinsed
    and drained

2 heaping tablespoons Dijon mustard,
    or more to taste
4 shallots, minced
Coarse salt
Freshly ground black pepper

Place the yolks in a food processor with the garlic and one-fourth of the lemon juice. With the food processor on, add the oil in a slow, thin stream until the mixture emulsifies and all the oil has been absorbed.

Add the cornichons, capers, mustard, and the remaining lemon juice. Pulse until the cornichons are chopped but the sauce is still chunky, 10–15 seconds.

Add the shallots and pulse for 1 or 2 seconds. Season to taste with salt and pepper.

Add more lemon juice or mustard if you want. If the flavors seem too concentrated or the remoulade seems too thick, loosen it up with 1–2 tablespoons very hot tap water.

You want it pourable and looser than store-bought mayonnaise. Trust your palate and adjust the recipe to suit it. Whichever way you go, don't be shy. You won't be using much of this sauce on the plate, so you want it to really make an impact.

❖ **IF MAKING IN ADVANCE,** this sauce will keep refrigerated for up to 3 days.

BRAISED CELERY
1 head firm, fresh celery, leaf end cut
   away and leaves reserved for garnish
1¹/2 cups Chicken Stock (page 23)
   or Basic Vegetable Stock (page 24)

Coarse salt
Freshly ground black pepper
2 cloves garlic, smashed

Separate the celery ribs and, using a vegetable peeler, gently remove the stringy outer part of the ribs. Cut the ribs on the bias into 3-inch lengths.

Pour the stock into a pot, season with salt and pepper, and add the garlic.

Add the celery and cook over low heat until slightly softened but still *al dente*, about 7–8 minutes. (If the stock doesn't cover the celery, add enough water to cover.)

Remove the celery from the liquid and let cool. Reserve the cooking liquid for another use such as soup or stock, or discard.

❖ **IF MAKING IN ADVANCE,** the celery can be refrigerated for up to 24 hours. **WHEN READY TO PROCEED,** allow to come to room temperature.

YUKON GOLD POTATOES
Coarse salt

4 medium Yukon Gold potatoes

Place the potatoes in a pot of heavily salted water and bring to a boil over high heat.

Cook until the potatoes are tender and easily pierced with a knife, about 15–20 minutes, depending on size.

Drain but do not rinse the potatoes.

As soon as they are cool enough to handle, slice the potatoes into ¹/2-inch discs. (Wipe the knife clean periodically as you slice or the starch will accumulate and drag as you work, marring the shapes.) Reserve.

SALMON AND ASSEMBLY
4 cups wood chips, such as applewood,
   cherrywood, or alderwood
4 6-ounce skinless salmon fillets

Oil for drizzling and grilling
Coarse salt
Freshly ground black pepper

Preheat the oven to 325°F.

Place the wood chips in a stainless steel bowl and add enough water just to cover them. Allow to soak for at least 30 minutes and preferably 2 hours.

Prepare an outdoor grill, letting the coals burn down until covered with white ash.

Scatter the soaked wood chips over the coals.

Season the salmon with salt and pepper, and drizzle it lightly with oil. Lightly oil the grill grate.

Place the salmon on the grill and cook to desired doneness. (It is difficult to specify an exact cooking time. If you like healthy grill marks, it needs about 3–4 minutes on one side, then 2–3 minutes on the other.) If you are not sure about how the fish is progressing, open one with a knife and take a peek inside. It should be cooked a bit inward from the edge but still opaque at the center. (Just be sure to serve yourself that one.)

Place the potatoes and celery in separate small pots and reheat over the grill.

To serve: Place the potato slices and celery in the center of a platter. Surround with the salmon fillets and pass the remoulade sauce alongside in a sauceboat.

For a more formal presentation, lay out the potatoes and celery decoratively on the plate, keeping the potato slices close enough to each other to create a "base" on which the salmon may rest. Place the salmon fillets on top of the potatoes. Drizzle the sauce over and around the salmon. Garnish the dish with the reserved celery leaves and serve the remaining remoulade sauce on the side in a sauceboat.

OPTIONS: This is the way I serve this dish at home, but if you want to simplify things, the salmon and remoulade sauce alone are a delicious combination.

WINE: Serve this with a pinot blanc.

GRILLED TROUT WITH SPAETZLE
AND BROWN BUTTER SAUCE

Serves 4

If there's one great example of how good fish on the bone can be, it's trout. Many people are put off by eating trout with the head on and bones in, but it is actually fairly easy to navigate your way around.

Be sure to follow the important direction of letting the spaetzle get nutty brown and crisp.

SERVE THIS WITH Braised Bibb Lettuce (page 271).

SPAETZLE
3/4 cup all-purpose flour
1/2 teaspoon coarse salt, plus more for
   boiling water
1/4 teaspoon baking powder
2 eggs

1/4 cup milk
1 heaping tablespoon Dijon mustard
1 tablespoon chopped chives
1/2 teaspoon freshly ground black
   pepper

In a mixing bowl, stir together the flour, salt, and baking powder.

In a separate bowl, lightly beat the eggs, then pour them over the dry ingredients. Work the mixture into a thick batter.

Add the milk, a little at a time, stirring until each addition is incorporated.

Stir in the mustard, chives, and pepper. Let rest for 15–20 minutes.

Bring a large pot of lightly salted water to a boil.

Set a colander with large holes over the pot. Pour one-third of the batter into the colander and push it through with a rubber spatula.

Allow the spaetzle to cook for about 1 minute. (They will rise to the surface when done.) Remove with a slotted spoon, shake off as much excess water as possible, and transfer to another strainer or a bowl lined with paper towels.

Repeat with the remaining batter.

BROWN BUTTER SAUCE
8 ounces (2 sticks) unsalted butter
2 tablespoons capers, rinsed and
    drained
1 tablespoon finely chopped flat-leaf
    parsley
Juice of 1 lemon

Melt the butter in a sauté pan over medium-high heat and continue to cook until it turns brown and nutty, 6–7 minutes.

Add the capers and parsley to the sauce, then add the lemon juice.

Remove from the heat and keep covered and warm.

TROUT AND ASSEMBLY
4 trout (12–14 ounces each), with
    heads and tails on
Coarse salt
Freshly ground black pepper
Olive oil for brushing fish
1 tablespoon unsalted butter

Preheat the oven to 325°F.

Season the trout inside and out with salt and pepper.

Prepare an outdoor grill, letting it burn down until covered with white ash. Make sure that there are at least 4–5 inches between the coals and the grate.

Brush the trout with oil before placing it on the grill to be sure that it won't stick. Grill slowly, 4–5 minutes per side. If unsure of doneness, after flipping, make an incision just behind the gill. (This is one of the thicker parts of the fish.)

Heat 1 tablespoon butter in a nonstick pan. Let it get good and hot, sizzling but not yet browned.

Add the spaetzle to the pan. Let cook for 30 seconds, then give them a toss and cook another 30 seconds. Cook until the spaetzle take on some brown color.

To serve, place the spaetzle in a bowl. Lay the trout on a platter and serve the sauce alongside in a sauceboat.

For a more formal presentation, place a trout in the center of each of 4 dinner plates and mound some spaetzle next to it. Spoon the brown butter sauce over and around the fish.

FOOD FOR THOUGHT—TROUT: They are part of the same family as salmon—the *Salmonidae* family. Some live exclusively in fresh water; others, such as rainbow trout, start their lives in fresh water but move to the ocean and become steelhead trout. Other members of this family include char and grayling.

OPTION: You can omit the spaetzle, and this dish will still be delicious.

BEER: Serve this with a crisp ale.

PORCINI-CRUSTED TUNA WITH WHITE BEAN PUREE AND MUSHROOM BROTH

Serves 4

Here is an example of some great contrasts. Coating a piece of super-fresh tuna with porcini powder (see Food for Thought) brings out the distinct qualities of both ingredients. And the white bean puree offers a moist, starchy complement. The dish is unified by the mushroom broth, which underscores the mushroom theme and is beautifully soaked up by the puree. You will need a spice mill for the powder. You can also use a coffee grinder, but clean it out well before and after. (And open the lid slowly after grinding; the superfine powder will rise like smoke if you don't.)

PORCINI POWDER
1¹/2-ounce package dried porcini
   mushrooms

Preheat the oven to 275°F. Spread the dried porcini on a cookie sheet, place in the oven, and allow to dry thoroughly, 10–12 minutes. Transfer to a grinder or spice mill and pulverize until it is powder.

❖ **IF MAKING IN ADVANCE,** this powder will keep for several months when stored in a cool, dry place.

PORCINI-CRUSTED TUNA
AND ASSEMBLY

24 sprigs beautiful, young, tender
   flat-leaf parsley
1 3¹/2-ounce package enoki mushrooms
2 tablespoons extra-virgin olive oil
Drizzle truffle oil
Coarse salt

Freshly ground black pepper
White Bean Puree (page 259)
4 tablespoons olive oil
1¹/2 cups Mushroom Stock
   (page 26)
4 8-ounce tuna "mignons"
   (see page 156)

Preheat the broiler.

In a small bowl, dress the parsley and mushrooms with the extra-virgin olive oil, truffle oil, salt, and pepper. Toss gently just to coat the parsley and mushrooms.

If the white bean puree is cold, allow it to come to room temperature, then gently reheat it in a sauté pan with 2 tablespoons olive oil in the following manner: Heat the oil over medium-high heat, then add the puree to the pan. Set aside, covered, to keep warm.

Warm the mushroom stock in a pot set over medium heat.

Season the tuna on all sides with salt and pepper, then with the porcini powder.

Heat the remaining 2 tablespoons olive oil in a 12-inch ovenproof sauté pan over high heat until almost smoking.

Place the tuna mignons in the pan and sear for 10–20 seconds on each side to brown and seal them. (Use tongs to turn the tuna onto various sides.)

Finish the tuna under the broiler for 1–2 minutes, depending on how well done you like your fish.

Serve the tuna on a platter with the parsley and mushrooms sprinkled on top. Pass the white bean puree in a bowl and the mushroom stock in a sauceboat alongside.

For a more formal presentation, mound some white bean puree in the center of each of 4 large dinner plates or bowls. Place a tuna steak in the center of the puree, toward the 6 o'clock position. (I like to cut a corner off each tuna using a sharp knife to show a little window into the ruby red rareness of the fish.) Place some parsley-mushroom salad behind the tuna, then spoon the mushroom stock around the puree. Drizzle the entire dish with truffle oil.

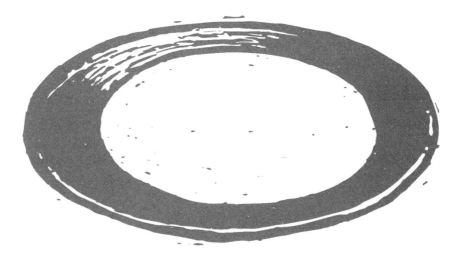

OPTIONS: If you prefer your fish very rare and with a cool center, take it out of the refrigerator just before cooking and omit the broiler step.

FOOD FOR THOUGHT—MAKING PORCINI POWDER: Porcinis have to be very dry to get a good yield when pulverized. If there is any moisture at all, they will simply ball up. Porcini powder will keep indefinitely, and I encourage you to keep some on hand because it adds a compelling element to a number of dishes: Toss some with some hot pasta, garlic, and olive oil, and you'll have something irresistible. You can also stir a bit into risotto and soups.

WINE: Serve this with a complex chardonnay or white Burgundy.

SEARED TUNA WITH CHICKPEA-EGGPLANT PUREE AND TOMATO VINAIGRETTE

Serves 4

This recipe is a bit out of character for me, but I created it to achieve a Mediterranean effect for the summertime. The tomato, olive oil, garlic, lemon zest, and black olives in the garnish all strongly suggest the Mediterranean, as does the sumac. Take the time to seek out this spice, available from Middle Eastern grocers. It gives off a pleasing lemony flavor and also provides a surprising visual effect: The tuna, which doesn't look particularly attractive when seared, becomes a beautiful reddish brown when crusted with the sumac.

TOMATO VINAIGRETTE	Coarse salt
3/4 cup Tomato Broth (page 27)	Freshly ground black pepper
1/2 cup extra-virgin olive oil	

Whisk the broth and oil together. (Do not emulsify.) Season with salt and pepper to taste.

❖ **IF MAKING IN ADVANCE,** this vinaigrette can be refrigerated in a tightly covered container for up to 2 days.

CHICKPEA-EGGPLANT PUREE	3 cups Chicken Stock (page 23), water, or a combination
2 large eggplants (may be omitted, but add an extra 1/2 cup chickpeas)	Freshly ground black pepper
3 tablespoons olive oil	3 tablespoons extra-virgin olive oil
Coarse salt	Juice of 2 lemons
1 cup canned chickpeas (see Food for Thought)	2 cloves garlic, minced
	1 heaping tablespoon tahini paste

Preheat the oven to 350°F.

Cut the eggplants in half lengthwise.

Score the exposed flesh, rub with the olive oil, and season with salt.

Place the eggplants on a cookie sheet and cook in the preheated oven until very soft, about 90 minutes.

While the eggplants are cooking, prepare the chickpeas: Place them in a small pot, cover with approximately 3 cups stock, and season with salt and pepper. Place over high heat, bring to a boil, then lower the heat and let simmer for 3–4 minutes. Drain.

Place the chickpeas in the bowl of a food processor and pulse a few times to break them down. Scrape the sides as you work to get an even mixture.

Drizzle the extra-virgin olive oil into the bowl and pulse to blend with the chickpeas.

Add the lemon juice, garlic, and tahini paste, and puree until smooth in texture. Season with salt and pepper and pulse again. Reserve.

Remove the eggplants from the oven, allow to cool, then scoop out the flesh.

Puree the eggplants in a food processor, season with salt and pepper, and fold into the chickpea puree.

❖ **IF MAKING IN ADVANCE,** this puree can be tightly covered and stored in the refrigerator for up to 3 days. **WHEN READY TO PROCEED,** allow to come to room temperature.

SEARED TUNA AND ASSEMBLY

1 cup loosely packed microgreens, sprouts, or any small lettuces available at gourmet grocers

Zest of 1 lemon, peeled in strips with a zester

10 Kalamata olives, pitted and sliced lengthwise into slivers

Few drops extra-virgin olive oil

Coarse salt

Freshly ground black pepper

4 8-ounce tuna "mignons" (see page 156)

6–8 tablespoons sumac (available from Middle Eastern grocers; paprika may be substituted)

2 tablespoons canola or vegetable oil

Preheat the broiler.

If refrigerated, allow the tomato vinaigrette to come to room temperature.

Gently reheat the chickpea puree over low heat. Remove from the heat and cover to keep warm.

Toss the microgreens, lemon zest, olives, and extra-virgin olive oil together in a bowl. Season with salt and pepper. Reserve.

Season the tuna on both sides with salt, pepper, and sumac.

Heat the canola oil in an ovenproof sauté pan until almost smoking. Place the tuna mignons in the pan and sear for 30–40 seconds on each side. If the mignons are particularly thick, sear the sides as well.

Finish under the broiler for 1–2 minutes, depending on how well done you like your fish.

To serve, place the greens in the center of a platter and surround with the tuna. Pass the chickpea puree in a bowl and the vinaigrette in a sauceboat, with a small spoon alongside for stirring.

For a more formal presentation: Spoon a mound of chickpea puree in the center of each of 4 dinner plates or large pasta bowls. Place a tuna mignon on top but toward the lower portion of the plate. Place some greens behind the tuna. Spoon the vinaigrette all around. Serve immediately.

FOOD FOR THOUGHT—CHICKPEAS: Because individual chickpeas are so small, attaining the smooth, creamy puree in a food processor requires making more than this recipe calls for. (After a few seconds a smaller quantity will simply elude the blade by sticking to the sides of the bowl.) Serve the extra puree cold with pita bread or put on the table in place of butter.

OPTIONS: If you prefer your fish very rare and with a cool center, take it out of the refrigerator just before cooking and omit the broiler step.

PEPPERED TUNA WITH PARSNIP PUREE, SHALLOT CONFIT, AND RED WINE SAUCE

Serves 4

This hearty, meatlike treatment of tuna is especially appropriate in the winter, although the red wine sauce is intense and pleasing year-round. The heat of the pepper is countered by the sweetness of the shallots and the parsnip puree, and the roundness of red wine sauce really pulls everything together. Special bonus effect: When the parsnip puree soaks up the red wine sauce, look out! They are spectacular together.

RED WINE SAUCE

1 tablespoon olive oil	1/2 cup white vinegar
1 tablespoon plus 1 teaspoon unsalted butter	2 teaspoons sugar
1 cup thinly sliced shallots	1 tablespoon black peppercorns
1/3 cup sliced garlic	1 bay leaf
3 1/2 cups (approximately) rich red wine such as zinfandel or pinot noir	2 sprigs thyme

---

In a saucepan, heat the oil and 1 tablespoon butter over low heat until almost smoking.

Add the shallots and garlic, and cook for 20–25 minutes, stirring occasionally with a wooden spoon and scraping any caramelized bits of shallot or garlic from the bottom of the pot.

Add the wine, vinegar, sugar, peppercorns, bay leaf, and thyme.

Raise the heat to high, bring to a boil, lower the heat, and simmer until reduced by one-third, 25–30 minutes. Pour the mixture through a fine-mesh strainer. Reserve the sauce and discard the solids.

❖ **IF MAKING IN ADVANCE,** cool, cover tightly, and refrigerate for up to 5 days. **WHEN READY TO PROCEED,** return to a boil and whisk in 1 teaspoon butter if you'd like to enrich the sauce. Season with salt only; there is already plenty of pepper.

SHALLOT CONFIT	1¹/₄ cups canola oil (approximate)
12 shallots, peeled and cut lengthwise into wedges	

Place the shallots in a small pot with just enough oil to cover and set over low heat.

Cook about 1 ¹/₄ hours, or until the shallots are sweet, tender, and deep golden brown. (Test by piercing with a sharp, thin-bladed knife.)

They can sit in the oil, off the heat, until ready to serve. At that point, drain well.

PEPPERED TUNA AND ASSEMBLY	Coarse salt
Parsnip Puree (page 261)	8 tablespoons coarsely ground black
4 8-ounce tuna "mignons" (page 156)	pepper
(see Food for Thought)	2 tablespoons canola or vegetable oil

Preheat the broiler.

If the parsnip puree has been refrigerated, reheat it in a double boiler set over simmering water.

Season the tuna on both sides with salt. Spread the pepper out on a plate and press the tuna on the pepper to give it a healthy *au poivre* coating.

Heat the oil in an ovenproof sauté pan until almost smoking.

Place the tuna mignons in the pan and sear for 1 minute. Turn the mignons over and sear for an additional 1 minute. If the mignons are particularly thick, sear the sides as well.

Finish under the broiler for 1–2 minutes, depending on how well done you like your fish.

To serve, place the shallots in the center of a platter and surround with the tuna. Pass the puree in a bowl and the red wine sauce in a sauceboat alongside.

For a more formal presentation, spoon a mound of parsnip puree in the center of each of 4 dinner plates or large pasta bowls. Arrange the shallots decoratively on top of the puree. Place a tuna mignon on top but toward the lower portion of the plate. Spoon the red wine sauce all around. Serve immediately.

FOOD FOR THOUGHT—SHOPPING FOR TUNA: Avoid tail cuts of tuna steaks. Those with white circular striations are from the back of the fish and tend to be tough.

OPTIONS: If you prefer your fish very rare and with a cool center, take it out of the refrigerator just before cooking and omit the broiler step.

WINE: Serve this with a zinfandel.

ROASTED SEA BASS WITH WILTED KALE
AND WHITE BALSAMIC VINAIGRETTE

🌿

Serves 4

Here is another meaty treatment of fish that is also ideal on a winter's day. The chewy kale and white balsamic vinaigrette create a perfectly balanced trio when paired with the fish. The white balsamic vinegar shows more restraint than plain white vinegar; it has the sweetness of balsamic vinegar but doesn't run roughshod over the other components of the dish. Whatever fish you chose to use (see Options), be sure to ask your fishmonger for thick fillets with the skin still on. This cooking technique results in a tender flesh and a nice crisp skin. If you don't want to eat the skin, simply peel it off before serving, but I wouldn't miss it for the world.

SERVE THIS WITH Red Lentil Mash (page 252). The delicate flavor of the lentils is a great vehicle for firm-fleshed white fish. You can also serve this with White Bean Puree (page 259).

WHITE BALSAMIC VINAIGRETTE	Juice of 2 lemons
2 heaping tablespoons old-fashioned	2/3 cup olive oil
French grain mustard	Coarse salt
1/2 cup white balsamic vinegar	Freshly ground black pepper

Place the mustard in a small nonreactive mixing bowl. Moisten with the vinegar, lemon juice, and oil.

Whisk the ingredients together. Season with salt and pepper to taste. Reserve.

❖ **IF MAKING IN ADVANCE,** this vinaigrette can be kept in the refrigerator for up to 24 hours.

> **WILTED KALE**
>
> 2 tablespoons olive oil
> 3 cloves garlic, thinly sliced
> 1 bunch (1½ pounds) fresh green kale,
>   stems and center stalks removed,
>   well washed, and left a little damp
>
> Coarse salt
> Freshly ground black pepper

In a large saucepot, warm the oil over medium heat.

Add the garlic to the pot and cook until it begins to sizzle, 2–3 minutes.

Add the slightly damp kale to the pot. (It will kick and spit a bit, which is what you want.) Season with salt and pepper, then stir constantly until the kale is well wilted and tender, 5–6 minutes. Taste and adjust the seasoning if necessary. (You may need to cook this in batches; if so, spread out each batch to cool on a cookie sheet and repeat until the process is done. This will prevent overcooking.)

❖ **IF MAKING IN ADVANCE,** this can be prepared the day before and stored in a tightly sealed container in the refrigerator.

> **ROASTED SEA BASS**
> **AND ASSEMBLY**
> 4 8-ounce sea bass fillets
>
> Coarse salt
> Freshly ground black pepper
> 2 tablespoons olive oil

Preheat the oven to 450°F.

If using fish with the skin on, score the skin with a razor blade or very sharp, very thin knife.

Season fish on both sides if skinned; if skin on, season flesh side only, after scoring.

Warm the oil in a 12-inch ovenproof sauté pan over medium-high heat.

Place the fish, skin side down, in the pan. Press down on the fish with a spatula to keep them from curling. Cook for 2 minutes, or until the skin is relaxed and starting to brown.

Transfer the sauté pan to the floor of the oven. (It will continue to sauté, but the heat of the oven will also cook the flesh. See Food for Thought.) Cook for 4–5 minutes, checking for doneness after 2 minutes. Baste the fish every minute as it cooks.

While the fish is cooking, reheat the kale and any other accompaniments.

To serve, place the kale in the center of a large platter and arrange the bass around it. Pass the sauce in a sauceboat alongside.

For a more formal presentation, place some kale in the center of each of 4 dinner plates. Place the fish, skin side up, on the kale and drizzle the vinaigrette over and around the fish.

FOOD FOR THOUGHT—COOKING SEA BASS: Pay careful attention to the cooking time here. Sea bass tend to be larger than other fish, producing thicker fillets that call for longer cooking times than you might be used to.

OPTIONS: You may substitute other firm-fleshed white fish such as halibut or cod for the sea bass. If you opt to do this, ask the fishmonger if the skin of the fish you select is edible. If not, remove it before serving.

In a restaurant setting we take some Veal Stock (page 32), season it with salt and pepper, and use it as a sauce. Then we spoon the vinaigrette over that; it separates rather nicely. If you like, incorporate this touch at home. You might also finish the dish with a sprinkling of minced browned bacon.

SEARED STRIPED BASS WITH TARRAGON, TOMATO, AND BLACK OLIVES IN A TOMATO BROTH WITH COUSCOUS

🌿

Serves 4

This is a dish I created for the first menu at Alison on Dominick Street. What makes it noteworthy are the enormous vibrant flavors created in such a light dish. The couscous is a perfect foil for the tomato broth; it soaks up the broth but is lighter than, say, potato puree, which would be much too imposing here. When reheating the tomato broth, add the garnish during the last minute to keep all the flavors, including that of the broth, distinct.

TOMATO BROTH	1/2 cup dry white wine
1 tablespoon olive oil	3 tablespoons white vinegar
1 medium carrot, cut into large dice	Sprig tarragon
1 rib celery, cut into large dice	10 black peppercorns
3 cloves garlic, smashed	1 bay leaf
4 tablespoons tomato paste	6 plum tomatoes, coarsely chopped
1 teaspoon sugar	Coarse salt

Warm the oil in a pot. Add the carrot, celery, and garlic to the pot and cook until softened, 5–7 minutes.

Add the tomato paste and sugar, lower the heat, and cook for 3–4 minutes.

Add the wine, vinegar, tarragon, peppercorns, bay leaf, and tomatoes. Mix together, season with salt, and cook for 2–3 minutes.

Add enough water to cover by 1 inch.

Raise the heat to high, bring to a boil, then skim the surface. Reduce the heat until the broth is just simmering. Simmer for 15–20 minutes, until the flavor is vibrant and round. Strain through a fine-mesh strainer. Reserve.

❖ IF MAKING IN ADVANCE, allow to cool and keep tightly covered in the refrigerator for up to 3 days or in the freezer for up to 2 months.

COUSCOUS	Coarse salt
1 cup dry couscous	

Place the couscous in a small stainless steel bowl.

Bring a few cups of lightly salted water to a boil.

Pour enough boiling water over the couscous to cover it by about 1/8 inch.

Cover the bowl with plastic wrap, pulling it tightly to form an airtight seal. The couscous will cook and absorb the liquid in 15–20 minutes. (See Food for Thought.)

Remove the plastic and fluff the couscous with the tines of a fork.

❖ IF MAKING IN ADVANCE, the couscous can be prepared up to this point and stored in a tightly covered container in the refrigerator for up to 3 days.

SEARED STRIPED BASS AND ASSEMBLY	2 tablespoons olive oil
1/4 cup Chicken Stock (page 23)	8 Kalamata olives, each pitted and cut into 8 thin crescent-shaped slivers
1/2 tablespoon unsalted butter	4 plum tomatoes, seeded and cut into 1/4-inch dice
4 7-ounce striped bass fillets with skin on (be sure to ask your fishmonger to remove the pin bones or do it yourself with a pair of tweezers)	1/2 teaspoon fresh tarragon leaves
	1 lemon, peeled, sectioned, and each section cut into thirds
Coarse salt	
Freshly ground black pepper	2 tablespoons finely minced chives

Place the tomato broth in a pot over low heat.

In a small saucepan over a low flame, heat the couscous with the chicken stock and butter, stirring to incorporate the ingredients, 3–4 minutes. Remove from the heat and cover to keep warm.

Score the fish skin with a razor blade or very sharp, very thin knife. Season with salt and pepper.

Warm the oil in a 12-inch nonstick sauté pan over medium-high heat. Add the fish to the pan, skin side down. Cook until light brown and crisp, 3–4 minutes.

Flip the fish and cook an additional 2–3 minutes. Check the fish for doneness by gently cutting one open at the center.

Add the olives, tomatoes, tarragon, and lemon to the tomato broth. (Do this at the last second because olives can take on an unpleasant flavor if overcooked.)

To serve, place the couscous in the center of a platter and arrange the fish around it. Sprinkle the chives over the top. Pass the sauce alongside in a sauceboat.

For a more formal presentation, spoon a mound of couscous in the center of each of 4 large bowls. Place a striped bass fillet on each bed of couscous. Spoon the sauce over and around the fish. Sprinkle some chives over each serving.

FOOD FOR THOUGHT—COUSCOUS: A good test of its doneness is to wait until the bottom of the bowl is warm but not hot to the touch.

WINE: Serve this with a Chablis.

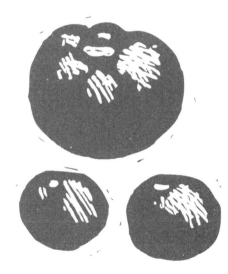

BACON-WRAPPED SEA SCALLOPS WITH ROASTED TOMATOES AND CABBAGE RISOTTO

Serves 4

As I mentioned previously, I usually enjoy risotto as an accompaniment, and here is a fine example. As a vehicle for roasted tomato and cabbage, and a counterpoint to the creamy scallops, risotto makes a wonderful team player here. The biggest challenge in this dish is having everything ready at the same time.

GETTING ORGANIZED: Keep in mind that the scallops cook very quickly, and have everything warmed and covered just before cooking them.

CABBAGE	8 ounces (2 sticks) unsalted butter
1 very firm head Savoy cabbage	Coarse salt
3 cloves garlic, thinly sliced	Freshly ground black pepper
2/3 cup Chicken Stock (page 23) or	
Basic Vegetable Stock (page 24)	

Remove the core from the cabbage and cut the head into 6 equal sections. Remove the outer leaves and feather them out a bit to give the leaves some air; this will help the braising liquid penetrate the cabbage.

Place the garlic, stock, and butter in a pot set over high heat. Bring to a boil and season with salt and pepper.

Add the cabbage to the pot, season again, lower the heat, and simmer, stirring occasionally, until it takes on a pale green color, about 20 minutes. Place on a cookie sheet, spread it out, and allow it to cool. (This will keep the contained heat in the cabbage from overcooking the vegetable.)

❖ **IF MAKING IN ADVANCE,** the cabbage can be cooled, covered, and refrigerated for up to 2 days.

OPTIONS: This is an amazing dish by itself. Taste it and just imagine how well it goes with such dishes as roast squab and quail.

ROASTED TOMATOES AND CABBAGE RISOTTO

1 quart Basic Vegetable Stock (page 24)

2 tablespoons unsalted butter (1 tablespoon is optional)

1 tablespoon olive oil

1 small Spanish onion, cut into 1/4-inch dice

1 clove garlic, thinly sliced

8 ounces (1 cup) Arborio rice

1/2 cup dry white wine

2–3 tablespoons Chopped Roasted Tomatoes (page 13), or to taste

1 tablespoon Roasted Garlic Puree (page 12)

2 tablespoons grated Parmesan cheese (optional)

Pour the stock into a pot and bring to a simmer over high heat. Lower the heat and allow the stock to continue to simmer.

In a large, heavy-bottomed pot, melt 1 tablespoon butter and warm the oil over medium-high heat.

Add the onion and garlic to the pot and cook, stirring continuously, for 5 minutes.

Add the rice and stir to coat with the butter and oil. Stir constantly until the rice turns opaque in the center, 3–4 minutes.

Add the wine and stir until it evaporates.

Add about 1 cup simmering stock and cook, stirring continuously, until the rice is almost dry. Continue to add stock by the cupful, stirring as you cook and adding more stock only when the previous addition has been absorbed. After about 15 minutes, begin adding the stock in smaller increments until you reach the desired consistency. The rice should be fully cooked, *al dente*, and have a pleasing, slightly creamy consistency.

❖ **IF MAKING IN ADVANCE,** leave out the final addition of stock. Spread the risotto out on a cookie sheet and allow it to cool. Transfer to an airtight container and set aside.

WHEN READY TO PROCEED, return the risotto to the pot, warm through, and add the final addition of stock.

Coarsely chop the braised cabbage and add it to the pot. Add the roasted tomatoes and roasted garlic puree, and stir to incorporate. If desired, add the cheese and remaining 1 tablespoon butter.

BACON-WRAPPED SCALLOPS AND ASSEMBLY	16 very thinly sliced bacon strips
16 diver scallops	2 tablespoons olive oil
Coarse salt	1¹/3 cups Smoked Pork Jus
Freshly ground black pepper	(page 25)
	8 sprigs fresh chervil

Preheat the broiler.

Lightly season the scallops on top and bottom with salt and pepper. Wrap each scallop with a slice of bacon, pressing down to get the bacon to adhere as much as possible.

Warm the oil in a nonstick pan over high heat.

Holding the scallop with kitchen tongs, place it seam side down in the pan to seal the seam.

Continue to cook for 1–2 minutes, then rotate. Cook the bacon on all sides and keep a close eye on it to make sure you cook it evenly all over. Finish by browning the top and bottom of the scallops, about 20 seconds per side.

Transfer the scallops to a cookie sheet and cook under the broiler for 1–2 minutes on each side. They should still be a bit opaque in the center.

To serve, create a disc of risotto (using a mold or forming it with a spoon) in the center of each of 4 large bowls. Place 4 scallops on top of each risotto disc and spoon the pork jus around it like a moat. Top each serving with 2 chervil sprigs.

OPTIONS: You may omit the bacon and/or replace the Smoked Pork Jus with Tomato Vinaigrette (page 166).

PAN-ROASTED SWORDFISH
WITH STEWED GREEN LENTILS,
SHERRY VINEGAR, AND ROASTED SHALLOTS

Serves 4

This nice wintry fish dish is being included here somewhat optimistically because at the time of this writing overfishing of swordfish is a concern. Should this problem persist, substitute mako, mahimahi, or sturgeon.

STEWED GREEN LENTILS

2 ounces bacon, minced (about 1/2 cup), or 2 tablespoons olive oil (see Note)

1/2 Spanish onion, cut into small dice

1 medium carrot, cut into small dice

2 celery ribs, cut into small dice

2 tablespoons olive oil

2 cups French green lentils (see Food for Thought)

5 1/2 cups Chicken Stock (page 23); if using canned, use half water and half chicken stock

1 tablespoon minced garlic

1 tablespoon chopped fresh thyme

1 tablespoon coarse salt, or more to taste

Freshly ground black pepper

In a heavy-bottomed pot, cook the bacon over medium heat until browned and some fat has rendered, about 5 minutes. (If not using bacon, warm the oil.)

Add the onion, carrot, and celery to the pot and cook until tender, 3–4 minutes.

Add the oil and lentils, and stir to coat all ingredients evenly.

Raise the heat to high and add the stock, garlic, thyme, and salt. (If using homemade stock, you may want to increase the salt slightly.) Season with pepper.

Bring to a boil, lower the heat, and allow to simmer for about 1 hour, or until the lentils are tender.

Serve directly from the pot, using a slotted spoon.

❖ **IF MAKING IN ADVANCE**, strain the lentils in a fine-mesh strainer but don't rinse, and spread out on a cookie sheet to cool. Refrigerate in an airtight container for up to 3 days.

OPTIONS: If you want to turn this into a lentil soup, add chicken stock to taste, making it as thick or as thin as you like.

NOTE: Before mincing the bacon, firm it by placing it in the freezer for 10 minutes.

SHERRY VINEGAR SAUCE	1 teaspoon sugar
1 tablespoon unsalted butter	Pinch coarse salt
3 large shallots, thinly sliced	1/2 teaspoon freshly ground black
5 cloves garlic, thinly sliced	pepper
1/3 cup water	3/4 cup Veal Stock (page 32)
1/3 cup very good quality sherry vinegar	

Melt the butter in a medium saucepan over medium heat. Add the shallots and garlic. Cook, stirring often, until nicely caramelized, 15–20 minutes, taking care not to burn them.

Deglaze the pan with the water and vinegar.

Add the sugar, salt, and pepper to the pan and cook until reduced by half, 3–4 minutes.

Add the stock, lower the heat, and simmer for 10–15 minutes, until the flavors are slightly intensified.

Strain, discard the solids, and reserve.

ROASTED SHALLOTS	1 tablespoon olive oil
8 medium shallots of uniform size,	Coarse salt
root end trimmed	Freshly ground black pepper

Preheat the oven to 350°F.

Place the shallots in a small stainless steel bowl and toss with the oil. Season lightly with salt and pepper.

Wrap the shallots snugly in aluminum foil and place in the oven for 30–35 minutes, or until tender.

Remove from the oven, cover to keep warm, and reserve.

SWORDFISH AND ASSEMBLY	**Freshly ground black pepper**
4 6-ounce swordfish steaks,	1 teaspoon olive oil
cut 1 inch thick	1 tablespoon unsalted butter
Coarse salt	

Preheat the oven to 375°F.

Season the swordfish on both sides with salt and pepper.

In an ovenproof sauté pan, warm the oil and butter over high heat.

Add the swordfish to the pan and cook for 1 minute.

Flip the swordfish and then place the pan in the oven for 1 1/2–2 minutes.

To serve, spread the lentils over the surface of a platter and place the swordfish fillets on top. Pass the shallots alongside the fillets and pass the sauce in a sauceboat.

FOOD FOR THOUGHT—LENTILS: The green lentils from the Puy region of France are the best: small, uniform in size, and with a deep green color. They are more flavorful than brown lentils.

OPTION: For a fancier presentation, arrange some lentils in the center of each of 4 dinner plates. Lay the swordfish on the beans and place 2 shallots alongside the fillet. Spoon some sauce around the plate.

SAUTÉED RED SNAPPER WITH BRAISED CABBAGE, CRISP POTATO, AND CAPER-SCALLION VINAIGRETTE

Serves 4

This dish is a study in complementary contrasts: the crunchy, starchy potato against the soft, leafy cabbage, the fatty snapper cut by the acid of the vinaigrette, the salty capers and the sweet scallions. The vinaigrette is highly acidic, so it is especially important not to overdress this dish.

CAPER-SCALLION VINAIGRETTE

3 tablespoons capers, rinsed
4 scallions, thinly sliced on the bias
Juice of 3 lemons

1/3 cup extra-virgin olive oil
Coarse salt
Freshly ground black pepper

Combine the capers, scallions, lemon juice, and oil. Season with salt and pepper to taste and set aside.

❖ **IF MAKING IN ADVANCE,** this vinaigrette can be kept covered in the refrigerator for 1 day.

BRAISED CABBAGE

4 ounces Chicken Stock (page 23)
   or low-sodium canned chicken broth
2 cloves garlic, peeled and minced
3 tablespoons unsalted butter

Coarse salt
Freshly ground black pepper
1 head Savoy cabbage, cored and
   coarsely chopped

In a large kettle or deep saucepan, bring the stock to a boil, lower to a simmer, and add the minced garlic.

Add the butter, using a whisk to incorporate it into the broth.

Season with salt and pepper to taste.

Add the cabbage leaves and braise the cabbage until tender, about 15–20 minutes, stirring occasionally to coat the leaves evenly with the cooking liquid.

Remove the cabbage from the pan with a slotted spoon or tongs, allowing the excess liquid to drain off. Reserve the cooked cabbage and discard the liquid.

CRISP POTATO	Freshly ground black pepper
2 Idaho potatoes, washed and unpeeled	1/3 cup canola or vegetable oil
Coarse salt	

Using a mandoline, the shredding blade of a box grater, or the shredding disc of a food processor, shred the potatoes. Gently squeeze the shredded potato between your hands to eliminate any excess moisture.

Divide the shredded pieces into 4 equal piles, about a handful each. Season lightly with salt and pepper.

Heat the oil over low heat in a nonstick sauté pan, ensuring that it does not become sizzling hot.

Place 1 pile of shredded potato into the oil. (If you hear a sizzling sound when the potato is placed in the pan, lower the heat until the sound becomes a gentle bubble.) Note that the potato will "float" in the oil. This is the desired effect; there is not much oil.

Using a metal spatula, press down on the potato to form a perfect circle and allow to cook gently for 3–4 minutes, or until lightly golden brown.

Remove the crisp potato from the pan and drain on paper towels.

Repeat the process with the remaining piles of shredded potato.

Set the crisp potatoes aside in a warm place.

❖ IF MAKING IN ADVANCE, the crisp potatoes can be stored in an airtight plastic container in the refrigerator for 1 day.

SNAPPER AND ASSEMBLY	Freshly ground black pepper
4 red snapper fillets (7–8 ounces each),	2–3 tablespoons extra-virgin olive oil
pin bones removed (see Note)	1 tablespoon unsalted butter
Coarse salt	

Warm the cabbage over medium heat.

Season the red snapper fillets with salt and pepper.

Heat the oil and butter in a nonstick pan over medium-high heat and sauté the snapper fillets, skin side down, until the skin is crispy, about 3–4 minutes.

Carefully flip the fillets and sauté an additional 1–2 minutes, until the fillets are done.

To serve, place the potatoes in the center of a platter and surround them with the snapper fillets. Pass the cabbage on a plate alongside and the sauce in a sauceboat.

For a more formal presentation, place some cabbage in the center of each of 4 dinner plates. Place 1 crisp potato on top of the cabbage and 1 snapper fillet on top of that. Drizzle the fillet with the caper-scallion vinaigrette and serve immediately.

FOOD FOR THOUGHT—COOKING SNAPPER: Let the fish cook on the skin side for two-thirds of the cooking time, which will crisp it nicely and cause less wear and tear on the flesh side. Also pick up the fillet with a spatula and crack it open slightly to see if the center is slightly pink; if so, it should be removed from the heat; the retained heat will complete the cooking process.

NOTE: You may substitute salmon or mackerel for the snapper in this recipe. You can also serve the snapper with Lemon Orzo (page 258) or White Balsamic Vinaigrette (page 172).

WINE: Serve this with a sauvignon blanc.

SEARED HALIBUT WITH CHANTERELLES AND CHANTERELLE JUS

Serves 4

This dish makes inventive use of the stems that usually get discarded from chanterelle mushrooms; they are used to make a jus.

SERVE THIS WITH Leek Puree (page 262) or Potato Puree (page 268).

CHANTERELLE JUS

2 tablespoons olive oil

1/2 small Spanish onion, coarsely chopped

6 cloves garlic, thinly sliced

1 small leek, white part only, coarsely chopped

Stems from 1 pound chanterelle mushrooms

1 ounce dried chanterelle or 1/2 ounce dried porcini mushrooms

6 sprigs thyme

1 bay leaf

1 tablespoon black peppercorns

1/2 cup dry white wine

1 tablespoon white vinegar

Warm the oil in a sauté pan over medium heat. Add the onion, garlic, and leek to the pan and sweat them in the oil until soft but not colored, about 5 minutes.

Add the mushroom stems, dried mushrooms, thyme sprigs, bay leaf, and peppercorns to the pan. Add the wine, vinegar, and just enough water to cover.

Raise the heat to high, bring to a boil, and skim the surface. Lower the heat to allow the liquid to simmer. Let cook until slightly reduced and the flavors are intensified, about 40 minutes.

Strain and reserve.

SEARED HALIBUT AND ASSEMBLY	Coarse salt
1 tablespoon extra-virgin olive oil	Freshly ground black pepper
1 tablespoon unsalted butter	4 6-ounce halibut fillets
1 clove garlic, minced	2 tablespoons vegetable oil
1 pound chanterelle mushrooms (stems removed to make jus above)	Truffle oil for drizzling
	2 tablespoons finely minced chives

Warm the extra-virgin olive oil, butter, and garlic in a sauté pan over medium-high heat.

Add the mushrooms to the pan, season with salt and pepper, and cook, stirring, until the mushrooms begin to give off their liquid, about 5 minutes. Cover to keep warm and set aside.

Season the halibut fillets on both sides with salt and pepper.

Warm the vegetable oil in a sauté pan over medium-high heat. Add the halibut to the pan and cook for 3–4 minutes, then flip and cook an additional 2 minutes. (To cook it more well done, finish under the broiler for 1 minute.) (See Food for Thought.)

Transfer the halibut to the center of 4 dinner plates. Place the mushrooms around the halibut and spoon the chanterelle jus all around. Drizzle the plate with the truffle oil and finish with a sprinkling of chives.

FOOD FOR THOUGHT—COOKING HALIBUT: Make sure when you sear the halibut that the oil is hot so that the fish takes on a deep golden color and provides some contrast to the snow-white flesh.

SOFT-SHELL CRABS WITH CORN AND GREEN ONION RISOTTO AND BACON DICE

❧

Serves 4

My favorite way to enjoy soft-shell crabs is between two pieces of white bread with tartar sauce, lemon, and onion. But this recipe runs a close second. It is a perfect summertime dish, and either component—the risotto or the crabs—is delicious in a number of other contexts.

3 ears corn, stripped (about 5 cups), with the "milk" from the cobs reserved
1 quart Chicken Stock (page 23)
2 tablespoons unsalted butter
1 tablespoon olive oil
1 small Spanish onion, cut into 1/4-inch dice
1 clove garlic, thinly sliced
8 ounces (1 cup) Arborio rice
1/2 cup dry white wine
4 scallions, equal parts white and green, roots removed, and finely chopped crosswise

Place 1 cup corn kernels and the "milk" in a blender and puree until smooth. Reserve.

Pour the stock into a pot and bring to a simmer over high heat. Lower the heat and continue to simmer.

In another large, heavy-bottomed pot, melt the butter and warm the oil over medium-high heat.

Add the onion and garlic to the pot and cook, stirring continuously, for 5 minutes.

Add the rice and stir to coat with the butter and oil. Stir constantly until the rice turns opaque in the center, 3–4 minutes.

Add the wine and stir until it evaporates.

Add about 1 cup simmering stock and cook, stirring continuously, until the rice is almost dry. Continue to add stock by the cupful, stirring as you cook and adding more stock only when the previous addition has been absorbed. After about 15 minutes, begin adding the stock in smaller increments until you reach the desired consistency. The rice should be fully cooked, *al dente*, and have a pleasing, slightly creamy consistency. (Leave this risotto a bit less "wet" than you usually would to allow for the addition of the corn puree.)

❖ **IF MAKING IN ADVANCE,** leave out the final addition of stock. Spread the risotto out on a cookie sheet and allow it to cool. Transfer to an airtight container and set aside. **WHEN READY TO PROCEED,** return the risotto to the pot, warm through, and add half of the final addition of stock. (The corn puree will provide the final bit of liquid.)

Add the remaining corn kernels to the pot, stir to incorporate, and let cook for 2 minutes. Add the corn puree and cook for another minute. Finish by stirring in the scallions.

SAUTÉED SOFT-SHELL CRABS AND ASSEMBLY	Coarse salt
	Freshly ground black pepper
4 ounces good-quality, double-smoked bacon, cut into fine dice (optional)	4 tablespoons olive oil for frying
8 soft-shell crabs (see Food for Thought)	2 tablespoons unsalted butter

If using, place the bacon in a sauté pan over medium-high heat. Cook until the bacon browns and the fat is rendered, about 5 minutes.

Transfer the bacon to paper towels to drain.

Season the crabs lightly with salt and pepper. Heat half of the oil and half of the butter in a sauté pan over medium-high heat.

Place 4 crabs, belly side down, in the pan and cook until slightly crisp, about 40 seconds.

Flip the crabs and cook until the other side is crisp, about another 40 seconds.

Transfer the crabs to paper towels to drain.

Wipe out the pan and repeat with the remaining oil, butter, and crabs.

Mound some risotto in the center of each of 4 dinner plates. Scatter some diced bacon (if using) over each serving and place a soft-shell crab on top of each plate.

OPTIONS: The bacon dice can be omitted.

FOOD FOR THOUGHT—BUYING AND CLEANING SOFT-SHELL CRABS: When choosing soft-shell crabs, make sure they are alive. Most fishmongers will clean them for you, but try to cook them the same day they are cleaned because they lose a lot of vital juices if kept too long. If you want to clean them yourself, here's how: Using a pair of kitchen shears, cut across the body to remove the eyes and mouth opening (that is, the face). Reach into the opening and pull out the little sack inside. (Often it's quite sandy.) Place the crab, belly down, on a work surface. Holding either end of the pointy shell, lift and remove the spongy gills. Flip the crab over, and you'll notice an armorlike tail piece that goes under to the belly and comes to a point; pull that away.

COOKING SOFT-SHELL CRABS: Sometimes when panfrying soft-shell crabs, things can get a little dangerous because the contained liquid in the legs and claws can explode. To avoid this, pierce the extremities with a pin.

SAUTÉED SKATE WITH BACON BUTTER

Serves 4

Here we go again with the bacon, but I can't help myself. This is a rich and satisfying fish dish for which most of the work can and should be done ahead of time.

SERVE THIS WITH Braised Bibb Lettuce (page 271), Braised Cabbage (page 184), or Potato Puree (page 268).

BACON STOCK AND	1¹/2 quarts water, or enough to cover
BACON BUTTER	1 large Idaho potato
2 tablespoons olive oil	4 cloves garlic, smashed
1 small carrot, quartered	4 tablespoons unsalted butter
¹/2 Spanish onion, coarsely chopped	Coarse salt
1 rib celery, quartered	Freshly ground black pepper
1 cup dry white wine	Juice of 1 lemon, or more to taste
2 tablespoons white vinegar	2 tablespoons Chopped Roasted
15 black peppercorns	Tomatoes (page 13)
1 bay leaf	2 tablespoons minced chives
2 sprigs thyme	
12 ounces bacon scraps (if you don't have any, your butcher may have them for sale)	

Warm the oil in a saucepan over medium-high heat. Add the carrot, onion, and celery to the pan and cook until softened, about 5 minutes.

Add the wine, vinegar, peppercorns, bay leaf, thyme, and bacon scraps. Add enough water to cover.

Raise the heat to high and bring to a boil. Lower the heat and simmer, skimming frequently, for 60 minutes.

❖ **YOU SHOULD MAKE THIS DISH AHEAD.** Strain it and refrigerate overnight. **WHEN READY TO PROCEED,** simply scrape the fat off the surface. You will be left with 2/3–1 quart stock.

Peel the potato and cut it into 1/4-inch dice.

Place the potato in a small pot, cover by 1 inch with cold water, and add the garlic. Bring to a simmer over medium heat and cook for 4–5 minutes, or until the potato is tender.

Drain, discard the liquid, and pick out and discard the garlic. Spread the potatoes out on a clean, dry surface and allow to cool.

Pour 2 cups bacon stock into a saucepan, reserving the rest for another use.

Bring to a boil over high heat and whisk in the butter. Season with salt, pepper, and lemon juice. Add the tomatoes, chives, and potato just before serving.

SAUTÉED SKATE AND ASSEMBLY	Coarse salt
4 boneless, skinless skate wings	Freshly ground black pepper
(7–8 ounces each; see Food	2 tablespoons unsalted butter
for Thought)	

Season the skate wings lightly with salt and pepper.

Melt the butter in a nonstick pan over medium-high heat, letting it sizzle and start to turn brown. Place the skate in the pan, cartilage side down, and cook for 1 minute. Flip and cook for another minute.

To serve, place the skate and any accompaniments on a large platter and pass the sauce alongside in a sauceboat.

FOOD FOR THOUGHT—BUYING AND WORKING WITH SKATE: Skate is hard to come by, so make a call to your fishmonger before planning to make this dish. Make sure that the skate's skin and cartilage are removed before you buy it and that it has a sweet smell. Sauté the skin side last to keep it from curling.

Poultry and Game

I am a big fan of poultry and game because you can take members of these groups in any number of directions with wildly varied results. Poaching, for example, yields a very gentle flavor, while roasting results in a rich and succulent bird. I especially love the unique diversity of game birds and the great variety of flavors that occur as you move from squab (rich, almost livery) to quail (full-flavored but not quite as intense) to guinea hen (distinct but milder than the other two). They are not as heavy as beef or pork but, in their own way, are just as satisfying.

Before we dive into the recipes, allow me to share a few thoughts on the poultry and game featured in this chapter:

Chicken

As far as I'm concerned, there is nothing better than roast chicken. There is a home-cooked feel to it that you rarely encounter in a restaurant because the technique doesn't lend itself to advance preparation, which is how many restaurant dishes are made.

There is no recipe for roast chicken in this chapter, but because this book advocates cooking ahead of time as much as possible, especially when entertaining, I wanted to share how we prepare roast chicken in advance at my restaurants without sacrificing any quality. Of course, a simple whole roast chicken is easier, but if you are making dinner for a large group, you might want to try my technique:

We separate chickens into leg and thigh pieces, and the breast with the wing tip still attached and the rib cage in, and then marinate them in a simple blend of garlic, lemon, olive oil, and herbs. While just a few hours will do the trick, I recommend a twenty-four-hour marination. Then we brown those pieces in a pan with butter and olive oil, starting with the skin side, taking it to a rich brown. Then we flip the pieces, toss a few crushed garlic cloves into the pan, and add whatever herbs are on hand. That goes into a 500°F oven; the heat helps speed the process and crisp the skin, as does basting every few minutes.

We take the chicken out when it is still rather pink at the bone, letting the contained heat continue to cook it and allowing the juices time to redistribute. When we are ready to serve it, we simply throw it on the grill or back in the oven to reheat it. The results replicate those of a crackling bird right from the oven, and you can obtain the same result in your home.

One other point about chicken: I strongly encourage you to buy whole chickens rather than boneless, skinless breasts, even for recipes that call for a breast only. Skin and bone are great sources of flavor, and the bones can be used to make stock. (In hopes of inspiring you to buy and butcher a chicken, instructions are featured in the sidebar on page 198. Keep in mind that once you have mastered butchering a chicken, you can tackle any bird with confidence.) It also pays to buy organic chickens. The flavor is superior to name-brand birds, and if you consider the difference in price, even the best are still less expensive than red meat or seafood.

Game Birds

There is nothing like the flavor of game birds. Although mass farming does dilute the flavor a bit because they are not necessarily feeding on what they would eat in the wild, the characteristics are still inherent in the birds and are certainly worth a try at home.

Game birds are easier to work with than you may think and worth whatever small obstacles they present. To me there is nothing that speaks so effortlessly of autumn and holidays.

Duck

Something I appreciate about duck is its high utilization quotient: Its liver is delicious sautéed, its legs can be made into confit, the breasts can be smoked, and even the neck skin can be used to make sausage casing.

There are various ways to approach a roast duck. If you can plan ahead sufficiently to buy the duck a day or two before you'll be cooking it, leave it uncovered in the refrigerator to dry out. Some people have been known to hang the duck to help the skin dry out. (Drying is particularly helpful if you have bought a duck wrapped in plastic.) Some very industrious people have been known to dip a duck in boiling water for a minute to force the pores of its skin to open before cooking. I have even heard that some people put their duck in the dishwasher on the rinse cycle for a minute or two.

If you would rather not roast an entire duck, buying and roasting just the breast is an easier and perfectly viable alternative. (Many gourmet markets now sell boneless breast on its own.) In these cases, I recommend *magret*, the very meaty breast of a Moulard (a cross between a Muscovy and Pekin, or Long Island, duck). Pekin ducks are not as flavorful as Muscovy or Moulard ducks, but they are a perfectly viable alternative and, if using only the breast, the leftover parts can be used in a number of other recipes and the bones can be employed in a stock. Before roasting a duck breast, I perforate the skin all over with a fork to assist in eliminating the fat. I start the duck, skin side down, in a pan over high heat and cook it until the skin takes on a dark, roasted appearance. Then I flip the breast, transfer it to a 500°F oven, and cook it, basting it with its own fat, until it is roasted and has a crisp exterior. This is the procedure used in this chapter, and you'll find that it produces superior results every time.

Capon, Guinea Hen, Quail, and Squab

In case you don't know, a capon is a rooster that has been neutered. It is a young bird that happens to grow very quickly, resulting in a large body that is still tender and juicy. I always prefer capon to turkey, even on Thanksgiving. (In fact, if you want to try something different next November, roast a capon and pair it with the Sausage and Fennel Seed Stuffing on page 269.)

Guinea hen, known as *pintade* in France, has delightful characteristics all its own. It stands up well to nicely seasoned accompaniments but isn't nearly as gamy as squab or woodcock. I think of it as a cross between a chicken and a pheasant. Something it shares in common with the latter is that it can dry out easily, so pay close attention whenever you pop one in the oven.

Quail, too, boasts a pronounced flavor that isn't gamy at all. Many specialty markets now sell semi-boneless quail, with the leg and wing bones still attached, and the skin intact. They are great for pan-roasting and grilling, and are well suited to a number of stuffings.

Squab is a dense, very red bird, referred to as *pigeon* in France. It is only a distant cousin of the pigeons that we shoo off our porches here. It is usually cooked to rare or medium-rare, and I wouldn't have it any other way.

Rabbit

These very lean animals are usually divided into two culinary classes: fryers and roasters. Fryers are younger rabbits that weigh only about two pounds and are ideal for sautéing and grilling. Roasters are older, and because they have been hopping around longer, they are tougher and therefore considered good for stewing. But I'll let you in on a secret: I only use fryers, and to preserve their delicate texture and flavor, cook them only until they're cooked and not a minute longer.

Butchering a Chicken

This technique is applicable to any bird that you want to quarter. Even if you have never considered yourself capable, don't be afraid to try it. Chickens are cheap, and even if you muck it up the first few times, it'll still taste great. If you really create a mess, make soup. There are some very easy ways to butcher a chicken, and this is the easiest one of all:

Lay the chicken on a cutting board with the cavity facing you. Using a little strength, insert a heavy chef's knife just to the right of the tail until it protrudes from the neck cavity. (If you look or feel inside, you'll locate the backbone and valleys of ribs falling down from it.) The knife tip should be on the same side of the neck as the butt of the knife is to the tail. Press down firmly, not in a sawing motion but with pressure on both the tip and the handle to sever the backbone from the thigh and rib cage. Repeat this step on the other side of the backbone, then remove it.

Now you have a bird with no backbone. Press it out, forcing it flat on your work surface with the skin side out, like a chicken pancake. The legs should be pointing outward at a 45-degree angle. Use your hands to get a sense of the division of the leg and thigh from the heart-shaped torso of the bird. Cut at a 45-degree angle to remove the legs and thighs.

This will leave you with the heart-shaped body before you. With your knife close to the breast plate (which divides the two breasts), score down one side, and press and remove the breast. You now have one breast with the wing tip attached. To finish the process, invert the last breast, rib side up. Locate the breast plate and remove it with a sharp downward motion of the knife as close to the breast plate as possible. Now all you need to do is separate the wing tips from the breast. Cut the first major joint down from the wing on both sides. You now have beautiful roaster pieces.

PAN-ROASTED CHICKEN WITH SOFT POLENTA AND ROASTED GARLIC JUS

🌿

Serves 4

The polenta in this recipe is noteworthy for two reasons: First, it's made with white rather than yellow cornmeal. Although white cornmeal can be difficult to find, I prefer its sweeter flavor and smoother texture to yellow. Second, this is also a very creamy polenta because it is made with a cornmeal-to-milk ratio of 1 to 5.

SERVE THIS WITH Braised Cabbage (page 184), mounded next to the polenta before saucing the plate, or Sautéed Spinach (page 230) or Wilted Kale (page 173).

SOFT POLENTA

2 1/2 cups milk

2 teaspoons coarse salt

1 teaspoon freshly ground black pepper

1 tablespoon unsalted butter

1 large clove garlic, minced

1/2 cup white cornmeal

Pour the milk into a saucepan and add the salt, pepper, butter, and garlic. Bring to a boil over high heat, reduce the heat to low, and whisk in the cornmeal. The resulting mixture will look very loose.

Cook, stirring frequently, for 12–15 minutes. Reserve or, if you like, leave over low heat and keep warm by stirring frequently, or transfer to a double boiler set over simmering water. (See Food for Thought.)

GARLIC CONFIT

2 heads garlic, divided into peeled cloves of about equal size (leave out particularly large or small cloves)

1 cup dry white wine

3 cups (approximately) Chicken Stock (page 23)

Coarse salt

Freshly ground black pepper

Sugar

Place the garlic and wine in an 8-inch sauté pan set over high heat. Cook until the wine evaporates, then add enough stock to cover.

Cook until the stock reduces to dry, about 8 minutes, then add enough to cover again and cook until reduced to dry.

Repeat a third time. The garlic should be tender when pierced with the tip of a sharp, thin-bladed knife. Season with salt, pepper, and sugar, and remove from the heat.

CHICKEN AND ASSEMBLY

2 small chickens (2–2½ pounds each), quartered
Coarse salt
Freshly ground black pepper
2 tablespoons olive oil
1 tablespoon unsalted butter
4 cloves garlic, smashed
Handful of herb sprigs, such as thyme, flat-leaf parsley, or sage
1 cup dry vermouth
¾ cup Dark Chicken Stock (page 32)
Sugar (optional)
2 cups Roasted Garlic Jus (page 31)

Preheat the oven to 425°F.

Season the chicken all over with salt and pepper.

Heat the oil and melt the butter in a large skillet over medium-high heat.

Add the chicken pieces to the pan, skin side down, and cook until the skin becomes deeply browned, 6–7 minutes.

Turn the pieces over, add the garlic and herbs (stems and all), and place the pan in the preheated oven. Cook for 6–8 minutes, or until the juices run clear when pierced with a knife at the leg joint.

Remove the pan from the oven and transfer the chicken to a cutting board. Reduce the oven temperature to 200°F.

When cool enough to handle, remove the breast plate from the chicken. Sever and French the leg by running a paring knife around the bone on the lower portion of the leg, 1 inch from the end, and removing the detached skin and meat.

Place the chicken parts on an ovenproof dish and keep warm in the oven while you continue with the recipe.

Drain the fat from the pan, leaving the herbs and garlic.

The next step may cause a bit of a flare-up, so use a heavy oven mitt and lean away from the stove as you do it: Add the vermouth to the pan and place the pan over medium-high heat. Cook until the vermouth has reduced by two-thirds, about 2 minutes.

Add the dark chicken stock to the pan and cook until reduced by one-third, 3–5 minutes.

Strain the sauce through a fine-mesh strainer. Taste and season with salt, pepper, and sugar if necessary.

To serve, arrange the chicken on a platter and put the polenta in a bowl. Pass the sauce in a sauceboat alongside.

For a more formal presentation, spoon a mound of polenta in the center of each of 4 dinner plates. Lean a piece of chicken against the polenta. Spoon the roasted garlic jus around the perimeter of the plate.

FOOD FOR THOUGHT—MAKING POLENTA IN ADVANCE: Making the polenta several hours ahead of time and keeping it, covered with waxed paper, in a double boiler over low heat is a great way to simplify the preparation of this dish. Cornmeal, even fine grinds, varies from company to company. If the ratio of 1 to 5 begins to look too thick, add some more warm milk 2–3 minutes after you start making it. Conversely, if after 6 or 7 minutes it looks too loose, add some more cornmeal and really work it in well with a whisk.

POACHED CHICKEN BREAST STUFFED
WITH GOAT CHEESE AND SPINACH

❧

Serves 4

This is a recipe that I cook at home myself—a versatile method for having a sophisticated meal on tap with very little last-minute prep work. This is a remarkable dish because it requires nothing but a pot of simmering water to cook it successfully; there is no butter, no oil, no sautéing, and no roasting. Yet the results are delicious. Here I've stuffed the chicken with goat cheese and spinach, but you can substitute Chopped Roasted Tomatoes (page 13), or any filling you like.

Avoid buying boneless, skinless chicken breast pieces if possible. You'll get the best results by purchasing a whole organic chicken and removing the breast yourself. (See the poultry introduction, page 194.)

SERVE THIS WITH a small salad for an ideal lunch.

SPINACH AND
GOAT CHEESE FILLING
2 tablespoons extra-virgin olive oil
1 large clove garlic, minced
1/4 cup Chicken Stock (page 23)
   or water

1 1/2 pounds spinach, stems removed
   and well washed in several changes
   of cold water
Coarse salt
Freshly ground black pepper
4 ounces high-quality fresh goat cheese,
   at room temperature

Heat the oil in a sauté pan over medium heat. Add the garlic and cook gently for 15–20 seconds, being careful not to let it color.

Add the stock and immediately put the spinach in on top of it. Cook, stirring quickly, because the spinach will cook down rapidly. Season with salt and pepper. Continue to cook for about 1 minute, then remove from the heat and spread out on a cookie sheet to cool.

When cool, transfer to a mixing bowl and gently combine with the goat cheese. Taste and adjust the seasoning if necessary.

❖ **IF MAKING IN ADVANCE,** store in a tightly covered container in the refrigerator for up to 24 hours.

CHICKEN AND ASSEMBLY	Coarse salt
4 large boneless, skinless chicken breasts	Freshly ground black pepper

Cover the chicken breasts, 1 at a time, with a sheet of plastic wrap and gently pound to a thickness of 1/2 inch. Season with salt and pepper.

Lay each breast in the center of a clean 12 × 18- or 20-inch piece of plastic wrap.

Place one-fourth of the cooled prepared filling in the center of each breast.

Wrap the plastic tightly around the breast and roll up the ends, turning tighter and tighter until the breast is in a cylindrical shape; take care to keep the plastic wrap tight around the roll.

Once the cylinder is formed, continue to twist the ends tightly until they are well sealed. Set aside and repeat with the other 3 breasts.

❖ **IF MAKING IN ADVANCE,** the stuffed chicken breasts can be refrigerated for up to 24 hours or frozen for up to several days. **WHEN READY TO PROCEED,** allow to come to room temperature.

To cook the chicken breasts, set a large pot of water over medium-high heat and bring to a simmer. Carefully place the wrapped chicken breasts in the water and poach for 15–16 minutes.

Remove the chicken breasts with tongs and allow to rest for 5 minutes.

Carefully remove the plastic, using a sharp knife or scissors. Cut the chicken on a bias into 1/2-inch-thick slices and serve.

SAGE AND WALNUT–STUFFED SADDLE OF RABBIT
WITH POTATO PUREE

Serves 4

In this recipe, saddle of rabbit is stuffed with an aromatic blend of bread crumbs, walnuts, and sage that is bound together with butter. The autumnal qualities of the stuffing make this a perfect fall dish.

SERVE THIS WITH haricots verts or Stewed Brussels Sprouts (page 267).

11 tablespoons (1 stick plus 3 tablespoons) unsalted butter	Freshly ground black pepper
2 cloves garlic, minced	6 tablespoons dry white wine
2/3 cup toasted and ground walnuts	1/2 cup Dark Chicken Stock (page 32)
1 teaspoon finely chopped fresh sage	1 teaspoon Roasted Garlic Puree (page 12) (optional)
5 tablespoons dry bread crumbs	4 cups Potato Puree (page 268), kept warm in a double boiler set over simmering water
4 boneless saddles of rabbit (6–7 ounces each)	
Coarse salt	

Preheat the oven to 400°F.

Place 8 tablespoons butter and half of the minced garlic in a sauté pan and cook over low heat until the butter is melted.

Create a stuffing by transferring the butter and garlic to a mixing bowl and adding the walnuts, sage, and bread crumbs. Stir to incorporate into a thick, malleable paste.

Score the fleshy flap on the outside of the rabbit saddles, lay a sheet of plastic wrap over them, and gently pound each one to an even thickness with a meat tenderizer or the bottom of a heavy pan.

Season the saddles inside and out with salt and pepper.

Spoon some of the stuffing onto the central portion of each saddle and wrap the flaps around it, folding one flap over the other. (See Food for Thought.)

Tie the saddles closed with kitchen string about 1 inch from each end and at the center, being sure to make it firm but not excessively tight.

Heat 2 tablespoons butter and the remaining minced garlic in an ovenproof sauté pan until the butter is melted.

Place the rabbit saddles in the pan and brown on both sides, about 1 minute per side.

Transfer the pan to the preheated oven and cook, basting frequently, until quite firm to the touch, 6–7 minutes.

Remove the pan from the oven and transfer the saddles to a clean, dry surface, keeping them covered and warm.

Pour the excess fat from the pan and return the pan to the stove over medium-high heat.

Add the wine and deglaze by bringing the wine to a boil and letting it reduce by half, 1–2 minutes.

Add the stock and let it reduce for 3–4 minutes.

Whisk the remaining 1 tablespoon butter and the roasted garlic puree (if using) into the sauce. Strain through a fine-mesh strainer and reserve.

To serve, place the rabbit saddles on a platter and the potato puree in a bowl. Pass the sauce alongside in a sauceboat.

For a more formal presentation, mound some potato puree in the center of each of 4 dinner plates and lean a rabbit saddle against it. Spoon the sauce around the plate.

FOOD FOR THOUGHT—KEEPING THE STUFFING IN: When folding the rabbit around the stuffing, make sure that the first turn is firm; you want the stuffing itself tightly contained in the center of the rabbit when it cooks.

WINE: Serve this with a full-bodied white such as a great California chardonnay.

PAN-ROASTED SQUAB WITH MUSHROOM SAUCE AND PARMESAN FLAN

Serves 4

his recipe achieves some very intense flavors with very little work. The flan and mushroom sauce play off each other very well because they both complement the rich, crispy squab. Take special care to make sure each component is hot when serving this dish.

SERVE THIS WITH Sweet Pea Stew (page 263). Its flavors complement the squab and the flan equally well.

MUSHROOM SAUCE	Coarse salt
1 cup Mushroom stock (page 26)	Freshly ground black pepper
1 cup Dark Chicken Stock (page 32)	Few drops truffle oil

Pour the mushroom stock into a saucepan over medium-high heat. Reduce by half, then add the dark chicken stock to the pot. Season to taste with salt and pepper. Drizzle some white truffle oil on top.

OPTION: Add 1 tablespoon freshly shaved black truffle to the sauce just before serving.

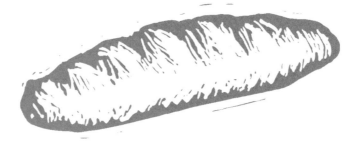

PAN-ROASTED SQUAB
  AND ASSEMBLY

4 tablespoons olive oil

1 tablespoon unsalted butter

4 squabs (about 12 ounces each),
    broken down into breast and leg
    (ask your butcher to do this or
    do it yourself; see page 198)

Coarse salt

Freshly ground black pepper

4 Parmesan flans (page 264)

Preheat the oven to 375°F.

Warm 2 tablespoons oil and 1/2 tablespoon butter in an ovenproof sauté pan over medium-high heat until the butter melts and the oil begins to sizzle.

Place the squab breasts in the pan, skin side down, and cook until the skin turns a deep golden brown, 3–4 minutes. Move the pan around to keep the squab from sticking.

Turn the breasts over and cook on the other side for 1 minute.

Transfer the squab breasts to a clean, dry surface and cover to keep warm.

Warm the remaining oil and butter in the pan, and cook the legs in the same manner.

Finish all the pieces by placing them on a cookie sheet; season with salt and pepper, and cook them in the preheated oven for 2–3 minutes for rare, a bit longer for more well done.

To serve, unmold 1 Parmesan flan in the center of each of 4 dinner plates. Form a ring with the 2 squab breasts and 2 legs, and spoon some sauce around the plate.

WINE: Serve this with a beautiful white Burgundy or a complex chardonnay or a red Rhône.

ROASTED DUCK WITH SWEET ONIONS AND TURNIPS

❧

Serves 4

The star of this dish is the sweet onion and turnip gateau—a versatile accompaniment that you can use in a number of contexts all winter long. Keep it in mind to pair with squab, chicken, and quail dishes.

JUNIPER AND SPICE SAUCE

2 cups red wine
2 tablespoons sugar
12 black peppercorns
3 juniper berries
1 piece star anise
2/3 cup inexpensive balsamic or
    white balsamic vinegar
1/2 cup Dark Chicken Stock or 1/3 cup
    Veal Stock (page 32)
Coarse salt
Freshly ground black pepper

Place the wine, sugar, peppercorns, juniper berries, star anise, and vinegar in a sauté pan over medium-high heat. Cook until reduced to a syrupy consistency, 5–7 minutes.

Add the stock to the pan and cook another 2 minutes. Season with salt and pepper, and reserve.

SWEET ONION AND TURNIP GATEAU

4 tablespoons unsalted butter, plus
    more for molds
4 large Spanish onions, thinly sliced
Sugar
3 medium turnips
Coarse salt
Freshly ground black pepper

Preheat the oven to 300°F.

Place 3 tablespoons butter and the onions in a sauté pan and cook over medium-high heat. Add a pinch of sugar. Cook, stirring often, until the onions are deeply caramelized and sweet, 35–40 minutes.

Meanwhile, peel the turnips. Using a paring knife, cut off the top and bottom. Using a mandoline or a very sharp knife and steady hands, slice the turnips into 1/8-inch-thick rounds as uniform in size as possible.

Melt the remaining tablespoon of butter in a sauté pan over medium heat.

Lay the turnip slices in the pan, being careful not to let them overlap.

Cook for 2 minutes, then flip and season with salt, pepper, and sugar. Cook another minute, then transfer to paper towels and let drain.

Lightly butter four 4-ounce ramekins or dome-shaped nonstick molds.

Set 1 turnip slice in the bottom, then overlap the slices around the side to cover the interior of the mold. Finish by tucking the last slice under the first.

Fill the molds with caramelized onion.

Bake for 7–8 minutes.

DUCK AND ASSEMBLY	Coarse salt
4 *magret* duck breasts (8–9 ounces each; see Note)	Freshly ground black pepper
	1 tablespoon (approximately) olive oil

NOTE: You can also ask the butcher to cut Pekin duck breasts. If you do, save the legs for Braised Duck Legs with Egg Noodles, page 133.

Preheat the oven to 375°F.

Puncture the duck breasts on both sides with the tines of a fork. Season with salt and pepper.

Use just enough oil to coat the bottom of a cold ovenproof sauté pan, using your finger to ensure even distribution.

Place the breasts in the pan, skin side down.

Cook over medium heat, draining the fat from the pan every few minutes, until the skin is a deep golden brown, about 15 minutes.

Drain the fat one last time, flip the breasts, and transfer to the preheated oven. Cook for 15 minutes, basting frequently with the fat that renders out and draining the fat if a surplus accumulates in the pan. You can remove it at this point or cook another 5 minutes.

Remove the duck to a cutting board and cut on the bias into thin slices.

Unmold 1 gateau in the center of each of 4 dinner plates. Lay slices of duck breast all around and spoon the sauce over and around the duck.

WINE: Serve this with a pinot noir.

ROAST QUAIL WITH BARLEY AND ROASTED TOMATOES

🌿

Serves 4

I n this great winter dish the rich quality of the quail is offset by the nutty flavor of the roasted barley. Notice how much impact the white vinegar has here; without it, this would be too dark and heavy.

Don't try to rush the barley. Follow the recommended cooking times and season as you go to get the proper depth of flavor.

BARLEY

1 1/2 tablespoons unsalted butter

1 tablespoon canola oil

2 large Spanish onions, halved and
   thinly sliced

Coarse salt

Freshly ground black pepper

1 tablespoon olive oil

8 ounces barley (1 1/3 cups)

6–8 cups Basic Vegetable Stock
   (page 24) or Mushroom Stock
   (page 26)

1 teaspoon light brown sugar

In a large sauté pan, warm 1/2 tablespoon butter and the canola oil over medium-high heat.

Add the onions, season with salt and pepper, and slowly cook until richly caramelized, about 30–40 minutes.

Remove from the heat and spread out on a cookie sheet to cool.

❖ IF MAKING IN ADVANCE, this step can be performed up to 1 week ahead of time. Refrigerate the cooled onions in an airtight container. (You can also prepare this entire component in advance; see instruction at the end of the recipe.) WHEN READY TO PROCEED, allow the onions to come to room temperature.

Finely chop the caramelized onions.

Heat the remaining 1 tablespoon butter and the olive oil in a sauté pan over low to medium heat. Add the barley to the pan and brown it slowly, about 20 minutes, stirring continuously to keep it from scorching. The barley will attain a deep, roasted flavor if you don't rush it.

Once the barley is browned, transfer it to a pot with the caramelized onions.

Add enough stock to cover by 1 inch.

Season with salt, pepper, and sugar. Cook over low to medium heat. Add stock when necessary to keep the mixture from drying out, but not so much that it looks like soup. (Think of it as you would a risotto, only adding stock when the last addition has been absorbed.) Cook for 25–30 minutes, or until the grain is tender but still a bit *al dente*.

Place the contents of the pan on a cookie sheet and spread it out so that it cools quickly. Reserve.

❖ IF MAKING IN ADVANCE, this component can be stored in an airtight container in the refrigerator for up to 5 days. WHEN READY TO PROCEED, reheat over a low flame, stirring to prevent scorching. (You may need to add a bit of stock when reheating to return the proper moisture to the barley.)

QUAIL AND ASSEMBLY
2 tablespoons Chopped Roasted
   Tomatoes (page 13)
2 tablespoons extra-virgin olive oil
2 teaspoons white vinegar
Roasted Shallots (page 182),
   skins removed and cut crosswise
   into 1/8-inch slices

1 cup Dark Chicken Stock (page 32)
2 tablespoons unsalted butter
8 whole boneless quail
   (about 6 ounces each)

Preheat the broiler.

Place the tomatoes in a small mixing bowl. Moisten with 1 tablespoon oil and the vinegar.

Prepare the shallots.

In a saucepan over medium-high heat, bring the stock to a simmer. Whisk in the tomatoes and shallots. Cover and keep warm over low heat.

Warm the remaining 1 tablespoon oil and the butter in a 12-inch sauté pan over medium-high heat.

Add the quail to the pan, 2–3 at a time, and cook about 1 minute on each side, just to brown the skin.

Transfer the quail, breast side up, to a roasting rack and repeat until all have been browned.

Place the rack under the broiler, about 6–8 inches from the heat source. Broil for 1 minute, then flip over and cook an additional 30–40 seconds for medium-rare to medium.

Place the barley on a platter and arrange the quail on top. Pass the sauce in a sauceboat alongside.

OPTION: Grilled squab can be substituted for the quail.

WINE: Serve this with a complex red wine such as a cabernet sauvignon.

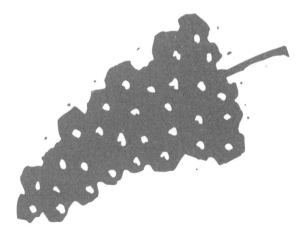

ROASTED LEG AND LOIN OF RABBIT WITH
SPRING ONIONS AND DRY VERMOUTH SAUCE

🌰

Serves 4

The technique employed by this recipe offers a method of "wet roasting" rabbit that produces a nice caramelization while keeping the leg moist.

SPRING ONIONS	1 tablespoon unsalted butter
24 spring onions, white part only, or pearl onions	Coarse salt
	Freshly ground black pepper

Place the onions in a sauté pan. Cover with water (see Note) and add the butter to the pan. Season with salt and pepper. Place over high heat and bring to a boil. Lower the heat and let simmer until the liquid has evaporated and the onions are covered with a glaze, 15–20 minutes.

NOTE: For a more flavorful effect, use Chicken Stock (page 23) instead of water.

ROASTED OYSTER MUSHROOMS	Freshly ground black pepper
1/2 cup olive oil	12 ounces oyster mushrooms, smaller
1 clove garlic, smashed	ones left whole, larger ones cut
Coarse salt	in half

Preheat the oven to 350°F.

Place the oil and garlic in a small mixing bowl and season with salt and pepper.

Dip the mushrooms in the oil, shake off any excess, and place on a cookie sheet.

Roast in the preheated oven until golden brown and starting to crisp around the edges, 15–18 minutes.

Remove from the oven and set aside, covered with aluminum foil to keep warm.

RABBIT, PAN SAUCE, AND ASSEMBLY	2 tablespoons olive oil
2 rabbit fryers, rear legs removed and loins boned out (ask your butcher to do this)	1/2 cup dry vermouth
	3 sprigs marjoram, plus 2 tablespoons fresh marjoram leaves
Coarse salt	4 cloves garlic, crushed
Freshly ground black pepper	1/2 cup Dark Chicken Stock (page 32)
3 tablespoons unsalted butter, at room temperature	

Preheat the oven to 450°F.

Season the rabbit legs with salt and pepper.

Warm 1 tablespoon butter and 1 tablespoon oil in a sauté pan over medium-high heat until the butter melts.

Add the legs to the pan and sear for 2–3 minutes on each side.

Drain all fat from the pan and deglaze with the vermouth.

Add the marjoram sprigs, garlic, and 1/2 tablespoon butter.

Transfer the pan to the preheated oven and cook, basting frequently, until the legs are quite firm to the touch and nicely glazed, 8–10 minutes.

Remove the pan from the oven. Transfer the legs to a clean, dry surface and cover to keep warm.

Return the pan with its cooking juices to the stove top and cook over medium-high heat until the liquid is reduced to a thick gloss, about 1 minute. (It may already have reduced to this point in the oven.)

Add the stock to the pan, raise the heat to high, bring to a boil, and reduce to a consistency that will lightly coat the back of a spoon. Finish by whisking in 1/2 tablespoon butter. Strain and reserve.

Warm 1 tablespoon butter and 1 tablespoon oil in a sauté pan over medium-high heat until the butter melts.

Add the loins to the pan and sauté for 2–3 minutes on each side, keeping them pink.

To serve, place 1 leg on each of 4 plates. Cut the loin on the bias into 2-inch slices and arrange decoratively around the leg. Reheat the mushrooms and onions in the sauce, spoon over and around the rabbit, and garnish with the marjoram leaves.

FOOD FOR THOUGHT—IS IT DONE? If you are unsure whether or not the leg is done, remove it from the pan and place skin side down on the cutting board. Run your knife along the thigh bone for a discreet peek inside.

WINE: Serve this with a pinot gris or sauvignon blanc.

ROAST DUCK WITH PORT AND
RED WINE VINEGAR REDUCTION

🌿

Serves 4

This recipe is a great lesson in how easy it is to roast duck. The port and red wine vinegar reduction beautifully cuts the fattiness of the duck. Be very careful when cooking not to over-reduce it; it should pour easily and have a powerful but not overpowering flavor. If it becomes too cloying or thick, whisk in some hot water.

SERVE THIS WITH Celery Root Puree (page 266) or Braised Endives (page 274).

RED WINE VINEGAR REDUCTION

1 tablespoon unsalted butter	1 teaspoon black peppercorns
1 teaspoon olive oil	1 bay leaf
1 cup thinly sliced shallots	Pinch ground cloves
1/2 cup sliced garlic	1 cup Dark Chicken or Duck Stock
2 cups ruby port (see Food	(page 32)
for Thought)	Coarse salt
1 cup red wine vinegar	Freshly ground black pepper

Warm the butter and oil in a sauté pan over medium-high heat.

Add the shallots and garlic to the pan and cook until the shallots are nicely caramelized, 10–12 minutes.

Deglaze with the port and vinegar. (Be careful, this might cause a brief flare-up.)

Add the peppercorns, bay leaf, and cloves, and cook until reduced by half.

Add the stock, raise the heat to high, and bring to a boil. Skim off any impurities that rise to the surface, lower the heat, and simmer until slightly thickened, about 20 minutes. Season with salt and pepper, strain, and reserve.

❖ **IF MAKING IN ADVANCE,** this sauce may be kept in the refrigerator, tightly covered, for up to 5 days. **WHEN READY TO PROCEED,** allow to come to room temperature and reheat gently over low heat.

ROAST DUCK AND ASSEMBLY
1 Pekin (Long Island) duck (about
  4 pounds), separated into breast
  and leg pieces (see page 198 or
  ask your butcher to do this)
	Coarse salt
	Freshly ground black pepper

Preheat the oven to 350°F.

Score the duck on both sides and season with salt and pepper.

Place the pieces, skin side down, in an ovenproof sauté pan and cook over medium-high heat until the fat begins to render and the skin turns a beautiful golden brown, about 15 minutes.

Flip the pieces, drain off some of the fat, and place in the preheated oven.

Cook the breast until firm to the touch, 15–20 minutes, basting every 5 minutes with the rendered duck fat and draining off some fat if an excessive amount accumulates.

Remove the breasts and keep warm.

Lower the oven temperature to 300°F and cook the legs an additional 20–25 minutes. They are ready when the juices run clear when a knife is inserted. If the leg and thigh bone feel springy, however, keep cooking.

Place a duck leg in the center of each of 4 dinner plates. Cut the breast on the bias into long, thin slices and surround the leg with them. Spoon the sauce over and around the duck.

WINE: Serve this with a red Burgundy.

FOOD FOR THOUGHT—SAVE THE GOOD STUFF FOR DRINKING: When you reduce a liquid, the flavors intensify, so an inexpensive port will do quite nicely here.

ROAST DUCK WITH AUTUMN FRUIT COMPOTE

Serves 4

This is a quintessential autumn dish that brings together succulent game and soft, sweet seasonal fruits.

SERVE THIS WITH Wild Rice Griddle Cakes (page 275) or wild rice.

---

4 magret duck breasts (8–9 ounces each; see Note)
Coarse salt
Freshly ground black pepper

1 tablespoon (approximately) olive oil
1 1/2 cups Autumn Fruit Compote (page 272), warmed

Preheat the oven to 375°F.

Perforate the duck breasts on both sides with the tines of a fork. Season with salt and pepper.

Use just enough oil to evenly coat the bottom of an ovenproof sauté pan.

Place the breasts in the pan, skin side down. Cook over medium heat, draining the fat from the pan every few minutes, until the skin is a golden brown, about 15 minutes.

Drain the fat one last time, flip the breasts, and transfer to the preheated oven.

Cook for 15 minutes, basting frequently with the fat that renders out and draining the fat if a surplus accumulates in the pan. You can remove it at this point or cook another 5 minutes for a slightly more well done duck. Remove to a cutting board and cut on the bias into thin slices.

Serve the duck on a platter and pass the compote alongside in a bowl.

NOTE: Alternatively, you can ask your butcher to cut Pekin duck breasts; if using the latter, save the legs for Braised Duck Legs with Egg Noodles, page 133.

ROAST GUINEA HENS WITH TRUFFLED POLENTA AND BUTTERNUT SQUASH

Serves 4

This dish is loaded with intense flavors—butternut squash prepared two ways (cubed and in chips), truffled polenta, and full-flavored roast guinea hens. Pay close attention to the guinea hens when cooking; they have a tendency to dry out.

I SERVE THIS WITH Stewed Brussels Sprouts (page 267).

BUTTERNUT SQUASH	2 tablespoons unsalted butter, cut into
1 small butternut squash	4 pieces
Coarse salt	1/4 cup canola oil

Cut the squash's neck and body apart. Remove the stem end from the neck, stand the neck on a cutting board, and use a knife to remove the skin. Cut the flesh into 1/2-inch dice and place in a shallow saucepan with just enough water to cover.

Season the water moderately with salt and dot with the butter.

Cook over low to medium heat until tender, about 15 minutes. Once tender, strain and set aside to cool.

❖ **IF MAKING IN ADVANCE,** the cooked, cooled squash can be covered and refrigerated overnight. **WHEN READY TO PROCEED,** reheat gently over medium heat.

Cut the bottom end off the body of the squash, stand it up on a cutting board, and use a knife to remove the skin. Scoop out the seeds, then set the body on its side and slice it very carefully and evenly into 1/16-inch rings. (You can also do this with a mandoline.)

Pour the oil into a large, shallow pan. Place the pan over medium-high heat and bring to a temperature of 325°F.

Fry the squash rings in the oil until crisp and golden, flipping them after 30 seconds. If the oil is getting too hot, turn off the heat.

Using tongs or a slotted spoon, transfer the rings to paper towels to drain. Season lightly with salt. Reserve.

❖ IF MAKING IN ADVANCE, the squash rings can be covered and refrigerated for up to 24 hours.

POLENTA	1 tablespoon unsalted butter
2 1/2 cups milk	1 large clove garlic, minced
2 teaspoons coarse salt	1/2 cup white cornmeal
1 teaspoon freshly ground black pepper	1 black truffle or 2 drops truffle oil

Pour the milk into a saucepan and add the salt, pepper, butter, and garlic. Bring to a boil over high heat, then lower the heat and whisk in the cornmeal. The resulting mixture will look very loose. (If you want a thicker polenta, add more cornmeal and a pinch more of salt and pepper.)

Cook, stirring frequently, for 6–7 minutes.

Shave the truffle into the polenta and stir gently to incorporate. Reserve or, if you like, leave over low heat and keep warm by stirring frequently. You can also transfer the polenta to a double boiler set over simmering water. (If reserving for more than a few minutes, wait until just before serving before shaving in the truffle.)

GUINEA HENS AND ASSEMBLY	2 tablespoons olive oil
2 guinea hens (2 pounds each), quartered (see Food for Thought)	2 tablespoons unsalted butter
	1 cup Dark Chicken Stock (page 32)
Coarse salt	1 tablespoon Roasted Garlic Puree
Freshly ground black pepper	(page 12)

Season the guinea hens with salt and pepper, and perforate their skins with the tines of a fork.

Heat the oil and butter in an ovenproof sauté pan over medium-high heat.

Add the guinea hen pieces to the pan, skin side down, and cook until browned, about 10 minutes.

Flip the pieces and transfer the pan to the preheated oven. Cook, basting every minute or so. After about 5 minutes, check for doneness by piercing the breast with a paring knife to see if it is just pink at the bone. When it is, remove the breasts and let the legs cook an additional 2 minutes.

Let the pieces rest for 5 minutes.

Meanwhile, in a saucepan, warm the stock over medium heat and stir in the roasted garlic puree. Add the butternut squash dice to the pot and warm through.

Remove the breastplate and ribs from the guinea hens, leaving the wing tip intact. Separate the thigh-leg pieces and French the leg by running a paring knife around the bone on the lower portion, 1¹/₂ inches from the end. Remove the detached skin and meat.

To serve, place the guinea hen pieces on a platter. Garnish with the squash rings. Serve the polenta in a bowl and pass the sauce alongside in a sauceboat.

For a more formal presentation, spoon some polenta in the center of each of 4 plates. Place 1 guinea hen breast on each mound of polenta. Place the thigh next to it and the leg behind it, sticking straight up. Spoon some squash rings between the guinea hen breast and thigh, and spoon some sauce around the plate. Garnish with the squash rings, draping one over the bone of the leg.

FOOD FOR THOUGHT—FAT REDUCTION: Because of the deposits of fat under the skin, guinea hens can "pop" when browned on the stove top. To prevent this, poke the small pockets of light yellow fat on the breast and leg with a sharp, thin-bladed knife. The fat will run out into the pan.

Meats

In my childhood household, my grandmother's forte was working Italian magic with inexpensive cuts of meat. The smell of something braising or stewing on the stove was always there. She would snip off the most tender pieces for me, content herself to gnaw on another bone. I thought she was being kind but know now that she was keeping the best part for herself.

The primal delights of meat take all of us back to the roots of hunting and gathering. Maybe that is why I'm rarely content to just cook a steak (and don't have any steak recipes here): it just seems too easy. I'm much more interested in taking lesser cuts and making them irresistible.

In the following pages you'll see why I love braising so much, not just in my recipe for Braised Lamb Shanks (page 225) but also in the ones for Braised Pork Shoulder (page 227) and Braised Short Ribs (page 241). These are the dishes I crave when the words "red meat" are uttered.

I also find the smoky char of a grill appealing and have presented it here in Grilled Top Sirloin of Lamb Marinated in Yogurt and Served with Couscous (page 246). No less intense an effect is created by pan-roasting the Veal Chop with Orzo, Swiss Chard, and Roast Garlic (page 234) and the Boneless Stuffed Saddle of Lamb (page 239).

I've also made room here for some cuts that I love, often surrounding them with a component that offers great contrast. Bacon-Wrapped Pork Tenderloin with Sautéed Spinach (page 229) pairs the delicate pork with smoky, fatty bacon—a truly sublime combination. And Porcini-Crusted Filet Mignon with Wilted Arugula (page 232) finds the filet surrounded with earthy mushroom powder that benefits as much as the meat does from the searing process.

For those of you who enjoy returning to childhood favorites as much as I do, there is a recipe for Meatloaf (page 248) that may make you remember it more fondly than you do already.

Last but not least, I have to put a word in for organ meats. They have never been terribly popular in this country, but they have come into vogue in recent years in a number of Italian and French restaurants. I was raised on them and love them. So humor me and try the Seared Calf's Liver with Sweet-and-Sour Onions and Red Wine Sauce (page 237) or the Honeycomb Tripe Slow-Cooked with Tomato, Bacon, and Onions (page 243). I can see you wincing from here, but trust me and do what my grandmother used to urge me to do: "Just try it."

BRAISED LAMB SHANKS

❧

Serves 6

This is without a doubt the most requested recipe I've ever created. Lamb shanks are one of the cuts of meat that benefit most from long, slow braising. Don't omit the step of turning the shanks every half hour; it causes them to caramelize even as they braise. If the braising liquid seems too reduced at the end of the cooking process, stir 1 cup of water into the liquid before straining.

SERVE THIS WITH Soft Polenta (page 199), Tomato-Thyme Risotto (page 148), Potato Puree (page 268), or White Bean Puree (page 259).

6 lamb foreshanks (see Food for Thought)	1 tablespoon black peppercorns
Coarse salt	3 anchovy fillets
Freshly ground black pepper	1 whole head garlic, cut in half
3 tablespoons plus 1/2 cup olive oil	2 cups red wine
2 ribs celery, roughly chopped	1 cup dry white wine
1 carrot, roughly chopped	1/3 cup white vinegar
1 large Spanish onion, roughly chopped	1 teaspoon sugar
1/2 cup tomato paste	2 cups Veal Stock (page 32) or
5 sprigs thyme	1 cup demi-glace (see Note)
1 bay leaf	2 cups Chicken Stock (page 23)

Preheat the oven to 325°F.

Season the lamb shanks liberally with salt and pepper. With a sharp knife, cut about 1 inch from the bottom (narrow end) of the shank bones down to the bone and all the way around; this will help expose the bone while cooking. Set aside.

Heat 3 tablespoons oil in a pot over medium-high heat. Add the celery, carrot, and onion to the pot, and cook until very soft, 8–10 minutes.

Add the tomato paste and cook 1–2 minutes.

Add the thyme, bay leaf, peppercorns, anchovies, and garlic, and cook another 2–3 minutes.

Add the red and white wine, vinegar, and sugar, raise the heat to high, and bring to a boil.

Lower the heat to medium and add the veal and chicken stocks. Leave over medium heat while you brown the shanks.

In a sauté pan over medium-high heat, brown the shanks well in the remaining 1/2 cup oil on both sides, about 1 minute for each of 3 sides. Use tongs to flip them over.

Transfer the shanks to a roasting pan and pour the stock mixture on top. Cover with aluminum foil and cook in the preheated oven for 1 hour. Remove the foil and cook for another 3 hours, turning the shanks over every half hour until the meat is very soft.

Remove the shanks from the braising liquid and strain the liquid. Skim any fat that rises to the surface and use the liquid as a sauce.

WINE: Serve this with any full-bodied red wine.

FOOD FOR THOUGHT—WHAT FORE? I use the foreshanks rather than the rear shanks because they are, as a rule, meatier.

NOTE: Demi-glace is veal stock that has been reduced by half. High-quality prepared versions are available at gourmet shops.

BRAISED PORK SHOULDER

🌿

Serves 4

This long-cooked dish is the perfect fare for a winter Sunday afternoon when it can braise throughout the early hours, be enjoyed as a late lunch, and then saved for other meals. It makes wonderful leftovers that can be put to use in sandwiches (shredded with some barbecue sauce is my favorite version) or in soups and stuffings.

SERVE THIS WITH Pickled Red Cabbage (page 254) and/or Spaetzle (page 160) or White Balsamic Vinaigrette (page 172).

1/2 pork shoulder (2–3 pounds), boned out and tied like a roast	2 ribs celery, roughly chopped
Coarse salt	4 tablespoons tomato paste
Freshly ground black pepper	1 bay leaf
4 cloves garlic, slivered, plus 10 cloves, crushed	Pinch dried thyme or oregano
1 cup olive oil	2 cups white wine
3 carrots, roughly chopped	2/3 cup white vinegar
1 Spanish onion, roughly chopped	2 cups Veal Stock (page 32), or 1 beef bouillon cube dissolved in 2 cups water

Preheat the oven to 300°F.

Season the pork shoulder liberally with salt and pepper, and stud it with the slivered garlic.

In a heavy-bottomed ovenproof saucepan or casserole, warm the oil over medium-high heat. Add the pork and brown on all sides, 2–3 minutes per side.

Transfer the pork to a clean, dry surface.

Add the carrots, onion, and celery to the pan and sauté for 3–4 minutes.

Add the tomato paste and cook for 5 minutes, stirring to coat the vegetables with the paste.

Add the crushed garlic, bay leaf, and thyme. Deglaze with the wine and vinegar. Add the stock, taste, and season with salt and pepper, being careful not to oversalt.

Gently immerse the pork in the liquid. If the liquid comes more than halfway up the pork, drain a bit off.

Cover the pan and transfer it to the preheated oven. Cook gently, turning the pork over in the pot every hour, for 2 1/2 hours, or until the meat appears very tender.

Remove the pot from the oven. Remove the pork and allow it to rest on a rack.

Strain the liquid through a fine-mesh strainer and reserve to use as a sauce.

Peel off and discard the pork's skin. Cut the meat in thin slices against the grain. Serve with the sauce alongside in a sauceboat.

BACON-WRAPPED PORK TENDERLOIN
WITH SAUTÉED SPINACH

Serves 4

The tenderloin is one of the leanest parts of the pig. This means that a quick-cooking technique will bring out all of its delicious flavor and that it can take on the qualities of the bacon without becoming unbearably heavy. The combination of smoky bacon and tender pink pork is sublime.

This is also a very convenient make-ahead recipe. After wrapping and browning the tenderloin, it can be held for up to one hour, then finished under the broiler or—for a more succulent and smoky variation—on the grill.

Don't let your butcher talk you out of slicing the bacon super-thin. He may warn you that it will melt away in the pan. Assure him that you know what you're doing and that you want it as thin as you've indicated.

SERVE THIS WITH White Bean Ravioli (page 143).

PEPPERCORN SAUCE
1 cup Veal Stock (page 32), Dark
    Chicken Stock (page 32),
      or braising liquid from Pork Confit
    (page 42)
2 tablespoons Chopped Roasted
    Tomatoes (page 13)

1 tablespoon canned green
    peppercorns, drained
1 teaspoon fresh marjoram leaves
Coarse salt
Freshly ground black pepper
3 tablespoons heavy cream

Pour the stock into a saucepan and bring to a boil over high heat.

Stir in the roasted tomatoes, peppercorns, and marjoram leaves. Season with salt and pepper.

❖ **IF MAKING IN ADVANCE,** this sauce can be cooled, covered, and refrigerated for up to 1 day. **WHEN READY TO PROCEED,** gently reheat, and add the cream.

SAUTÉED SPINACH

1 pound spinach

3 tablespoons olive oil

2 small cloves garlic, thinly sliced

Coarse salt

Freshly ground black pepper

Wash the spinach and shake off the excess water.

Warm the oil in a sauté pan over medium-high heat and add the garlic.

When the garlic begins to sizzle, add the spinach to the pan and cook, stirring continuously, until it softens and steams. Season with salt and pepper. Once it is completely cooked down, about 1 minute, transfer to a cookie sheet and allow to cool.

PORK TENDERLOIN

AND ASSEMBLY

2 1/2 pounds pork tenderloin (see Note)

Coarse salt

Freshly ground black pepper

Ground coriander

Garlic powder

5 ounces bacon, very thinly sliced

4 sprigs marjoram for garnish

NOTE: Many gourmet stores now sell packaged pork tenderloin, usually two to a package. They work fine for this recipe.

There will be some silver skin on the surface of 1 side of the tenderloin. Slide a thin-bladed knife under this skin and remove it. (Hint: The knife will slide more easily in one direction than the other.)

Remove about 1/2 inch off the tapered end of the tenderloin to form a perfect cylinder. Season with salt, pepper, a light sprinkling of ground coriander, and a pinch of garlic powder.

Lay the bacon strips in an overlapping line on a sheet of parchment paper.

Place 1 piece of tenderloin across the short ends of the bacon (perpendicular to the strips) and roll to cover with the bacon.

Repeat with the other tenderloin segments.

❖ **IF MAKING IN ADVANCE**, the bacon-wrapped tenderloin can be covered with plastic wrap and refrigerated for up to 2 days. **WHEN READY TO PROCEED**, allow to come to room temperature.

Preheat the oven to 425°F.

Place the tenderloin, seam side down, in a cold nonstick pan and set over medium-high heat.

As the temperature in the pan increases, brown the tenderloin well on the first side for 2–3 minutes or just until the seal holds.

Turn and cook all sides, about 2 minutes per side.

Transfer the pan to the preheated oven and cook for 8–10 minutes, turning the pieces after 5 minutes to ensure even cooking. (See Food for Thought.)

To serve, set a mound of spinach in the center of each of 4 dinner plates. Cut each pork tenderloin section in half and stand the pieces up next to the spinach. Spoon the sauce around and garnish with a sprig of marjoram.

FOOD FOR THOUGHT—PINK PORK: I prefer to eat (and serve) pork on the pink side. Although concern over trichinosis once led people to cook all pork well done, this is no longer a necessary precaution because pigs are raised in more sanitary conditions.

PORCINI-CRUSTED FILET MIGNON
WITH WILTED ARUGULA

❧

Serves 4

Usually when I have a steak, I'll opt for a rib eye or porterhouse because I like a bone and marbleized meat. But sometimes there is nothing like a buttery filet mignon; it offers all the charms of all meat with very little work. When cooking filet mignon, I often choose a pan-seared version to seal in as much of the juice as possible. In this recipe the porcini crust makes that searing a source of distinct flavor.

SERVE THIS WITH Potato Gratin (page 256) or Potato Puree (page 268).

WILTED ARUGULA	
2 tablespoons olive oil	1 pound arugula, washed and left
1 clove garlic, minced	a little wet

Place the oil and garlic in a sauté pan and warm over medium heat.

When the garlic begins to sizzle, add the arugula to the pan and cook until wilted but still vibrant, about 1 minute.

Turn the arugula out on a cookie sheet to cool.

PORCINI-CRUSTED FILET MIGNON	Porcini Powder (page 163)
4 filets mignons (7–8 ounces each)	4 tablespoons unsalted butter
Coarse salt	2 tablespoons olive oil
Freshly ground black pepper	

Preheat the oven to 450°F.

Season the filets on all sides with salt and pepper, then dredge in the porcini powder. Shake off the excess powder.

Melt 2 tablespoons butter and the oil in a large ovenproof sauté pan over medium-high heat.

Add the filets to the pan and sear on all sides, about 1 minute per side.

Drain the grease from the pan, temporarily removing the filets if necessary.

Add the remaining 2 tablespoons butter, return the filets, and transfer the pan to the preheated oven. Cook for an additional 3–4 minutes for rare or 5–6 minutes for medium rare, basting every minute or so.

To serve, mound some arugula in the center of each of 4 plates and place a filet alongside.

VEAL CHOP WITH ORZO, SWISS CHARD, AND ROAST GARLIC

Serves 4

There are two types of veal chop: One, a loin chop, resembles a junior version of a beef T-bone steak with both the shell and the tenderloin represented. The other, the veal chop that most of us associate with the name, is a big, round ball of meat on the end of a single bone. This is also known as a rib chop. You can use either version in this recipe. Rib chops tend to be more expensive than loin chops, so choose according to your budget. (Personally, I happen to love the more economical loin chop.) In this recipe and elsewhere it is usually a good idea to have the chop cut thickly and to sear it well when cooking.

There is not a lot of razzle-dazzle in the preparation of the veal chop in this dish. The real star of the plate is the timbale of orzo, Parmesan cheese, and Swiss chard—a versatile and surprisingly easy to prepare side dish that you'll enjoy having in your repertoire.

If you don't have a mold for the orzo, any small ovenproof ceramic vessel, such as a ramekin, will work fine.

ORZO, PARMESAN, AND SWISS CHARD TIMBALE

2 tablespoons olive oil

1 clove garlic, minced

1 bunch red Swiss chard, tough outer stems removed

2 1/2 cups dry orzo

Coarse salt

6 tablespoons grated Parmigiano-Reggiano cheese, or more to taste

Freshly ground black pepper

Place the oil and garlic in a sauté pan over medium heat.

When the garlic begins to sizzle, add the Swiss chard and cook until wilted but still vibrant, about 2 minutes.

Turn the Swiss chard out on a cookie sheet to cool.

Bring a pot of salted water to a boil. Add the orzo and cook until *al dente*, about 7 minutes.

Strain the orzo well but do not rinse. (You want to keep it starchy to bind the timbale.) Spread the orzo out on a cookie sheet and place in the refrigerator to cool. Once chilled, transfer to a mixing bowl and sprinkle on the cheese.

Squeeze out the excess liquid from the Swiss chard, roughly chop it, and add it to the bowl.

Stir to incorporate and season with salt and pepper (mostly with pepper because the cheese is salty).

Lightly oil four 6-ounce molds. Pack the orzo–Swiss chard mixture into the molds.

❖ **IF MAKING IN ADVANCE,** the timbales can be covered with plastic wrap and refrigerated for up to 24 hours. (In fact, this will help them set.) **WHEN READY TO PROCEED,** allow to come to room temperature.

Preheat the oven to 325°F.

If the molds are covered with plastic wrap, remove it and replace it with waxed paper.

Bake the timbales in the preheated oven for 12–14 minutes or microwave for 1–2 minutes on high. Let cool for 1 minute to facilitate unmolding.

GARLIC CONFIT SAUCE	1 tablespoon fresh oregano leaves
1 cup Veal Stock (page 32)	12 cloves Roasted Garlic (page 12)
2 tablespoons Chopped Roasted	Coarse salt
Tomatoes (page 13; optional)	Freshly ground black pepper

Pour the stock into a saucepan. Bring to a simmer over medium heat.

Stir in the tomatoes, oregano, and garlic. Simmer gently for 2–3 minutes, until the flavors are incorporated. Season with salt and pepper.

4 veal chops, rib or loin cut, at least
    1 inch thick (10–12 ounces each;
    see headnote)
Coarse salt
Freshly ground black pepper

1 tablespoon unsalted butter
1 tablespoon olive oil
1 tablespoon fresh thyme leaves
4 cloves garlic, unpeeled
4–8 sprigs oregano for garnish

Preheat the oven to 425°F.

Season the chops on all sides with salt and pepper.

In a large ovenproof sauté pan, melt the butter and warm the oil over medium-high heat.

Add the chops to the pan and brown them on one side, about 2 minutes.

Flip the chops. Add the thyme leaves and garlic.

Transfer the pan to the preheated oven and cook for 8–10 minutes for medium-rare, basting every 1 or 2 minutes.

To serve, arrange the veal chops on a platter and garnish with oregano sprigs. Unmold the timbales on a plate. Pass the sauce alongside in a sauceboat.

For a more formal presentation, unmold 1 timbale in the twelve o'clock position on each of 4 dinner plates, about 1 inch below the rim. Lay a veal chop at the six o'clock position, with the bone jutting toward one o'clock. Spoon some sauce around the veal chop. Garnish with the oregano sprigs.

OPTION: If you don't want to make a timbale, prepare the orzo and Swiss chard, toss them together, and top with grated Parmesan cheese.

SEARED CALF'S LIVER WITH SWEET-AND-SOUR ONIONS AND RED WINE SAUCE

Serves 4

As I've mentioned, childhood recollections of food are crucial in shaping our flavor and taste memories. I don't know of many kids who jumped up and down when their mother announced, "We're having liver for dinner," but I love it. Always have. Always will. The delicate quality of fresh calf's liver in no way resembles that nasty, bloodred beef liver of days gone by. To pay it the proper respect, when you purchase calf's liver, get it freshly cut from your butcher; don't trust anything presliced and wrapped with an expiration date on it. I like liver that is cut at least 3/4 inch thick. Since liver is very sensitive to heat, this helps prevent overcooking.

SERVE THIS WITH Sautéed Spinach (page 229), Potato Puree (page 268), or any other potato preparation.

SWEET-AND-SOUR ONIONS AND SAUCE	
2 large Spanish onions	2/3 cup sugar
2 cups red wine	Coarse salt
2/3 cup white vinegar	Freshly ground black pepper
	2 tablespoons grenadine (optional)
	1 cup Duck or Veal Stock (page 32)

Cut the onions in half lengthwise, leaving intact as much of the root end as possible, then cut each half into thirds.

Pour the wine, vinegar, and sugar into a large, shallow saucepan.

Add a pinch of salt, a healthy dose of black pepper, and the grenadine (if using).

Set the pan over high heat, bring to a boil, and reduce by two-thirds.

Lower the heat to medium, place the onion wedges in the pan, and simmer until tender but still toothsome, about 10 minutes. Remove the onions from the pan, set aside, and keep warm.

Add the stock to the onion cooking liquid and cook for 1 or 2 minutes. Season with salt and pepper and reserve.

SAUTÉED CALF'S LIVER

2 pounds calf's liver, cut into 1-inch-thick slices (see Food for Thought)
Coarse salt
Freshly ground black pepper

1 tablespoon unsalted butter
2 tablespoons olive oil
4 teaspoons Dijon mustard
6 tablespoons finely chopped roasted pistachio nuts

Preheat the broiler.

Season the calf's liver with salt and pepper.

Place the butter and oil in a sauté pan over high heat and warm until the butter ceases to sizzle.

Add the calf's liver to the pan and cook until rare, about 40–50 seconds per side. (Don't overcrowd the pan; do this in batches if necessary.)

Remove the pan from the heat and pat the liver dry with paper towels.

Lightly coat the liver with a thin layer of mustard (using your fingers is the best way to do this). Press the pistachio nuts into the surface on 1 side only.

To finish, cook under the broiler, about 8–10 inches from the heat source to avoid burning the nuts, for 2–3 minutes.

To serve, place the liver in the center of each of 4 dinner plates, fan some of the onions around, and spoon some sauce over the top.

WINE: Serve this with a Barbaresco.

FOOD FOR THOUGHT—CHOOSE ORGANIC: As is true with most organ meats, it is a wise choice to buy organic whenever possible because the artificial hormones fed to commercial livestock today lodge in the liver.

BONELESS STUFFED SADDLE OF LAMB

❧

Serves 4

I love boneless saddles of lamb because they bring with them a built-in pocket for stuffing. When roasted and cut into slices, it is visually dramatic. When selecting boneless saddles of lamb, ask your butcher to trim the outside of the saddle of any excess fat and be sure that you ask him to leave the flaps intact. These are what you will use to wrap the stuffing in place and hold it together.

SERVE THIS WITH White Bean Puree (page 259).

STUFFED LAMB	Coarse salt
8 ounces (2 sticks) plus 2 tablespoons unsalted butter	Freshly ground black pepper
3 cloves garlic, finely minced, plus 4 cloves garlic, smashed	2 boneless saddles of lamb (about 1½ pounds each; ask the butcher to trim the flap for stuffed loin)
3 tablespoons finely chopped flat-leaf parsley	1 tablespoon olive oil
1½–2 cups dry bread crumbs	2 tablespoons coarsely chopped thyme sprigs (stems and all)

Preheat the oven to 425°F.

Melt the 2 sticks of butter with the minced garlic in a small saucepan over low heat until infused.

Add the parsley and 1½ cups bread crumbs to the pan. Use a wooden spoon to stir together, adding more bread crumbs if necessary to form a malleable solid.

Transfer the contents of the pan to a bowl and allow to cool slightly. Taste and adjust the seasoning.

Using a paring knife, score the saddle flaps on both sides with a crosshatch pattern.

Spoon half of the stuffing onto the central portion of the saddle and wrap the flaps around it, folding one flap over the other.

Tie the saddle closed with kitchen string at 1-inch intervals, being sure to make it firm but not excessively tight.

Repeat with the other saddle.

Melt the remaining 2 tablespoons butter and the oil in an ovenproof sauté pan over medium-high heat.

Add the lamb to the pan and brown on all sides, about 2 minutes per side.

Remove the pan from the heat and add the smashed garlic cloves and thyme.

Transfer the pan to the oven and cook, basting occasionally and turning every few minutes, until nicely browned, about 12–15 minutes for rare.

Remove from the oven and let rest for 5 minutes before removing the string and slicing.

FOOD FOR THOUGHT—BONELESS SADDLE OF LAMB: The meat of the saddle is an extended part of the rack. Although not quite as tender, it is equally full flavored.

BRAISED SHORT RIBS

❧

This recipe captures all the soul-nourishing qualities of beef stew but does so with the beef still on the bone. It is extremely adaptable in that you can serve it simply with some braising liquid and roasted vegetables; or chill, slice, and grill it; or make it the basis of a satisfying sandwich (page 90). You can also chop it and stuff ravioli with it.

Keep the bone side up while cooking to ensure that the meat stays submerged and moist while cooking. For a dynamic presentation, skip the step of removing the bone and slice the short rib with the bone in.

SERVE THIS WITH Mushroom Stock (page 26) and some simple roasted vegetables.

2 pieces short ribs, with 3 ribs in each piece (about 2 1/2 pounds each)	1 tablespoon black peppercorns
Coarse salt	3 anchovy fillets
Freshly ground black pepper	1 whole head garlic, cut in half
Garlic powder	2 cups red wine
3 tablespoons plus 1/2 cup olive oil	1 cup dry white wine
2 ribs celery, roughly chopped	1/3 cup white vinegar
1 carrot, roughly chopped	1 teaspoon sugar
1 large Spanish onion, roughly chopped	2 cups Veal Stock (page 32) or demi-glace
1/2 cup tomato paste	2 cups Chicken Stock (page 23) or water
5 sprigs thyme	
1 bay leaf	

THE DAY BEFORE COOKING, score the fat covering the bones and season with salt, pepper, and garlic powder. Cover with plastic wrap and keep in the refrigerator overnight.

Preheat the oven to 325°F.

Warm 3 tablespoons oil in a pot over medium-high heat.

Add the celery, carrot, and onion to the pot, and cook until very soft, about 5 minutes.

Add the tomato paste and cook for 1–2 minutes.

Add the thyme, bay leaf, peppercorns, anchovies, and garlic, and cook another 2–3 minutes.

Add the red and white wine, vinegar, and sugar, raise the heat to high, and bring to a boil. Lower the heat to medium and add the veal and chicken stocks. Leave over medium heat while you brown the ribs.

Pour the remaining oil into a sauté pan and place over medium-high heat. Add the ribs to the pan and brown on both sides, about 1 minute per side. Use tongs to flip them over.

Transfer the ribs to a roasting pan, bone side up, and pour the braising liquid over the top.

Cover the roasting pan with aluminum foil and cook in the preheated oven for 1 hour.

Remove the foil and cook for 3 more hours, or until the bones are easy to remove and the meat is very soft. Turn the ribs over during the last 15 minutes to brown them a bit.

Remove the ribs from the braising liquid and strain. Skim off all the fat you can from the liquid and pass as a sauce.

WINE: Serve this with a zinfandel or shiraz.

Honeycomb Tripe Slow-Cooked with Tomato, Bacon, and Onions

Serves 4

I love tripe, which is a distinct taste memory of my childhood. (See Food for Thought.) It is where my entire flavor base was formed—there is pronounced sweetness, acid, and salinity, and lots of earthy flavor. Here I've taken my grandmother's simple recipe and given it a little more intensity. I don't sell much of this in my restaurants, but people who know and love tripe go gaga for it and are rewarded with seconds, just as at home.

You may want to order the tripe in advance since it is not always available. Frozen will work just fine, but leave plenty of time to let it thaw.

This recipe is a three-step process, but you can make a big batch; freezing the finished dish actually makes the tripe more tender. I recommend doing it in stages: Make the base one day and the tripe the next.

SERVE THIS WITH Soft Polenta (page 199) or white rice.

TRIPE BASE

1 tablespoon olive oil

1 pound double-smoked bacon, cut into 1-inch-square lardons

6 carrots, sliced thickly on the bias

2 large Spanish onions, cut in half lengthwise, cut again lengthwise, and then cut into 1-inch chunks

6 ounces tomato paste

Few pinches sugar

8 plum tomatoes, cut into sixths and seasoned with salt, pepper, and sugar

10 cloves garlic, thinly sliced

3 cups flavorful red wine such as pinot noir, cabernet sauvignon, zinfandel, or shiraz

3/4 cup white vinegar

1 tablespoon red pepper flakes

1 tablespoon chopped fresh thyme leaves

1 tablespoon chopped fresh marjoram leaves

1 bay leaf

Coarse salt

Freshly ground black pepper

Warm the oil in a large sauté pan over medium-high heat. Add the bacon and cook until it browns and renders down, about 5 minutes.

Add the carrots and onions to the pan and cook for 5–6 minutes.

Reduce the heat to low. Add the tomato paste and sugar, give a good stir, and cook for 4–5 minutes, stirring to ensure that the paste doesn't scorch on the bottom of the pot.

Add the tomatoes and cook for 1–2 minutes. Add the garlic, wine, vinegar, red pepper flakes, thyme, marjoram, and bay leaf, and season with a pinch of sugar, salt, and pepper.

Raise the heat to high, bring to a boil, lower the heat, and taste. The liquid should have an acidic edge, and you should taste the sweetness of the tomato and carrot. If too acidic, add about 1 cup water. If too sweet, add about 1 tablespoon white vinegar. Continue to simmer for 30 minutes over medium heat.

❖ **IF MAKING IN ADVANCE,** this mixture can be cooled and stored in the refrigerator for up to 48 hours.

TRIPE	2 tablespoons black peppercorns
3 tablespoons olive oil	1 teaspoon dried thyme
2/3 large carrot, roughly chopped	1 tablespoon fresh thyme leaves
1 large Spanish onion, roughly chopped	1 bay leaf
3 ribs celery, roughly chopped	4–5 pounds honeycomb tripe
3 cups dry white wine	Coarse salt
1 cup white vinegar	

In a large stockpot, warm the oil over medium-high heat. Add the carrot, onion, and celery, and sweat until warmed through, about 2 minutes.

Pour the wine into the pot and add the vinegar, peppercorns, thyme, and bay leaf. Raise the heat to high and bring to a strong simmer.

Add the tripe and just enough cold water to cover by 2 inches. Season well with salt.

Lower the heat and bring the liquid to a gentle simmer. Cook, covered, until the tripe is quite tender, about 3 hours. Check every hour or so and add enough water to bring the level back to cover if necessary. (Here is a test to check for doneness: Pull a piece of tripe out of the pot. Get your fingers very cold in a bowl of ice water and pinch the tripe. If your fingers easily pierce the meat and meet in the middle, it's done.)

Carefully remove the tripe from the liquid. Refresh in ice water until cool enough to handle.

Discard all but 1 quart of the cooking liquid.

When the tripe is cool enough to handle, cut it into desired shapes or strips. (I like triangles.)

Place the pieces in the base and soften the flavor of the base with half of the cooking liquid. Cook over low heat for 45 minutes so the tripe can absorb the flavor of the sauce. (If you would like a more intense tripe flavor, by all means add more cooking liquid.)

❖ **IF MAKING IN ADVANCE,** this can be cooled and frozen for up to 3 weeks.

CHILI OIL

For a quick and easy accompaniment, serve this chili oil on the side.

2 tablespoons Chopped Roasted Tomatoes (page 13)	Coarse salt
1 teaspoon fresh thyme leaves	Freshly ground black pepper
2 cloves garlic	Pinch sugar
1 heaping tablespoon tomato paste	1 tablespoon red pepper flakes
2/3 cup white vinegar	Pinch cayenne pepper
	1 cup olive oil

Place all the ingredients in a blender and process until emulsified. (The emulsification may not hold; it doesn't matter.) Serve alongside the tripe and let people drizzle over their own serving. This oil is also delicious with soft polenta.

BEER: Serve this with ice-cold beer.

FOOD FOR THOUGHT—TRIPE: Tripe is the lining of a cow's stomach; the honeycomb variety is the most desirable for its texture and flavor.

GRILLED TOP SIRLOIN OF LAMB MARINATED IN YOGURT AND SERVED WITH COUSCOUS

Serves 4

This is a Middle Eastern–inspired lamb dish that I occasionally serve as a special. The dual effects of the yogurt marinade and the heat of the grill soften the meat to a luscious texture that really shows off the lamb's qualities.

As with all roasted and grilled meats, let the lamb rest for a few minutes before slicing or serving. Be sure to do this on a rack. If you don't have a rack, invert a salad plate on a dinner plate and stand the meat on the salad plate to let the juices drain.

SERVE THIS WITH Cauliflower and Roasted Tomatoes (page 273).

COUSCOUS
1 cup dry couscous

Coarse salt

Place the couscous in a small stainless steel bowl. Bring a few cups of lightly salted water to a boil. Pour enough boiling water over the couscous to cover it by about 1/8 inch.

Cover the bowl with plastic wrap, pulling it tightly to form a hermetic seal. The couscous will cook and absorb the liquid in 15–20 minutes. (A good test of doneness is to wait until the bottom of the bowl is warm but not hot to the touch.) Remove the plastic wrap and fluff the grains with the tines of a fork.

❖ **IF MAKING IN ADVANCE,** the couscous can be prepared up to this point and stored in a tightly covered container in the refrigerator for up to 3 days.

LAMB AND ASSEMBLY
1 cup plain yogurt (low-fat may
   be used)
3 tablespoons fresh lemon juice
2 cloves garlic, minced

1/2 teaspoon coarse salt
1 teaspoon freshly ground black pepper
4 pieces top sirloin of lamb
   (6–7 ounces each)

CURRY OIL

❧

Moisten 3 tablespoons curry powder with 3 tablespoons warm water to make a paste. Stir in 1 1/3 cups of a neutral oil such as grapeseed and let steep overnight. Pour off the oil that rises to the top *but don't discard it*. That's your curry oil.

In a mixing bowl, stir together the yogurt, lemon juice, garlic, salt, and pepper. Place the lamb in a nonreactive vessel and pour the marinade over it. Cover tightly with plastic wrap and refrigerate overnight.

Prepare an outdoor grill, letting the coals burn until covered with white ash. (If using a gas grill with dual settings, set one side on high and the other on low.)

Lightly oil the grill to prevent the lamb from sticking.

Lift the lamb out of the marinade and shake off any excess. Pat dry.

Place the lamb pieces directly over the coals (the hottest part of the grate) and grill for 2 minutes on each side.

Move the lamb to the outside perimeter of the grill grate (the cooler part of the grill) and cook for an additional 2 minutes for rare or 4–5 minutes for medium.

Transfer the lamb to a rack and allow to rest for 2–3 minutes.

While the lamb is resting, place the couscous in a medium-sized nonstick pan and reheat over the grill until warmed through, about 1 minute. (Be mindful of the pan handle over the flame of the grill.)

Slice the lamb as thinly as possible. Mound some couscous in the center of each of 4 plates. Arrange overlapping slices of lamb decoratively over the couscous and spoon some Cauliflower and Roasted Tomatoes (page 273) on one side.

OPTION: For a sauce, dilute 1 cup braising liquid from the lamb shanks (page 225) with 3 tablespoons cauliflower liquid or Veal Stock (page 32). Curry Oil (see sidebar) is also a wonderful accompaniment.

WINE: Serve this with a rioja.

MEATLOAF

❧

Serves 4

Two of my favorite cooks, Timmy and Lev, came up with this recipe for Sunday dinner at one of the restaurants where I've cooked. When they finished concocting it, they decided to drape thin slices of bacon over it (wonder where they got that idea) just prior to baking. It is also quite tasty without the bacon.

I love meatloaf that has been cooled and then grilled; it adds additional flavor and texture.

SERVE THIS WITH Potato Puree (page 268).

1 tablespoon olive oil	1 cup milk
1 medium Spanish onion, finely chopped	2 pounds ground meat (equal parts beef, pork, and veal is ideal, but any combination will work)
3 cloves garlic, minced	2/3 cup crushed saltine crackers
2 eggs, beaten	1/4 cup minced flat-leaf parsley
1/2 teaspoon fresh thyme leaves	1 tablespoon coarse salt
3 tablespoons plus 1 teaspoon Dijon mustard	1 teaspoon freshly ground black pepper
2 tablespoons Worcestershire sauce	6 ounces thinly sliced bacon (optional)
1/2 teaspoon Tabasco sauce	

Preheat the oven to 350°F.

Warm the oil in a sauté pan over medium-high heat. Add the onion and garlic, and sauté until translucent, about 5 minutes. Remove from the heat and allow to cool.

In a mixing bowl, stir together the eggs, thyme, mustard, Worcestershire sauce, Tabasco sauce, and milk.

Place the ground meat in another bowl and pour the egg mixture over the meat. Add the saltines, parsley, and cooled onion and garlic to the bowl. Season with salt and pepper. Knead the meat together with the other ingredients until well blended. (If you like, cook a small portion of the mixture in a pan, then taste and adjust the seasoning to suit your taste.)

Transfer to a baking pan and form into a loaf. If using the bacon, place the slices crosswise across the top and tuck them under the loaf. Bake in the preheated oven for 1 hour, or until an instant-read thermometer inserted in the center of the loaf reads 160°F. Remove from the oven and let rest for 5 minutes before slicing.

OPTION: If you plan to grill the meatloaf as suggested in the headnote, let it cool for several hours. (If you attempt to grill it when warm, it will break apart and fall through the grate.) If you want to give the meatloaf a bit of a glaze, try the following recipe:

MEATLOAF GLAZE
1/3 cup ketchup
1/2 teaspoon Tabasco sauce
2 tablespoons light brown sugar
2 tablespoons white vinegar
1/2 teaspoon freshly ground black
   pepper

Stir the ingredients together in a mixing bowl and apply to the meatloaf slices as they grill.

Accompaniments

This chapter shares some of my favorite side dishes and accompaniments. Since many of the recipes in this book offer suggestions for pairings, leaving the final decision up to you, here are some thoughts about the composition of a dish. They are offered to guide you in determining when and where to use the recipes that follow.

When I sit down to design a dish, my thoughts are initially focused on the central item, usually the protein. (Some other chefs have been very successful taking the opposite approach and beginning with the accompaniment.) I then try to think of what I would like to eat alongside the primary element—usually no more than two or three accompaniments that get along well.

My first consideration is usually textural—I prefer dishes that have some kind of cohesion. For example, if I think of chicken, I think of mashed potatoes, vegetables, and a sauce to tie it together. If I think of a grilled sturgeon, my mind goes to something softer and lighter than potatoes, such as Leek Puree (page 262). With meats I like more assertive accompaniments such as Potato Gratin (page 256) or even Pickled Red Cabbage (page 254), which might overpower certain fish or poultry.

Usually my dishes have at least one soft component. I think they're wonderful for soaking up juices and allow a great deal of flexibility in the eating.

When unsure of what component to add to a dish, consider the sauce. You'll obviously need a sauce that complements the protein, so think about how that sauce will fare with the accompaniments. If you can't imagine dunking a spoonful of the side dish into the sauce, it is probably a bad idea. On the other hand, if the side dish and sauce seem almost as if they could be served together without the protein, you are probably on to something.

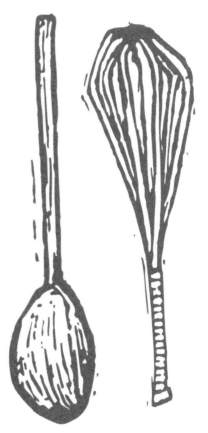

As much as I enjoy textural harmony, I also love temperature contrasts. There is nothing like it to make a dish inherently interesting. Think about how great the balance is in a hot fudge sundae or a falafel sandwich. When making a decision about this aspect of a dish, my advice is to keep each individual component at its own ideal temperature, the way you would choose to eat it on its own. Just be sure to choose ingredients that won't overwhelm each other when one is hot from the oven and the other cold and crisp from the refrigerator.

RED LENTIL MASH

Makes 4 side-dish servings

After overcooking countless batches of red lentils, I decided to be creative with the overcooked mess that I often found in my pot. I realized that I like the texture of these lentils because they come out somewhere between mashed potatoes and very thick soup. Their delicate flavor is an especially great vehicle for firm-fleshed white fish.

Don't rush the introduction of stock to the beans. Like a risotto, you don't want too much liquid in the pot at any given time.

1 3-ounce piece slab bacon (optional)	8 ounces red lentils, picked over
5 tablespoons extra-virgin olive oil, or 7 tablespoons if not using bacon	1 tablespoon chopped fresh thyme leaves
1 medium carrot, finely diced (1/3 cup)	1 bay leaf
1 large Spanish onion, finely diced (1/3 cup)	5 cups Chicken Stock (page 23) or Basic Vegetable Stock (page 24)
1 rib celery, finely diced (1/3 cup)	Coarse salt
4 cloves garlic, thinly sliced	Freshly ground black pepper

Render the bacon (if using) in a saucepan over low heat for 5 minutes. If not using bacon, warm 2 tablespoons oil over medium heat.

Add the carrot, onion, celery, and garlic to the pan and cook, stirring occasionally, until the vegetables are quite tender, 4–5 minutes.

Add the lentils, thyme, bay leaf, and 5 tablespoons oil and stir to coat the lentils.

Add enough stock to cover by 1/2 inch. Season with salt and pepper. Stir thoroughly. Taste and adjust the seasoning. Raise the heat to high, bring the stock to a boil, and then lower the heat to let the stock simmer for 8–10 minutes.

Add 1/4 cup stock to the pot. When that stock has been absorbed by the lentils, add another 1/4 cup. Continue to cook, stirring occasionally and taking care to scrape the bottom of the pan because the lentils have a tendency to stick. Continue adding stock in 1/4-cup increments until all the stock has been used or until the lentils have just a little bite left to them. The final mixture should have a slightly soupy quality.

Strainer the cooked lentils over the sink. Carefully shake the strainer so that most of the liquid drains off.

Place the lentils on a cookie sheet, spreading them out and allowing them to cool thoroughly. (Pick out and discard the bay leaf.) Warm over low heat when ready to serve.

❖ **IF MAKING IN ADVANCE,** these lentils may be stored for 2–3 days in a tightly sealed container in the refrigerator. **WHEN READY TO PROCEED,** allow to come to room temperature and warm over low heat.

PICKLED RED CABBAGE

Makes 4 side-dish servings

I'm not one to take a visual approach to food, but I have to say that this cabbage is positively stunning. It also has a pleasant tang that complements Braised Pork Shoulder (page 227) or Bacon-Wrapped Pork Tenderloin (page 229).

1 1/2 tablespoons coarse salt	1/2 cup grenadine
1 medium head red cabbage, shredded in a processor or cut by hand into chiffonade	2 cups red wine vinegar
	Freshly ground black pepper
	1 teaspoon caraway seeds

Put 2 quarts water and salt in a large pot and bring to a boil over high heat. Add the cabbage and blanch for 1 minute. Drain and run cold water over the cabbage, tossing it as you do to cool the entire batch. Drain well.

Pour the grenadine and vinegar into a large pot and bring to a boil over high heat. Cook until the mixture is reduced by two-thirds, 8–10 minutes. Season with pepper and add the caraway seeds to the pot, stirring to distribute them.

Add the cabbage, lower the heat to medium-high, and stir to coat with the reduction.

Cook until the cabbage softens a bit and takes on the flavor of the reduction, about 10 minutes. Serve immediately.

❖ **IF MAKING IN ADVANCE,** allow to cool and store in an airtight container in the refrigerator for up to 2 days. **WHEN READY TO PROCEED,** reheat gently over medium heat.

Smoked Onion Jam

Makes about 1 quart

This powerfully flavored jam is a perfect accompaniment to meats and roast game, and is also good for stirring into soups or spread on toast.

4 cups wood chips, such as applewood, cherrywood, or alderwood	1/2 cup plus 1 tablespoon olive oil
6 Spanish onions, cut in half with skins on	3 tablespoons unsalted butter
	Pinch sugar if needed
	Dash sherry vinegar

Preheat the oven to 325°F.

Place the wood chips in a stainless steel bowl and add enough water just to cover them. Allow to soak at least 30 minutes but preferably 2 hours.

Rub the onion halves with 1/2 cup oil. Place on a cookie sheet and roast in the preheated oven until they are tender but still hold their shape, about 30 minutes.

Meanwhile, prepare an outdoor barbecue, letting the coals burn until covered with white ash. Scatter the soaked wood chips over the coals.

Remove the onions from the oven and place on the edge of the grill grate, as far from the heat as possible. Cover and cook for 35–40 minutes.

Remove the onions from the grill and, when cool enough to handle, peel the skins back. Cut each onion crosswise into 1/2-inch slices.

In a saucepan over medium heat, heat the butter and remaining 1 tablespoon oil. Add the onions and cook, stirring regularly, until nicely browned and caramelized, 35–40 minutes. Taste toward the end, and if the smoke has made too much of an impact, add the sugar. Finish with a dash of sherry vinegar.

❖ **IF MAKING IN ADVANCE,** this jam can be cooled and stored for up to 1 week in a tightly covered container in the refrigerator.

Potato Gratin

Makes one 12-inch gratin, 6–8 servings

This is my version of a classic potato gratin. By infusing the cream with thyme, bay leaves, peppercorns, and garlic, it transmits an intense flavor throughout the dish. Having both long-cooked and barely cooked garlic in the mix creates a sublime depth of flavor. I particularly enjoy this with grilled or roasted meat.

- 1 pint heavy cream
- 4 sprigs fresh thyme
- 2 bay leaves
- 15 black peppercorns
- 15 cloves garlic, smashed
- Coarse salt
- Freshly ground black pepper
- 5 medium Idaho potatoes, peeled and cut into 1/8-inch-thick slices, ideally with a mandoline
- Unsalted butter for baking dish

Place the cream in a saucepan over high heat.

Add the thyme, bay leaves, peppercorns, and 12 cloves garlic. Season with salt and pepper. Bring to a boil, then immediately lower to a simmer. (If the cream starts to boil over, tame it with a few drops of cold water.)

Simmer for 15–20 minutes, until the cream takes on all the flavors. In the final few minutes of cooking, add the remaining 3 cloves garlic. Drain the cream, discard the solids, and reserve.

IF MAKING IN ADVANCE, it can be made up to this point 24 hours ahead of time and kept, covered, in the refrigerator.

Preheat the oven to 375°F.

Lightly butter a 12-inch circular baking dish.

Cover the surface with a layer of potato slices.

Dust lightly with salt and pepper, and spoon some of the cream mixture over the top.

Repeat with another layer of potatoes, seasoning, and cream. Continue layering until the gratin attains a height of about 2 inches. Press down gently on the potatoes to bring the cream up over the top.

Cover snugly with aluminum foil and place in the preheated oven. Bake for 35–40 minutes. Remove the foil and cook just until the top is browned or the gratin is done. (The gratin is done when a thin knife slips easily into its center.)

OPTION: For a variation, alternate layers of potato with slices of celery root or parsnip.

LEMON ORZO

❧

This powerful lemony side dish is especially appropriate for grilled fish. If the sauce base seems very lemony, that's all right because it will be diffused by the orzo.

Coarse salt	1 teaspoon Dijon mustard
8 ounces dried orzo	Juice of 2 lemons
2/3 cup heavy cream	Freshly ground black pepper
1 small clove garlic, finely minced	3 tablespoons Chopped Roasted
12 tablespoons (1 1/2 sticks) unsalted	Tomatoes (page 13)
butter	1 teaspoon chopped fresh oregano

Bring a pot of salted water to a boil. Add the orzo and cook until *al dente*, 6–7 minutes. Drain.

Meanwhile, pour the cream into a small saucepan and add the garlic. Bring to a boil over high heat, then immediately lower the heat and whisk in the butter, 1 piece at a time, until completely absorbed.

Blend for a few seconds with an immersion blender to reinforce the emulsion.

Whisk in the mustard and lemon juice, and season to taste with salt and pepper.

❖ **IF MAKING IN ADVANCE,** the sauce and orzo can be made 1 hour in advance. **WHEN READY TO PROCEED,** the orzo can be reheated over low heat with a few tablespoons of water.

Transfer the orzo to a mixing bowl and toss with the sauce. Add the tomatoes and oregano, and serve.

White Bean Puree

☙

Makes about 3 cups

This puree is delicious with fish dishes and forms the basis of an unusual ravioli. Be sure to keep the beans at just a simmer to prevent them from rupturing, and keep them covered with liquid to prevent them from drying out.

1¹/2 cups dry Great Northern beans	1 bay leaf
1 medium white onion, cut into ¹/4-inch dice	6 cups (approximately) Chicken Stock (page 23) or water
1 medium carrot, cut into ¹/4-inch dice	Coarse salt
1 rib celery, cut into ¹/4-inch dice	Freshly ground black pepper
2 cloves garlic, 1 smashed and 1 minced	¹/3 cup heavy cream
2 sprigs thyme plus 1 teaspoon fresh thyme leaves	Few drops extra-virgin olive oil

Soak the beans overnight or place in a pot, cover with water, and bring to a boil over high heat. Remove from the heat and set aside, covered, for 1 hour.

Drain the beans and transfer them to a 2-quart saucepan with the onion, carrot, celery, smashed garlic, thyme sprigs, bay leaf, and 5 cups stock.

Season with salt and pepper, and bring to a boil over high heat. Immediately lower the heat and simmer for 90 minutes, or until very tender. If the mixture becomes dry, add some of the remaining 1 cup stock.

Drain in a colander. Pick out and discard the thyme sprigs and bay leaf.

Warm the beans in a sauté pan over medium heat.

Add the cream, thyme leaves, and minced garlic to the pan and season with salt and pepper.

Raise the heat to high, bring to a boil, then lower to a simmer and add the vegetables to the pan.

Cook until the cream is reduced and is almost dry on the beans and the beans are heated through, 4–5 minutes.

Transfer the bean mixture to a food processor and process until smooth, adding a few drops of oil. Adjust the seasoning if necessary and pulse just to combine.

❖ **IF MAKING IN ADVANCE,** cool the puree in a large stainless steel bowl set in another bowl filled with ice water. Transfer to an airtight container and refrigerate up to 2 days. Bring to room temperature and warm in a pan over medium-high heat.

Parsnip Puree

This is a surprising alternative to mashed potatoes. It has a particular affinity with powerful sauces such as the Red Wine Sauce on page 169.

It is crucial that the parsnips be as dry as possible before pureeing. If they are still wet after pureeing, cook the puree for a minute or two in a nonstick pan over medium-high heat to evaporate the lingering moisture.

---

2 pounds parsnips, peeled and cut into
    1-inch dice
4 cups Chicken Stock (page 23)
    or water
1 tablespoon coarse salt, or more
    to taste

1 clove garlic, smashed
1/2 tablespoon unsalted butter
    (optional)
Freshly ground black pepper

Place the parsnips in a saucepan and add just enough stock or water to cover.

Add the salt and garlic to the pan. Bring to a boil over high heat, lower the heat, and let simmer. Cook the parsnips until quite tender when pierced with the tip of a thin, sharp-bladed knife, about 20–25 minutes.

Meanwhile, preheat the oven to 300°F.

Once the parsnips are cooked, drain and discard the liquid. Place the parsnips in the preheated oven and allow to dry for 15–20 minutes to concentrate the flavor and remove the water.

Remove the parsnips to the bowl of a food processor, and puree. If the puree seems a bit woody, pass it through a strainer, pushing down on it with a rubber spatula to extract as much puree as possible. If desired, finish by stirring in the butter. Season to taste with salt and pepper.

❖ **IF MAKING IN ADVANCE,** this puree can be kept warm over very low heat in a double boiler for up to 1 hour.

LEEK PUREE

Makes 4 side-dish servings

The fresh, aromatic flavor of leeks lends this puree an attractive, light quality. Make sure the leeks are very well cooked so that they will puree easily. If the leeks have a particularly woody center, increase the quantity of leeks to get more of the usable vegetable.

---

8 fresh leeks, white parts and 1 inch of green
3/4 cup Chicken Stock (page 23)
6 tablespoons unsalted butter

3 cloves garlic, smashed
Coarse salt
Freshly ground black pepper

Slice the leeks lengthwise and cut crosswise into 1/2-inch pieces. Rinse well in several changes of cold water.

In a large saucepan or small stockpot, place the stock, butter, and garlic. Place over medium-high heat and cook until the butter melts and starts to bubble. Add salt and pepper. Add the leeks to the pot and season again. Cook, stirring occasionally, until the leeks are very tender and army-green, 30–35 minutes. Remove the leeks from the heat and drain well. Transfer to a food processor and puree. Adjust the seasoning if necessary.

❖ **IF MAKING IN ADVANCE,** this puree can be kept in a tightly covered container in the refrigerator for up to 3 days. **WHEN READY TO PROCEED,** allow to come to room temperature and reheat gently in a sauté pan.

SWEET PEA STEW

✿

Makes 4 side-dish servings

If you love the flavor of fresh peas, you'll love this hearty accompaniment. If serving right away, I like to mash the peas a bit with a fork to really combine the flavors.

4 strips bacon, cut into small dice,
    or 1 tablespoon unsalted butter
1/2 Spanish onion, finely minced
3 cloves garlic, thinly sliced
1/2 cup Chicken Stock (page 23) or
    Basic Vegetable Stock (page 24)
	Coarse salt
	Freshly ground black pepper
	Sugar
	2 cups freshly shucked peas or frozen
	    petits pois, defrosted

Have an ice water bath ready.

Place the bacon in a sauté pan and cook over medium-high heat until nicely browned and some fat has rendered. (If not using bacon, melt the butter in a sauté pan over medium-high heat.)

Add the onion and garlic to the pan and cook until softened and beginning to take on some color, 4–5 minutes.

Add the stock, raise the heat to high, and cook until reduced almost to the point of dryness, 4–5 minutes. Taste and season with salt, pepper, and a pinch of sugar.

Meanwhile, bring a pot of lightly salted water to a boil and add the peas. Blanch for 1 minute, or until tender. Place in the ice water to stop the cooking and set the color. If you have successfully synchronized your cooking, you may skip the shock step and add the peas directly to the sauté pan with the bacon, onions, and garlic.

Toss well to thoroughly integrate the flavors. Remove from the heat and reserve.

❖ **IF MAKING IN ADVANCE,** this stew can be kept in a tightly covered container in the refrigerator for up to 3 days. **WHEN READY TO PROCEED,** allow to come to room temperature and reheat gently in a sauté pan.

PARMESAN FLAN

❧

Makes 4 flans

One of the things I love about flans is that they take a supporting element such as a vegetable, herb, or spice and make it substantial.

Something else I love about them is that that once you've mastered the basic technique, you can make them with just about anything. Some of my favorites are built around porcini powder, saffron, roast garlic, and truffle. (See Options.) Because Parmesan cheese is salty, be particularly careful when seasoning this flan.

---

1 pint heavy cream	Coarse salt
4 eggs	Freshly ground black pepper
3 heaping tablespoons grated	1–2 tablespoons unsalted butter for
Parmigiano-Reggiano cheese	coating ramekins
1 clove garlic, finely minced	

Preheat the oven to 300°F.

In a small mixing bowl, whisk together the cream, eggs, cheese, and garlic. Season with salt and pepper, bearing in mind that the cheese is salty. If desired, perform a taste test and adjust the quantities of cheese or seasoning to suit your own palate. (See Food for Thought.)

Butter four 4-ounce ramekins.

Divide the flan mixture evenly among the ramekins and set them in a roasting pan with enough water to come two-thirds of the way up the sides.

Cover the pan with aluminum foil and poke holes all over the foil with the tines of a fork.

Cook in the preheated oven for 30 minutes. Check for doneness by removing the foil. If they are firm in the center, remove them from the oven. If not, return and check at 5-minute intervals until they are firm.

❖ **IF MAKING IN ADVANCE,** simply cool thoroughly and cover with plastic wrap. **WHEN READY TO PROCEED,** gently reheat in the same manner or on top of the stove in a pan of simmering water until heated through, 7–8 minutes. (Test by inserting a knife in the center of 1 ramekin. When it comes out warm to the touch of a lip, it's done.)

OPTIONS: You can also make 1 large flan by simply pouring the mixture into a larger container. Allow about 10 minutes additional cooking time.

You can use this same recipe to make other flans by substituting the following for the cheese or in partnership with a reduced quantity of the cheese:

PORCINI

Add 2 teaspoons Porcini Powder (page 163) and 1 tablespoon chopped Roasted Wild Mushrooms (page 46), patted dry. Reduce cheese by half.

SAFFRON

Add 1/4 teaspoon saffron and omit the cheese for a great accompaniment to seafood.

CURRY

Add 1 teaspoon curry powder and omit the cheese for an Indian-themed accompaniment to poultry.

ROAST GARLIC

Stir in 3 tablespoons Roasted Garlic Puree (page 12) and omit the cheese for a potent accompaniment to roast meats.

TRUFFLE

Shave in some fresh black or white truffle and reduce the cheese by half for an outrageous flan that could stand by itself as a course.

FOOD FOR THOUGHT—TASTE TEST: If you want to check your flan's seasoning level but don't want to taste raw eggs, cook a cupful of the mixture in a nonstick pan over high heat, taste, and adjust the seasoning accordingly.

CELERY ROOT PUREE

❧

Makes 4 side-dish servings

This puree has particular affinity with roast duck. When shopping for celery root, density is important. Regardless of its size, it should feel heavy in your hand.

2 pounds firm, heavy knobs celery root, peeled and cut into 1-inch cubes	Freshly ground black pepper
	Sugar
Coarse salt	2 tablespoons unsalted butter

Preheat the oven to 250°F.

Place the celery root in a saucepan with just enough water to cover. Season with salt, pepper, and a pinch of sugar. Add the butter to the pan and place over high heat. Bring to a boil, then lower the heat and let simmer. Cook until tender, 20–25 minutes.

Strain the celery root and turn it out onto a baking sheet. Place the sheet in the preheated oven for 10 minutes to dry it out. (This will make the puree a bit thicker and concentrate the flavor.)

Transfer the celery root to the bowl of a food processor and puree until smooth.

❖ **IF MAKING IN ADVANCE,** chill in a bowl set in an ice water bath, cover, and refrigerate for up to 3 days. **WHEN READY TO PROCEED,** allow to come to room temperature and reheat gently in a sauté pan.

OPTION: If you like the texture of cooked celery root and prefer a chunky mash to a smooth puree, simply puree about 40 percent of the celery root and then combine the chunks with it.

STEWED BRUSSELS SPROUTS

Makes 4 side-dish servings

I like my Brussels sprouts cooked, and I mean good and cooked. This recipe gently stews them, creating a wonderful bed for game birds.

3 ounces bacon, roughly chopped	Coarse salt
1/2 Spanish onion, finely chopped	Freshly ground black pepper
4 cloves garlic, thinly sliced	Sugar
1 1/2 cups Chicken Stock (page 23)	1 pound Brussels sprouts

Place the bacon in a sauté pan and cook over medium-high heat until the bacon browns and some fat has rendered.

Add the onion and garlic to the pan and cook until translucent, about 5 minutes.

Add the stock and season with salt, pepper, and a pinch of sugar. Cook until the stock is reduced by half, 7–8 minutes.

Bring a pot of salted water to a boil. Add the sprouts and cook until tender but still a bit toothsome, about 4 minutes.

Drain the sprouts and refresh them under cold water. Transfer to a cutting board and quarter them.

Add the sprouts to the pot with the bacon-onion-stock mixture and stew gently until quite tender, 20–25 minutes.

❖ **IF MAKING IN ADVANCE,** this can be cooled, covered, and refrigerated for up to 3 days. **WHEN READY TO PROCEED,** allow to come to room temperature and reheat gently in a sauté pan.

POTATO PUREE

❧

For truly great mashed potatoes, you need to use cold, cubed butter and hot milk to attain the best possible emulsion. The key is to dice the butter as fine as possible so that you don't have to overwork the potatoes to distribute the ingredients.

2 pounds Idaho potatoes, peeled and cut into 1-inch cubes Coarse salt 1 cup milk, or more to taste	8 tablespoons (1 stick) cold unsalted butter, or more to taste, cut into small dice

Preheat the oven to 250°F.

Place the potatoes in a pot and cover with cold water. Season liberally with salt. Set over high heat, bring to a boil, and lower the heat slightly to maintain a strong and steady simmer. Cook until tender but not breaking apart, 12–15 minutes. Drain the potatoes very well in a colander and transfer to a cookie sheet.

Place the cookie sheet in the oven and cook until thoroughly dried out, 7–8 minutes. (Move them around from time to time to allow any water on the cookie sheet to dry.)

Place the milk in a pot and warm over medium heat.

Using a ricer or potato masher, puree the potatoes to a thick paste, taking care not to overwork them.

Using a rubber spatula, fold one-third of the butter into the potatoes. Then fold in one-third of the hot milk. Continue to work in the butter and milk in this fashion, using a gentle folding motion rather than aggressive stirring. Once all the butter and milk have been incorporated, season to taste.

❖ **IF MAKING IN ADVANCE,** these potatoes can be kept over very low heat in a double boiler for up to 2 hours. (The waxed paper that you removed from the butter makes a wonderful cover for them while being kept in this way; it will keep a film from forming over the top of the puree.)

SAUSAGE AND FENNEL SEED STUFFING

✿

Makes 8 side-dish servings

ake this once, and you may find it has become your traditional family
Thanksgiving stuffing. It's also delicious with any poultry or game bird. The
sausage and fennel seed make quite an impact.

---

1 pound coarsely ground pork butt
Coarse salt
Freshly ground black pepper
Ground coriander seeds
Sugar
4 cloves garlic, finely chopped
1 large Spanish onion, cut into fine dice
1/2 head celery, cut into fine dice
1/3 cup dry white wine
2 cups Chicken Stock (page 23),
   or more if needed

1 loaf sourdough bread, crusts
   removed, cut into 1-inch cubes,
   and well toasted (about 12 cups)
2 tablespoons fresh thyme leaves,
   or more to taste
1 tablespoon fresh marjoram leaves,
   or more to taste
4 tablespoons fennel seeds, or more
   to taste

Preheat the oven to 350°F.

In a mixing bowl, liberally season the pork with salt, pepper, coriander seeds, and sugar.

Add the garlic to the bowl and knead the mixture together. Let cure for 1 hour. Brown a portion of the sausage in a pan, taste, and adjust the seasoning as you see fit.

Brown the sausage in batches in a deep-sided pan.

Remove the sausage to a large bowl and set aside, but let the rendered pork fat remain in the pan.

Add the onion and celery, and cook until translucent, about 5 minutes.

Add the wine and cook until nearly evaporated, about 2 minutes.

Accompaniments ✿ 269

Add the stock and cook until reduced by half, 8–10 minutes.

Transfer the contents of the pan to the bowl with the sausage. Add the toasted bread cubes, thyme, marjoram, and fennel seeds, and knead together.

Transfer to a shallow baking dish and bake until warmed through and dry on top, 35–45 minutes.

OPTIONS: You can also cook this stuffing in the cavity of a turkey.

Stuffing is a personal thing. Season to your heart's content, adding significantly more fennel seeds, marjoram, and/or thyme to suit your taste.

BRAISED BIBB LETTUCE

Makes 4 side-dish servings

In this dish, soft Bibb lettuce is further tenderized as it cooks in hot stock for a versatile accompaniment to fish and poultry.

8 small (about the size of a tennis ball) heads Bibb lettuce, well washed (see Food for Thought)	Coarse salt
	Freshly ground black pepper
	1 clove garlic, smashed
3 cups Chicken Stock (page 23)	2 tablespoons unsalted butter

Preheat the oven to 350°F.

Place the lettuce in a baking pan large enough to hold it in a single layer with little excess room.

Pour the stock into a saucepan set over high heat and season with salt and pepper. Add the garlic to the pan. When the stock reaches a boil, whisk in the butter.

Pour the hot stock over the lettuce. (It should come at least halfway up the lettuce; a bit higher is all right.)

Cover the pan with foil and place in the preheated oven. Cook for 20 minutes.

Remove the foil, turn the heads 180 degrees, replace the foil, and return to the oven to cook until the heads are entirely softened, another 5–10 minutes. (Test for doneness by piercing with a sharp, thin-bladed knife.)

Remove the lettuce from the oven. Take the heads out of the braising liquid and set aside to cool. If you like, cool, degrease, and freeze the braising liquid and use it at another time to cook leeks or use as a soup base.

FOOD FOR THOUGHT—WASHING BIBB LETTUCE: Remove a few of the outer leaves. Fill a bowl with cold water and dip the lettuce "headfirst" into the water. Agitate it a little and repeat 3 or 4 times. As the lettuce loosens up, use your fingers to open the leaves a bit and allow the water to reach the deepest portion of the lettuce.

AUTUMN FRUIT COMPOTE

Makes 2 1/2–3 quarts

When the apples drop in fall, I start thinking about making this. It fills the house with the wonderful scents of cinnamon and nutmeg, which I associate with fall and winter cooking. I make a big batch of this compote because it keeps for up to a month. I use it for everything from an accompaniment to game to a filling for tarts. I also love it warmed over brioche French toast.

The amount of liquid the dried fruits will absorb is often anyone's guess. If you feel that the mixture is too dry after adding liquid, add more wine or water, or a combination. It should have the texture and appearance of mincemeat.

2 1/2 cups dry white wine	Pinch salt
2/3 cup white vinegar	6 cups assorted dried fruits (2 cups
1 cup light corn syrup	each) such as cranberries, currants,
1 cup freshly squeezed orange juice	prunes, golden raisins, or apricots;
Zest of 1 orange	larger fruits should be cut into
1 tablespoon freshly grated nutmeg	1/2-inch dice
1 tablespoon ground cinnamon	6 Granny Smith apples, peeled, cut
1 tablespoon ground allspice	into 1/2-inch dice, and tossed with
Pinch freshly ground black pepper	the juice of 1 lemon

Pour the wine, vinegar, corn syrup, orange juice, orange zest, nutmeg, cinnamon, allspice pepper, and salt into a large pot. Bring to a boil over high heat. Taste it. It should have some sweetness but be high in acid and spice.

Add all the fruit to the pot. Lower the heat and cook over low-to-medium heat for 40 minutes, stirring from time to time to prevent scorching. Taste it. If you want to add some more of this or that, go right ahead.

Transfer the contents of the pot to a cookie sheet and allow to cool.

Place in a jar with a tight-fitting lid and chill. Because of the white wine and vinegar, this will keep for up to 1 month in the refrigerator.

272 ✤ *Welcome to My Kitchen*

CAULIFLOWER AND ROASTED TOMATOES

Makes 4 side-dish servings

This side dish, enlivened with roasted tomatoes and curry powder, is well suited to Middle Eastern dishes such as the lamb on page 246.

Coarse salt	Splash dry white wine
1 large head cauliflower, separated into	Splash white vinegar
equal-sized florets	1/2 teaspoon curry powder
2 tablespoons olive oil	2 Chopped Roasted Tomatoes
1/2 Spanish onion, roughly chopped	(page 13)
2 cloves garlic, thinly sliced	Freshly ground black pepper

Bring a pot of salted water to a boil. Add the cauliflower florets to the pot and blanch for 45 seconds. Drain and run under cold water to stop the cooking. Drain again and reserve.

In a sauté pan, warm the oil over medium-high heat. Add the onion and garlic to the pan and sweat for 2–3 minutes.

Add the wine, vinegar, curry powder, and roasted tomatoes.

Season with salt and pepper, and stir well. Cook for 1 minute, just to heat the ingredients through.

Add the cauliflower and cook until tender, another 15–20 minutes. Adjust the seasoning and serve.

BRAISED ENDIVES

❧

Makes 4 side-dish servings

This is an especially appropriate side dish for fish, but it also works well with poultry and game.

4 Belgian endives	Sugar
1 quart Chicken Stock (page 23) or	3 tablespoons unsalted butter, cut into
Basic Vegetable Stock (page 24)	6 pieces
Coarse salt	1/2 lemon
Freshly ground black pepper	

Preheat the oven to 325°F.

Place the endives in a baking dish.

Pour the stock into a pot and season with salt, pepper, and a pinch of sugar. Bring to a boil over high heat, then pour over the endives.

Dot the endives with the butter and squeeze the lemon over them to help prevent discoloration.

Cover the baking dish with aluminum foil and place in the preheated oven. Cook until the endives are tender but firm, about 25 minutes. Test for doneness by inserting a paring knife toward the root end; the endive should still offer a bit of resistance. Remove from the cooking liquid and serve.

❖ **IF MAKING IN ADVANCE,** the endives can be cooled and refrigerated for up to 24 hours in their cooking liquid, but allow the liquid to cool first. **WHEN READY TO PROCEED,** drain off the cooking liquid, allow to come to room temperature, and reheat gently in a sauté pan.

WILD RICE GRIDDLE CAKES

🌿

These cakes are an original way to present wild rice. I especially like them with duck and other game.

1 tablespoon unsalted butter	1/2 cup milk
1 small Spanish onion, minced	3 eggs, beaten
6 ounces wild rice	Pinch nutmeg
2–3 cups Chicken Stock (page 23)	1/2 teaspoon baking powder
Coarse salt	1/3 cup all-purpose flour
Freshly ground black pepper	

Melt the butter in a saucepan over medium-high heat. Add the onion and cook until translucent, about 5 minutes.

Add the wild rice and enough stock to cover it. Season with salt and pepper. Lower the heat to medium and cook for 20–25 minutes, adding more stock as necessary to keep the rice covered until it has softened a bit but is still *al dente*.

Drain the rice and turn it out onto a cookie sheet to cool.

❖ **IF MAKING IN ADVANCE,** the rice can be covered and refrigerated for up to 2 days. **WHEN READY TO PROCEED,** allow it to come to room temperature.

In a mixing bowl, stir together the milk, eggs, nutmeg, baking powder, and flour. Add the rice to the bowl and toss together to form a rice batter.

Warm a nonstick skillet over medium-high heat.

Ladle 1/4-cup portions of rice batter onto the pan and cook for 2 minutes, or until golden, on 1 side. Flip and cook 1 minute on the other side, or until golden.

Remove the griddle cakes as they are done and keep covered and warm.

Vinaigrettes
and
Mayonnaises

CREAMY MUSTARD VINAIGRETTE

Makes 1¹/2 cups

1 egg yolk	2/3 cup olive oil
2¹/2 tablespoons Dijon mustard	Coarse salt
6 tablespoons sherry vinegar	Freshly ground black pepper

In a stainless steel bowl, whisk together the egg yolk and mustard. Add 1 tablespoon vinegar and whisk well. Add the oil slowly in a thin drizzle, whisking to form an emulsion. Slowly whisk in the remaining vinegar. Season with a pinch of salt and several grinds of pepper.

RED WINE VINAIGRETTE

Makes about 1¹/2 cups

Use this to dress tomatoes and pique their flavor. There is a lot of vinegar in the recipe, so use the vinaigrette sparingly.

¹/2 cup plus 2 tablespoons red wine vinegar	Pinch sugar
1 teaspoon dried thyme leaves	2 teaspoons coarse salt
1 teaspoon dried oregano leaves	2 teaspoons freshly ground black pepper
1 clove garlic, minced	1 cup olive oil

Place all the ingredients in a mixing bowl and whisk together.

SHERRY VINAIGRETTE

❧

Makes 1 cup

This is a good, basic salad dressing.

3 tablespoons Dijon mustard	3/4 cup olive oil
1 egg yolk	Coarse salt
4 teaspoons sherry vinegar	Freshly ground black pepper

In a mixing bowl, whisk together the mustard and the egg yolk. Whisk in 1 teaspoon vinegar, then slowly whisk in the oil to form a thick emulsion. Whisk in the remaining vinegar and season to taste with salt and pepper. If you feel the vinaigrette would benefit from a bit more sherry and/or mustard, by all means add them to suit your taste.

CREAMY ANCHOVY VINAIGRETTE

❧

Makes about 1 1/2 cups

This creamy dressing, reminiscent of a Caesar, is good with assertive salad greens, leftover roasted fish, and fresh vegetables.

3 egg yolks	3 anchovy fillets
Juice of 2 lemons	1 tablespoon capers, rinsed
2 cloves garlic, finely minced	1 tablespoon grated Parmesan cheese
1 tablespoon Dijon mustard	Coarse salt
1 1/2 cups olive oil	Freshly ground black pepper

Place the egg yolks, one-fourth of the lemon juice, garlic, and mustard in the bowl of a food processor. Turn on the machine and slowly drizzle in the oil in a thin stream until it emulsifies. With the machine still running, add the anchovies, capers, cheese, and remaining lemon juice. Stop the machine and taste. Season with salt, if necessary, and pepper. Restart the machine and drizzle in 2 tablespoons hot tap water.

DUCK LIVER VINAIGRETTE

Makes about 2 cups

I don't know how I came up with this—the pairing of duck liver and anchovies is unusual—but the results are great. This is especially delicious with assertively flavored grilled fish such as red snapper and pompano.

3 duck livers (about 1 ounce each); chicken livers can be substituted	2 anchovy fillets
	3 cloves garlic, thinly sliced
Coarse salt	1/2 cup sherry vinegar
Freshly ground black pepper	2 tablespoons Dijon mustard
1 1/2 cups olive oil	1 egg yolk

Season the duck livers liberally with salt and pepper. In a stainless steel or cast iron sauté pan, warm 1 tablespoon oil until very hot. Add the duck livers, anchovies, and garlic, and sauté quickly over high heat for 30–40 seconds, tossing frequently and taking care to brown the livers on all sides. Add 1 tablespoon vinegar to the pan and deglaze. Toss for an additional 10 seconds.

Immediately transfer the contents of the pan to the bowl of a food processor. Add the mustard, turn the machine on, and puree. Have the remaining oil in one hand and the egg yolk in the other. Add the oil in a thin drizzle while simultaneously adding the yolk. Once all the oil has been absorbed, add the remaining vinegar. Remove the vinaigrette from the bowl of the processor and strain through a fine-mesh strainer.

LEMON-GARLIC-PARSLEY VINAIGRETTE

Makes 1 1/2 cups

The fresh flavor of this vinaigrette and the ease of preparation (no whisking) make it a useful last-minute option to have in your repertoire.

2 cloves garlic, finely minced	Coarse salt
Juice of 3 lemons	Freshly ground black pepper
2 tablespoons minced flat-leaf parsley	Sugar
1 1/3 cups olive oil	

Place all the ingredients in a glass container with a tight-fitting lid. Shake well and pour as needed.

BASIC MAYONNAISE

Makes 1 3/4 cups

I call this a basic mayonnaise, but it does not resemble any store-bought mayonnaise you've ever seen. It is much creamier and thicker, in the classic French tradition.

STORING MAYONNAISE: All mayonnaises in this chapter can be kept in the refrigerator for up to 1 week. Let the mayonnaise cool in an open container in the refrigerator before covering it to make sure no warmth is retained. Also, return it to the refrigerator immediately after each use.

3 egg yolks	Coarse salt
Juice of 1/2 lemon	Freshly ground black pepper
1 1/3 cups olive or canola oil	

Place the yolks and lemon juice in the bowl of a food processor. Turn the machine on and slowly drizzle in the oil until the mixture is thick and emulsified. Season with salt and pepper.

❖ IF MAKING IN ADVANCE, chill the mayonnaise, uncovered, in the refrigerator, then cover and refrigerate for up to 1 week.

OPTION: You can also make this mayonnaise by beating the ingredients together with a whisk, but using a processor will save time.

ROASTED GARLIC MAYONNAISE

Stir into the mayonnaise 2 tablespoons Roasted Garlic Puree (page 12), a pinch of sugar, and 1 teaspoon Dijon mustard.

HERB MAYONNAISE

Process 1 tablespoon fresh chervil, 1 tablespoon chopped fresh chives, and 1 tablespoon fresh tarragon into the mayonnaise. Then blend in 2 tablespoons heavy cream. Adjust the seasoning.

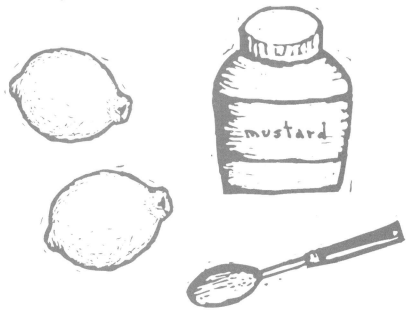

LEMON-CAYENNE AIOLI

🌿

Make about 1³/₄ cups

When made properly, this dressing should be very assertive yet thin. The flavor will vary somewhat based on the quality of the mustard and the vibrancy of the lemon juice.

3 egg yolks	¹/₂ teaspoon cayenne pepper
Juice of 1 lemon, or more to taste	Coarse salt
1 cup olive oil	Freshly ground black pepper
2 tablespoons (approximately)	
Dijon mustard	

Place the egg yolks and about 1 teaspoon lemon juice in the bowl of a food processor. Turn on the machine and pour the oil into the bowl in a thin stream, whisking to create an emulsion. Add 1 tablespoon mustard, 2 tablespoons lemon juice, and the cayenne, and season with salt and pepper. Taste and add more mustard or lemon juice if necessary.

TOMATO-ARMAGNAC MAYONNAISE

🌿

Makes 1¹/₂ cups

This intense and flavorful mayonnaise is ideal for any number of sandwiches. You might even try it on your next hamburger.

3 egg yolks	1 shallot, finely minced
1/2 clove garlic, minced	5 cornichons, finely minced
Juice of 1/2 lemon, or more to taste	1 teaspoon fine imported tomato paste
1 cup olive oil	2 tablespoons Armagnac
3 tablespoons Chopped Roasted	Coarse salt
Tomatoes (page 13)	Freshly ground black pepper

Place the egg yolks, garlic, and lemon juice in the bowl of a food processor. Turn the machine on and slowly drizzle in the oil until the mixture is thick and emulsified. Add the tomatoes, shallot, cornichons, tomato paste, and Armagnac, and process just enough to blend. Season with salt and pepper.

MUSTARD MAYONNAISE

Makes 1 1/2 cups

3 egg yolks	2 tablespoons Dijon mustard
1 clove garlic, mashed and minced	Coarse salt
Juice of 1/2 lemon, or more to taste	Freshly ground black pepper
1 cup olive oil	

Place the egg yolks, garlic, and lemon juice in the bowl of a food processor. Turn the machine on and slowly drizzle in the oil until the mixture is thick and emulsified. Add the mustard and process. Season with salt, pepper, and more lemon juice if necessary.

TRUFFLE MAYONNAISE

❦

Makes 1¹/2 cups

This intense mayonnaise can be used to dress meats, fish, or poultry. A little of it goes a very long way.

3 egg yolks	**1 tablespoon grated black truffle**
¹/2 clove garlic, mashed to a paste	**Coarse salt**
Juice of ¹/2 lemon	**Freshly ground black pepper**
1¹/3 cups olive or canola oil	

Place the egg yolks, garlic, and lemon juice in the bowl of a food processor. Turn the machine on and slowly drizzle in the oil until the mixture is thick and emulsified. Blend in the truffle and 1 tablespoon hot tap water. Season with salt and pepper.

Desserts

To be perfectly honest, I don't have a treasure trove of dessert secrets to share. Most chefs don't—the sweet stuff is usually handled by our pastry counterparts. But I have always felt strongly about one aspect of dessert: From the soul-satisfying side of things, if you can evoke a feeling of childhood, you have your diner hooked. I think this is because when we were kids, sweets were much more important to us. Our taste buds mature, and we gravitate to more sophisticated things, but that love of sweets never seems to go away. I guess it's an emotional connection—desserts remind us of simpler times.

From the standpoint of organizing a meal, appetizers at the beginning and desserts at the end create a perfect symmetry because desserts, like starters and salads, can be more intense and entertaining than main courses. Moreover, the entirely new set of flavors introduced in this category keeps the meal interesting while also signaling its end. Whether it is a sweet sorbet or a rich, creamy chocolate mousse, it's hard to imagine eating anything after dessert.

I've always found the techniques employed in dessert-making fascinating. For example, the sheer number of recipes that can be made from some variation on sugar, eggs, butter, and flour is astounding: from buttercream to crème anglaise to meringue to a variety of dough.

What follows are the desserts I've presented in a number of restaurants, and a few I make at home. Most of them are little twists on classics, such as Prune-Walnut Bread Budding (page 287) in place of bread pudding, Crème Fraîche Panna Cotta with Passion Fruit–Mint Sauce (page 292) in place of regular panna cotta, and Goat Cheese Cake (page 312) instead of . . . well, you get the idea.

As much as anywhere else, desserts are a place to juxtapose contrasting elements. What makes a hot fudge sundae so great? The cool, creamy vanilla ice cream and the thick, warm hot fudge. Well, that same basic yin-yang dynamic occurs if you serve vanilla ice cream with the Molten Chocolate Cakes on page 305. And the Raspberry and Ginger Sundae (page 300) is a medley of contrasts that will keep your palate guessing about what the next bite will bring all the way to the bottom of the bowl.

Because I am a big believer in second helpings of dessert and in having leftovers in the refrigerator, many of the following recipes are designed to serve more people than the savory dishes in the book.

I've tried to keep these desserts relatively simple so that even if you aren't an experienced baker, you'll enjoy making them as much as you enjoy devouring them.

PRUNE-WALNUT BREAD PUDDING

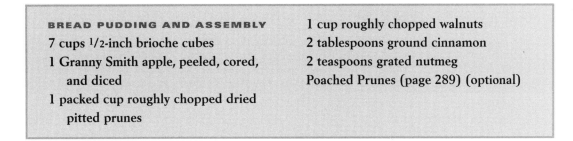

Serves 8

Bread pudding can be adapted to any number of variations. (When I was at Cascabel, the pastry chef, Lincoln Carson, made a chocolate bread pudding that would blow you away.) Here, a simple custard helps the autumnal flavors of prunes, walnuts, apples, cinnamon, and nutmeg infuse toasted brioche cubes. This is a great make-ahead recipe that is especially appropriate during the winter months.

Go out of your way to find brioche—it's ideal here—and don't over-toast the cubes; you want them firm but not impenetrable.

CUSTARD	3/4 cup sugar
1¹/2 cups milk	1 vanilla bean
1¹/2 cups heavy cream	2 eggs plus 6 egg yolks

Place the milk, cream, sugar, and vanilla bean in a saucepan and bring to a boil over high heat.

Meanwhile, in a small mixing bowl, whisk the eggs and yolks together.

As soon as the creamy mixture reaches a boil, remove the pot from the heat.

Add a small quantity of the creamy mixture to the egg mixture and whisk it in. Then whisk in the remaining creamy mixture in increments.

Strain the mixture through a fine-mesh strainer and allow to cool. You should have about 3¹/2 cups.

BREAD PUDDING AND ASSEMBLY	1 cup roughly chopped walnuts
7 cups ¹/2-inch brioche cubes	2 tablespoons ground cinnamon
1 Granny Smith apple, peeled, cored, and diced	2 teaspoons grated nutmeg
1 packed cup roughly chopped dried pitted prunes	Poached Prunes (page 289) (optional)

Preheat the oven to 350°F.

Arrange the brioche cubes in a single layer on a cookie sheet and toast in the pre-heated oven for 5 minutes.

In a large bowl, combine the brioche cubes, apple, prunes, walnuts, cinnamon, and nutmeg.

Pour the custard over the contents of the bowl and let sit for 10 minutes to allow the cubes to soak up the custard.

Transfer the soaked cubes to a 2-quart gratin dish set in a water bath and cook until set, 35–40 minutes.

To serve, spoon the warm dessert into individual dishes, with poached prunes on the side if desired.

OPTION: This custard recipe can be adapted to other fruits such as bananas or fresh overripe berries in the summer.

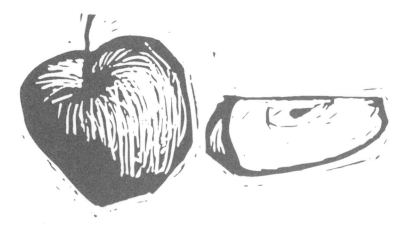

POACHED PRUNES

Serves 4 with ice cream, or 8 with Prune-Walnut Bread Pudding

I f you think of prunes as a geriatric breakfast treat, this recipe will expand your horizons. The dried plums swell up with the flavors of the poaching liquid, becoming irresistibly sweet and succulent.

1 cup dry white wine	1/8 teaspoon ground black pepper
1/2 cup sugar	Pinch fine salt
1 cinnamon stick	3 teaspoons vanilla extract
6 whole cloves	2 packed cups dried pitted prunes

Place the wine, sugar, cinnamon stick, cloves, pepper, salt, and vanilla extract in a saucepan over high heat. Bring to a boil and let boil for 1 minute.

Add the prunes to the pot, return to a boil, and then lower the heat until the liquid is at a gentle simmer. Poach the prunes, stirring occasionally and gently, until soft and plump, 8–10 minutes.

Remove the prunes with a slotted spoon. Strain the syrup and reserve for drizzling.

Serve with ice cream or as a side to Prune-Walnut Bread Pudding (page 287).

CHOCOLATE POTS DE CRÈME

❧

Serves 8

This fancy French version of chocolate pudding, once mastered, can be adapted to create any number of variations. (See Options.) Monitor the pots de crème carefully while they bake to ensure they don't dry out in the oven.

1 cup milk	1 cup finely chopped bittersweet
1 cup heavy cream	chocolate (3½ ounces), ideally
3 tablespoons sugar	Valrhona extra bitter 61%
1 whole vanilla bean	3 egg yolks, lightly beaten
	Tuiles (page 294) (optional)

Preheat the oven to 325°F.

Pour the milk and cream into a saucepan, add the sugar and vanilla bean, and bring to a boil over high heat.

Place the chocolate in a stainless steel mixing bowl and pour the boiling liquid over it. Stir until the chocolate is melted and thoroughly incorporated.

Add a little of the hot chocolate mixture to the egg yolks and whisk together. Continue to add in small increments, whisking as you go.

Strain the mixture through a fine-mesh strainer.

Divide the mixture among eight 4-ounce ramekins set in a water bath and bake in the preheated oven until set, 25–30 minutes. You can also bake the mixture in a 1-quart soufflé dish set in a water bath for approximately 45 minutes.

Serve with Tuiles (page 294) if desired.

CINNAMON-CHOCOLATE

Add 2 cinnamon sticks to the pot with the milk and cream.

WHITE CHOCOLATE MINT

Add 1 tablespoon plus 1 teaspoon mint extract to the pot with the milk and cream and use white chocolate instead of bittersweet.

MOCHA

Add 4 teaspoons ground instant espresso to the pot with the milk and cream.

CARAMEL

Make caramel by heating 1/2 cup sugar and 2 tablespoons water together in a pot. Spoon 1 tablespoon hot caramel into the bottom of each ramekin and pour the chocolate mixture over it before baking.

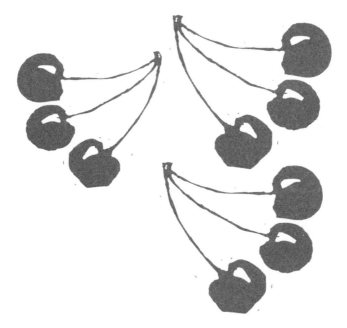

GRAPEFRUIT CAMPARI GRANITÉ

❧

Makes 4 cups, 4–6 servings

This is a frozen variation on a time-honed aperitif. It doesn't get much simpler than this.

3 cups fresh or canned grapefruit juice	3/4 cup simple syrup (2/3 cup water
1/2 cup Campari	with 1/2 cup sugar cooked to
	a boil and turned off)

Whisk together all the ingredients in a shallow container and freeze. Once frozen, scrape with a fork to form granité. Spoon into individual bowls.

OPTIONS: You can also pulse the frozen mixture in a food processor. This will create a slushier texture than scraping. This recipe also lends itself to experimentation with other flavors including lemon and orange or even juice concentrates such as cherry and cranberry.

CRÈME FRAÎCHE PANNA COTTA WITH PASSION FRUIT–MINT SAUCE

❧

Serves 6

Here, the Italian classic panna cotta (Italian for "cooked cream") gets a new, tart edge with the addition of crème fraîche. The passion fruit–mint sauce adds a sweet lift to the heavy cream.

Use the exact amount of gelatin indicated. A properly made panna cotta should just barely hold together, and an excessive amount of gelatin will give it too much body.

PASSION FRUIT-MINT SAUCE
1 cup simple syrup (²/3 cup water with
   ¹/2 cup sugar cooked to a boil and
   turned off)
¹/2 vanilla bean

¹/3 packed cup fresh mint leaves
³/4 cup melted passion fruit sorbet
2 heaping tablespoons passion fruit
   pulp and seeds (from 1 passion
   fruit; see Food for Thought)

Make a mint syrup by infusing the simple syrup, vanilla bean, and mint leaves overnight in the refrigerator. Strain. (If you'd like to speed the process, bring the syrup and vanilla bean to a boil and pour over the mint leaves. Strain and let cool.) You should have about 1 cup syrup.

In a mixing bowl, whisk together the melted sorbet, passion fruit, and 5 tablespoons mint syrup.

CRÈME FRAÎCHE PANNA COTTA
   AND ASSEMBLY
1¹/2 cups heavy cream
1 cup milk
¹/2 cup buttermilk

¹/2 cup sugar
1 vanilla bean
1 cup crème fraîche
3 teaspoons powdered gelatin

Place the cream, milk, buttermilk, sugar, and vanilla bean in a saucepan and bring to a boil over high heat. Remove from the heat and whisk in the crème fraîche. Strain through a strainer.

Add the gelatin to the hot cream mixture, stirring to dissolve.

Pour evenly into 6 bowls (about 1¹/3 cups each) or into a 1-quart soufflé dish. Chill to set for at least 2 hours. Serve with about 2 tablespoons passion fruit–mint sauce on top of each serving.

FOOD FOR THOUGHT—PASSION FRUIT: Fresh passion fruit has a dark, slightly wrinkled look. To remove seeds and pulp from a passion fruit, cut the fruit in half crosswise and scoop them out.

TUILES

Makes 12–16 cookies

These thin cookies are a traditional garnish to many French desserts. When just out of the oven, these are wonderfully malleable and can be formed into any number of shapes. Simply draping them over a rolling pin can yield a handsome cylindrical version. If they start to firm up more quickly than you can mold them, just return them to the oven for a few moments and they will soften.

1¼ cups confectioners' sugar
1 cup all-purpose flour
Seeds from ½ vanilla bean

4 egg whites
6 tablespoons unsalted butter, melted

In a mixing bowl, mix the sugar, flour, and vanilla seeds together.

Slowly whisk in the egg whites to form a paste.

Whisk in the melted butter and blend well.

Cover and chill for at least 2 hours.

Preheat the oven to 375°F.

On a nonstick cookie sheet, place 2-tablespoon portions of batter, evenly spaced and in whatever shapes you desire.

Bake in the preheated oven until lightly golden, 4–5 minutes.

Remove from the oven and allow to cool flat, or remove with a metal spatula and shape as you like.

OPTIONS: For chocolate tuiles, reduce the flour to ¾ cup and add ¼ cup unsweetened cocoa powder to the batter. For almond tuiles, add 1 teaspoon almond extract to the batter and sprinkle 2 tablespoons chopped blanched almonds on the batter after it is on the cookie sheet.

CHOCOLATE HAZELNUT CAKE

Serves 6–8

This is my favorite chocolate cake recipe. As a kid I loved a Funny Bone, a mass-produced cake with peanut butter filling that was covered in what I believed to be chocolate. This replicates those flavors, which went beautifully together.

1½ cups (7½ ounces) finely chopped bittersweet chocolate (ideally, Valrhona extra bitter 61%)
6 tablespoons unsalted butter, at room temperature

6 eggs, separated, plus 1 egg white
7 tablespoons sugar
1 cup hazelnut flour or almond flour (available at specialty food markets)

Preheat the oven to 350°F.

In a double boiler set over simmering water, melt the chocolate and butter together.

In a mixing bowl, whisk together the egg yolks and 5 tablespoons sugar.

Add a little of the hot chocolate mixture to the egg yolks and whisk together. Continue to add in small increments, whisking as you go.

In a separate bowl, whip the egg whites and the remaining 2 tablespoons sugar until soft peaks form.

Fold the resulting meringue into the chocolate-egg mixture, then fold in the flour.

Divide the mixture evenly between two 8-inch cake pans and bake until springy to the touch, 12–15 minutes. Remove the layers from the oven and allow to chill thoroughly.

HAZELNUT BUTTERCREAM
6 egg yolks
½ cup sugar
3 tablespoons water

12 ounces (3 sticks) unsalted butter, completely softened but not melted
¾ cup hazelnut paste (available at specialty food markets)

Place the egg yolks in the bowl of an electric mixer.

Cook the sugar in the water until it reaches soft ball stage, 6–7 minutes. If you have a candy thermometer, cook until you obtain a reading of 240°F. Dip a spoon into the sugar mixture, then dip the sample in ice water. When the sugar solution has a thick, malleable quality—rather than dissolving in the water—you have reached the soft ball stage.

Start whisking the egg yolks when the sugar is almost ready.

Slowly pour the sugar into the yolks as soon as it reaches the desired temperature. Whip until the bowl feels cool to the touch.

Add the butter a little at a time until all is incorporated. You will need to scrape down the sides of the bowl periodically to ensure an even integration of ingredients.

Add the hazelnut paste. You should have about 3 1/2 cups buttercream, enough to fill and coat an 8-inch cake.

❖ IF MAKING IN ADVANCE, the buttercream can be frozen for up to 2 weeks.

CHOCOLATE GLAZE AND ASSEMBLY	
1 1/2 cups finely chopped bittersweet chocolate (Valrhona extra bitter 61%)	8 tablespoons (1 stick) unsalted butter
	2 teaspoons light corn syrup

Melt the ingredients together in a double boiler set over simmering water. Makes about 1 1/4 cups glaze, enough to cover an 8-inch cake. Keep warm in a double boiler set over low heat.

Spread the buttercream 1/2 inch thick over the top of one chilled layer, leaving the sides unfrosted.

Place the other layer on top. Put in the refrigerator and let chill for at least 2 hours. (To speed the process, put it in the freezer for 30 minutes or until the frosting is quite firm to the touch.)

Remove the cake from the refrigerator and place it on a rack with a cookie sheet beneath it.

Pour the hot chocolate glaze over the cake and gently rock the cookie sheet back and forth in a seesaw motion to encourage the chocolate to run over the sides.

Transfer the rack to the refrigerator and chill until the chocolate firms up.

Remove the cake from the refrigerator, cut into wedges, and serve, ideally at room temperature.

OPTIONS: You can omit either the hazelnut buttercream or the chocolate glaze, and this dessert will still be delicious.

The chocolate that collects on the cookie sheet can be kept in plastic wrap for snacking or rolled into balls, dusted with cocoa powder, and served as a tasty truffle.

LEMON POUND CAKE WITH LEMON CURD AND BLACKBERRY COMPOTE

Serves 6

In this recipe, lemony pound cake is complemented with a creamy lemon curd and blackberry compote, a wonderful combination in the summertime.

2 cups all-purpose flour	1 1/4 cups sugar
8 ounces (2 sticks) unsalted butter	Zest of 5 lemons
Pinch fine salt	Juice of 2 lemons
Seeds from 1 vanilla bean	
3 eggs plus 5 egg yolks	

Preheat the oven to 350°F.

In a mixing bowl, beat the flour, butter, salt, and vanilla seeds together until light and fluffy.

In another bowl, whip together the eggs, egg yolks, and sugar until pale yellow and thick.

Add the lemon zest and juice, then fold the eggs into the flour-butter mixture.

Place the mixture in a 2-pound loaf pan and bake in the preheated oven until a knife inserted in the center of the cake comes out clean, 60–65 minutes. Alternatively, bake in two 8-inch cake pans until springy to the touch, about 30 minutes.

LEMON CURD	8 ounces (2 sticks) unsalted butter, at
1 cup fresh lemon juice	room temperature, cut into 16 pieces
1 cup sugar	5 egg yolks

Place the juice, sugar, and butter in a saucepan and bring to a boil over high heat.

Place the egg yolks in a mixing bowl and beat lightly.

Add a little of the hot mixture to the egg yolks and whisk together. Continue to add in small increments, whisking as you go.

Place in a pot over high heat and cook, stirring, until the mixture thickens and starts to bubble.

Carefully strain the mixture through a fine-mesh strainer. Cover with plastic wrap. Set aside and allow to cool.

BLACKBERRY COMPOTE	Juice of 1 lemon
2 pints fresh blackberries	Pinch fine salt
3 tablespoons sugar, or to taste (depending on berries)	

or

1 12-ounce bag frozen blackberries, at room temperature	Juice of 1 lemon
1/4 cup sugar, or to taste	Pinch fine salt

Place the berries, sugar, lemon juice, and salt in a saucepan over medium-high heat. Cook until the berries start to break down and the sauce thickens a bit, about 10 minutes. Be careful to leave it chunky.

OPTION: You may also use raspberries in this compote. Just be sure to check the amount of sugar.

ASSEMBLY

Cut the pound cake into slices. Lay 1 slice on each of 6 plates, spoon some lemon curd over the cake, and top with the berry compote.

OPTION: GINGER POUND CAKE

To make a ginger pound cake, omit the lemon zest and add 2 tablespoons ground ginger to the flour.

RASPBERRY AND GINGER SUNDAE

Serves 6

Everyone loves the combination of cake and ice cream, so I decided to put the two together in a coupe.

RASPBERRY-GINGER SAUCE

1 12-ounce bag frozen raspberries, thawed, or 2 pints fresh raspberries; for fresh reduce sugar to 3 tablespoons or to taste

2 tablespoons water

1/4 cup sugar, or to taste

2 tablespoons light corn syrup

2 tablespoons finely chopped fresh ginger, from about a 1 1/2-inch piece (no need to peel)

Juice of 1 lime

Pinch fine salt

In a blender, puree the raspberries and water together.

Transfer the mixture to a saucepan and add the other ingredients. Bring to a boil over high heat.

Lower the heat and cook until the sauce thickens, about 10 minutes.

Strain through a fine-mesh strainer. You should have about 1 cup sauce.

CARAMEL SAUCE

1 cup sugar

1/4 cup water

1 1/2 cups heavy cream

Pour the sugar and water into a saucepan set over medium heat and cook, swirling (but not stirring) the pot, until the mixture begins to take on a light amber color. Continue to cook until it attains a dark color, about 15–20 minutes. (Be very careful; the mixture could burn if overcooked. If it starts to burn, immerse the bottom of the pot in some lukewarm water to cool it quickly.)

Turn off the heat and carefully add the cream. It will bubble on contact. Once the bubbling stops, return to low heat and cook, stirring, for 1 minute, until the caramel sauce is formed.

ASSEMBLY
1 Ginger Pound Cake (see Option, page 299)

1 pint vanilla ice cream, slightly softened

Drizzle some raspberry sauce into the bottom of each of 4 sundae bowls. Add a slice of ginger pound cake and a scoop of vanilla ice cream. Top with caramel sauce.

OPTION: If you don't feel like making pound cake, buy a high-quality commercial version. To add ginger flavor to it, thinly slice a 2-ounce piece of ginger and simmer it with 3 tablespoons sugar and 1/2 cup water in a saucepan. Drizzle the resulting syrup over the cake slices.

MAPLE CRÈME BRÛLÉE

Serves 6

As much as I love the classic vanilla crème brûlée, this variation has much more character and flavor. For best results use a blowtorch instead of the broiler. Many gourmet specialty shops sell small propane torches designed expressly for this purpose.

2¹/4 cups heavy cream	¹/4 cup plus 3 tablespoons sugar
³/4 cup milk	¹/2 cup maple sugar (available from
¹/2 vanilla bean or ¹/2 teaspoon	specialty stores)
vanilla extract	8 egg yolks

Place the cream, milk, vanilla, and sugar in a saucepan and bring to a boil. Off the heat, add the maple sugar to the pot.

Place the egg yolks in a mixing bowl and beat lightly. Add a little of the hot mixture to the egg yolks and whisk together. Continue to add in small increments, whisking.

Strain through a fine-mesh strainer and allow to cool.

Preheat the oven to 325°F.

Divide the cooled mixture among six 4-ounce ramekins set in a water bath. Bake in the preheated oven until set, about 30 minutes. Remove from the oven and let cool.

❖ IF MAKING IN ADVANCE, the desserts can be refrigerated, uncovered, for up to 24 hours. WHEN READY TO PROCEED, soak up any moisture on the surface with a paper towel or paper napkin.

To caramelize: Sprinkle 2 teaspoons sugar evenly over each ramekin. Turn at a slight angle to allow any excess sugar to fall off (ideally onto the next one you'll be coating). Set under a very hot broiler until brown and bubbly, about 4 minutes. If using a blowtorch, ignite the flame and hold 3 inches from the surface of the dessert. Melt the sugar by moving the torch in a circular motion. As areas turn amber in color, focus the flame on another area of the dessert until it attains a uniform color. Serve immediately.

PISTACHIO-FIG TART

❧

This dessert was first developed by Paula Smith, the first pastry chef at Alison. I've tinkered with it over the years to create the recipe featured here. Let the tarts cool slightly but remove them from the pans while still warm. They are much easier to handle this way.

CITRUS CRÈME FRAÎCHE

1 cup crème fraîche

Zest of 1/2 orange, finely minced

Zest of 1 lemon, finely minced

Zest of 1 lime, finely minced

Place all the ingredients in a mixing bowl. Stir together and let chill 1 hour before serving. You should have 1 1/4 cups.

NOTE: Use this as a lively topping for any number of desserts.

PISTACHIO CRUST

2 cups ground unsalted pistachio nuts

1 cup plus 2 tablespoons sugar

2 1/4 cups all-purpose flour

2 teaspoons baking powder

Seeds from 1 vanilla bean or 1 teaspoon
   vanilla extract

Zest of 2 lemons

8 ounces (2 sticks) plus 2 tablespoons
   unsalted butter, at room temperature

1 egg plus 2 egg yolks

In a bowl, stir together the nuts, sugar, flour, baking powder, vanilla seeds or extract, and lemon zests.

Add the butter to the bowl and stir until fully incorporated.

Whisk in the egg and egg yolks 1 at a time.

Cover the dough with plastic wrap and chill for 30 minutes. You should have about 4 1/2 cups dough, enough for one 9-inch tart or eight 4-inch tarts.

VARIATION: You can substitute hazelnuts or walnuts for the pistachios.

FILLING	1 tablespoon plus 1 teaspoon ground
2 packed cups dried figs, stems	cinnamon
removed	Juice and zest of 1 lemon
1 1/2 cups water	1/2 teaspoon freshly ground
3/4 cup sugar	black pepper
2 teaspoons ground cloves	Pinch fine salt

Place all the ingredients in a saucepan and bring to a boil over high heat. Lower the heat and simmer until the figs are tender and the liquid has thickened and reduced, about 50 minutes.

Let cool and puree. You will have about 1 1/2 cups filling.

ASSEMBLY

For a 9-inch tart: Spray a tart pan that has a removable bottom with nonstick spray. Press half of the dough into the bottom of the tart pan. Chill well. Spread all the filling on the dough. Chill well.

Preheat the oven to 350°F.

Spread the remaining half of the dough over the filling (This is most easily done using wet fingers). Alternatively, roll out the dough, cut into strips, and arrange in a lattice pattern.

Bake in the preheated oven until golden brown, 45–50 minutes.

For 4-inch single-serving tarts: Coat the tart pans with nonstick spray. Let the dough come to room temperature.

Scoop 1/4 cup dough into the bottom of each tart pan and let chill before spreading evenly over the surface.

Spread 3 tablespoons filling into each tart. Chill well.

Preheat the oven to 350°F.

Spread 1/4 cup dough over the filling in each pan (most easily done using wet fingers).

Bake in the preheated oven until golden brown, 30–35 minutes.

Top with the citrus crème fraîche and serve.

MOLTEN CHOCOLATE CAKES

❧

Serves 6

About ten years ago it seemed that every New York City restaurant had its version of a "molten chocolate cake": small, cupcake-sized desserts that were sliced open at the table to reveal a hot liquid center. Although many people took a crack at them, my hat goes off to my former pastry chef, Lincoln Carson, who may not have been the originator of the species but produced the best one I've ever had. His recipe is included here. I recommend serving it with vanilla ice cream.

Do not overcook the cakes. Essentially, they are created by intentionally undercooking. You will need six 4-ounce foil ramekins, which are available in shops that sell bakeware. The foil ramekins are crucial to this effect because they allow the outside to cook more quickly, before too much heat reaches the center.

1¹/₃ cups finely chopped bittersweet chocolate (ideally, Valrhona extra bitter 61%) 13 tablespoons (1 stick plus 5 tablespoons) unsalted butter, at room temperature	6 eggs and 6 egg yolks ³/₄ cup sugar ¹/₂ cup plus 2 tablespoons all-purpose flour 6 teaspoons unsweetened cocoa powder

In a double boiler, melt the chocolate and butter together.

In a mixing bowl, whip the eggs, egg yolks, and sugar together until pale yellow and thick.

Pour the chocolate mixture into the egg mixture and whisk until semi-incorporated.

Add the flour to the bowl and whisk until all ingredients are just incorporated; take great care not to overmix.

Cover the batter and chill in the refrigerator for 2 hours.

Preheat the oven to 425°F.

Spray six 4-ounce foil ramekins with nonstick spray. Coat the interior of the ramkeins with cocoa powder and shake out the excess.

Place the batter in a pastry bag (no tip needed) and pipe into the ramekins, or use a spoon to do so.

Bake in the preheated oven until just starting to crack on top, 10–12 minutes.

Remove from the oven and let rest for 1 minute before turning the cakes out of the ramekins. Serve immediately.

NOTE: This recipe can also be made in a 9-inch springform, but it will not be as runny in the center. Adjust the baking time to 22–25 minutes.

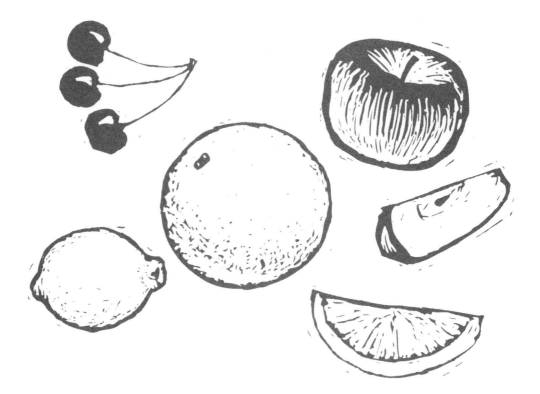

Crostata with Apricots and Sour Cherries

Makes one 10-inch crostata

This rustic dessert, created by my longtime assistant and good friend Lisa Reilly, is a charmingly unfinished pie that can be adapted to accommodate your favorite fruits.

CRUST
1 1/2 cups all-purpose flour
2 tablespoons sugar
1/2 teaspoon fine salt
1/2 cup chopped walnuts
4 tablespoons unsalted butter
1 egg yolk
3–4 tablespoons water

In the bowl of an electric mixer, place the flour, sugar, salt, and nuts.

Add the butter, turn on the mixer, and mix until well blended.

Add the egg yolk and mix.

Add the water and continue to mix until the dough comes together when pinched.

Cover the dough with plastic wrap and chill.

APRICOT-CHERRY FILLING
3/4 cup sugar
Zest and juice of 2 lemons
Zest and juice of 1 orange
1 whole vanilla bean
3 cups quartered dried apricots
3 cups dried sour cherries
2 cups toasted walnuts

Place 6 cups water, sugar, zests, juices, and vanilla bean in a saucepan. Bring to boil and let reduce for 10–12 minutes.

Add the apricots and cherries to the pan and cook until they are plump and the syrup is thick, about 20 minutes.

Strain the contents of the pan through a colander set over a bowl and reserve the liquid for drizzling. Fold the walnuts into the apricot-cherry mixture.

<table>
<tr><td>ASSEMBLY
Egg wash (1 egg yolk beaten with 1
    teaspoon cold water)</td><td>Sugar for sprinkling</td></tr>
</table>

Preheat the oven to 350°F.

Roll out the dough to form a 12-inch circle. (Since this is a rustic tart, it doesn't need to be a perfect circle.) Place the circle on a cookie sheet.

Spread the filling on the dough, but not all the way to the edges.

Fold the edges of the dough over the filling. Work your way around the perimeter, overlapping the edges as you form them.

Brush the exposed dough with egg wash and sprinkle with sugar.

Bake the tart in the preheated oven until golden brown, 35–40 minutes. Remove from the oven, allow to cool slightly, and drizzle with the reserved fruit liquid.

PLUM FINANCIER WITH HAZELNUT CRUST AND BROWN BUTTER CURD

Makes one 9-inch dessert

This classic dessert lets the flavor and character of the plums really shine. A financier crust is traditionally made with crushed almonds, but I use hazelnuts for their more pronounced flavor.

HAZELNUT DOUGH

2 cups ground hazelnuts
1 cup plus 2 tablespoons sugar
2¼ cups all-purpose flour
2 teaspoons baking powder
Seeds from 1 vanilla bean or 1 teaspoon
  vanilla extract

Zest of 2 lemons
8 ounces (2 sticks) plus 2 tablespoons
  unsalted butter, at room temperature
1 egg plus 2 egg yolks

In a bowl, stir together the ground nuts, sugar, flour, baking powder, vanilla seeds, and lemon zest.

Add the butter and stir until fully incorporated.

Whisk in the egg and egg yolks 1 at a time.

Cover the dough with plastic wrap and chill for 30 minutes. You should have about 4½ cups dough, enough for one 9-inch tart.

PLUM FINANCIER

1 recipe Brown Butter Curd (page 311)

8–10 plums, halved, pitted, and cut into
  thin slices but attached at the ends
½ cup toasted chopped hazelnuts

Preheat the oven to 350°F.

Spread the hazelnut dough over the bottom of a 9-inch tart pan.

Spread the brown butter curd over the dough.

Starting around the edge of the pan, fan the plum halves out over the curd and gently press down to cover the surface of the pan. Work your way toward the center of the pan until the entire surface is covered with plums.

Sprinkle the nuts around the outer edge of the tart.

Place the pan in the oven and bake until the crust is golden and the tart is bubbly, 30–35 minutes.

Remove from the oven and allow to cool before serving.

OPTION: Pears, apples, or peaches can be substituted for the plums.

BROWN BUTTER CURD

Makes 2 cups

This is a versatile filling well suited to simple fruit tarts. It's a sturdier alternative to custard.

Seeds from 1 vanilla bean	1 pound (4 sticks) unsalted butter
1 cup sugar	3 eggs
1/4 cup plus 2 tablespoons all-purpose flour	

Combine the vanilla seeds, sugar, and flour in the bowl of a mixer.

In a sauté pan, melt the butter over medium heat and cook until nutty and brown, but do not allow it to burn.

Slowly pour the melted butter into the sugar-flour mixture and mix until blended and cool.

Add the eggs, 1 at a time, and mix until incorporated.

Strain the mixture through a strainer. (The mixture will thicken as it cools, ultimately yielding 2 cups.)

❖ **IF MAKING IN ADVANCE,** cover and keep in the refrigerator for up to 24 hours. Be sure to stir gently before using.

GOAT CHEESE CAKE

This dessert brings the popular flavor of goat cheese to the classic format of a cheesecake. As you'll see, the combination is a winning one. Use a mild goat cheese; this isn't the place for the assertive flavor of an aged product.

12 ounces cream cheese, at room temperature	1 teaspoon vanilla extract
4 ounces goat cheese (1 small log), at room temperature	1 teaspoon anise extract
	2 cups sour cream
3/4 cup sugar	3 eggs

Preheat the oven to 325°F.

In a mixing bowl, mix the cream cheese and goat cheese together until well combined. (Scrape down the sides of the bowl as you work to ensure an even distribution of ingredients.) Stir in the sugar, vanilla extract, and anise extract, then mix in the sour cream. Add the eggs, 1 at a time, stirring until each one is well incorporated.

Pour the mixture into a 9-inch springform pan, wrap the bottom of the pan snugly with aluminum foil, set in a water bath, and bake in the preheated oven until set, 45–55 minutes. Remove from the oven, take the pan out of the water bath, and let cool before serving.

❖ **IF MAKING IN ADVANCE,** keep tightly covered in the refrigerator for up to 2 days.

OPTION: If you prefer a more conventional cheesecake, replace the goat cheese with cream cheese.

NAPOLEON MINUTE

❧

Makes 4 servings

If you love napoleons, here is an unconventional recipe that captures all of their trademark charms. I learned to make it when I worked as a pastry assistant in Paris. Once the filling is made, you should use it as soon as possible because its consistency at room temperature is ideal. If you make it in advance, return it to room temperature and then beat it lightly with a wooden spoon.

PASTRY CREAM AND FILLING

2 cups milk
2 teaspoons vanilla extract
5 egg yolks

3/4 cup sugar
1/2 cup all-purpose flour
8 ounces (2 sticks) unsalted butter,
    at room temperature

Pour the milk and vanilla extract into a saucepan and bring to a boil over high heat.

In a mixing bowl, whisk the egg yolks and sugar together until the sugar dissolves.

Whisk in the flour.

Add a little of the hot milk mixture to the egg mixture and whisk together. Continue to add in small amounts, whisking as you go.

Return the combined mixture to the pot and cook over low heat, stirring constantly, until very thick, about 15 minutes. Take care not to let the mixture scorch. If the mixture appears lumpy at this point, strain it through a fine-mesh strainer, pushing it down with a rubber spatula.

Allow to cool to room temperature or chill until ready to use. This is your pastry cream.

NOTE: If you'd like to flavor the pastry cream, add 1–2 tablespoons of any flavored liqueur at this point.

Whip the butter in an electric mixer until very fluffy, 7–8 minutes. Scrape down the sides from time to time to guarantee a uniform mixture. (When properly whipped, the butter will have doubled in volume and taken on the appearance of thick whipped cream.) Check to be sure the butter and pastry cream are at comparable temperatures. If they are not, wait for the cream to come to room temperature. Fold the butter into the pastry cream and hold at room temperature.

PUFF PASTRY AND ASSEMBLY
1 sheet store-bought puff pastry, cut into twelve 4-inch squares

4 tablespoons sugar
Confectioners' sugar for sprinkling

Preheat the oven to 375°F.

Prick the puff pastry squares all over with a fork.

Sprinkle each square with 1 teaspoon sugar.

Bake the squares between 2 cookie sheets (to weight them down) until golden brown, 15–20 minutes. Remove from the oven and allow to cool.

Lay 4 of the squares, sugar side up, in front of you.

Place a dollop (about 6 tablespoons) of pastry cream in the center of each square. Top each one with another square, sugar side up, and press down gently.

Place another dollop on top of each square, add the final 4 squares, and press down gently again, ensuring that the cream spreads out to the sides.

Use a knife to smooth out any cream that oozes out. Shake confectioner's sugar over the top of each napoleon and serve.

OPTION: If you like, add berries or chocolate chips to the cream in each layer.

Index